WomanWitness

OTHER PUBLICATIONS
BY THE AUTHOR

Books

Preparing the Way of the Lord
God-With-Us: Resources for Prayer and Praise
Why Sing? Toward a Theology of Catholic Church Music
An Anthology of Scripture Songs
WomanPrayer, WomanSong: Resources for Ritual
WomanWord: Women of the New Testament
WomanWisdom: Women of the Hebrew Scriptures: Part One

Records/Cassettes/Published Music Collections

Joy Is Like the Rain
I Know the Secret
Knock, Knock
Seasons
Gold, Incense, and Myrrh
In Love
Mass of a Pilgrim People
RSVP: Let Us Pray
Songs of Promise
Sandstone
Remember Me
WomanSong
EarthSong

Music resources are available from Medical Mission Sisters
77 Sherman Street/Hartford, CT 06105/203-233-0875/203-232-4451

WomanWitness

A Feminist Lectionary
and Psalter

Women of the Hebrew Scriptures

PART TWO

Miriam Therese Winter

Illustrated by Meinrad Craighead

CROSSROAD • NEW YORK

1992

The Crossroad Publishing Company
370 Lexington Avenue, New York, NY 10017

Printed in the United States of America

Cover illustration and text illustrations: Meinrad Craighead

Manufactured in the United States of America
Typesetting output: TEXSource, Houston

Library of Congress Cataloging-in-Publication Data

Winter, Miriam Therese.
    WomanWitness : a feminist lectionary and psalter : women of the Hebrew scriptures: part two / Miriam Therese Winter ; illustrated by Meinrad Craighead.
        p. cm.
    ISBN 0-8245-1141-7 (pbk.)
    1. Women in the Bible. 2. Women—Prayer-books and devotions—English. 3. Bible. O.T.—Devotional literature. I. Title.
    II. Title: Woman witness.
    BS575.W55 1992
    264'.34—dc20   91-37708
                                                              CIP

Contents

Psalms

PREFACE

I REMEMBER CLEARLY how it all began. I felt like a female Jonah, eager to escape an impossible task. Find all the women in the Bible? Reconstruct their stories? Create ritual contexts to preserve their legacies? Yet the women themselves commissioned me, and their presence on the edge of my consciousness kept me from running scared. It was an enormous challenge. There were times when the project swallowed me up, spit me out, and left me feeling the full effects of a spiritual death and resurrection. It encompassed the whole of me, head and heart, and transformed my perspective. In any intimate relationship, one is bound to be changed. We entered into relationship, the biblical women and I, and now in some deep, inexplicable sense, they will always be with me as soul sisters, spirit guides, and friends.

I began by reading the Bible again, painstakingly, book by book. I saw new meanings as a result of my biblical/theological education, feminist orientation, extensive reading, and lived experience in the barrios, villages, and urban centers of Africa, Asia, and Latin America, of North America, Europe, and Australia. Then I sat with the narratives of the women and watched them come to life.

What happened to me in the writing is sure to happen to others who choose to reflect prayerfully with these biblical witnesses and wrestle with the questions they raise. Like me, others will cross the line separating past stories from our own. As I encountered heroines such as Deborah, Judith, and Vashti, I learned to look more intentionally for the heroic in myself. As I agonized with violated women, mourned the rape of Dinah, Tamar, and the Levite's concubine, decried the destruction of Cozbi and the ritual sacrifice of Jephthah's Daughter, I felt an assault to my own integrity as a female in my tradition. The abuse of a sister anywhere has become an abuse of me. I was drawn to poet and prophet, to music-maker and truth-teller, to the women who shaped the rituals, in the circles of their experience, in their own intuitive way. I was touched by the extraordinary witness of ordinary women, by Achsah and Orpah and Abishag, by the woman who anointed the head of Jesus, by the woman at the well. I am still intrigued by the anonymity of individual women and the secrets they have retained: Eve's daughters, Isaiah's wife, the sisters of Jesus, and his mother's sister whom I met at the foot of the cross. I am grateful for the many in ministry whose leadership still inspires: Miriam the sister of Moses, Mary Magdalene, Dorcas, Phoebe. These and others model for me possibilities in the years ahead.

In the company of this cloud of witnesses, I am questioning present praxis and its basis in tradition on a far deeper level than I had ever done before. How much of what is normative stems from an arbitrary infrastructure of power and control? What does intimidation have to do with the transforming ways of God? How can any human agency presume to excommunicate anyone from the orbit of redeeming grace? These are not ephemeral concerns raised by a disenchanted radical fringe. They are biblically based inquiries, perennial issues of prophetic persons on behalf of systemic justice in all aspects of life. They underlie the questions posed to the community by Jesus and, vicariously, to us. "Who do people say that I am? Who do *you* say that I am?" (Mk 8:27, 29)

With *WomanWitness*, the three-volume series encompassing all the women of the Bible is complete. *WomanWisdom* is the companion volume for women of the Hebrew scriptures. The women of the New Testament are all included in *WomanWord*. This volume contains an index of all the women and a listing of all the psalms indexed according to theme. There is also a lectionary calendar that will serve as a guide to encountering the women in a systematic way. It is intended to facilitate personal reflection and integrative prayer.

I am grateful to so many people as I write these final lines, especially to the biblical women who gave so freely to me; to Meinrad Craighead, whose powerful images enable these spirited women to become more visible to us; to John and Mary Ellen Eagleson, not only my favorite editors, but feminists and friends; to my global community of Medical Mission Sisters who continue to confirm that we are one world, and that our gifts benefit everyone.

This series is a thanksgiving offering to the One Who created us in Her image and rejoices in all that is female, Whose blessing extends to all women and men and to all the created universe through Her Spirit of shalom.

———— ◇ ————

CHRONOLOGY

The Dawn of Civilization
        Eve's Daughters

B.C.E.

1800–1700   The Age of the Matriarchs/Settlements in Canaan
        Lot's Daughters / Dinah / Tamar

1700–1600   Israelites go down into Egypt
        Potiphar's Wife / Jochebed / Shiprah and Puah
        Pharaoh's Daughter

c. 1280   The Wilderness Sojourn
        Shelomith

c. 1250–1020   Conquest of Canaan/Period of the Judges
        Rahab / Mahlah, Noah, Haglah, Milcah, Tirzah / Achsah
        Deborah / Jael / Samson's Mother / Delilah
        Micah's Mother / Ichabod's Mother / Jephthah's Daughter
        Virgin Daughter / Ruth and Naomi

c. 1000–961   Monarchy of David
        David's Mother / Merab / Bathsheba
        David's Daughter Tamar

c. 961–922   Empire of Solomon
        Two Mothers / Queen of Sheba / Temple Singers

c. 922–722   Divided Kingdom
        Northern Kingdom of Israel
        Queen Mothers / Jezebel / Samaritan Mothers
        Lo-ruhamah
        Kingdom of Judah
        Queen Mothers: Naamah / Maacah / Azubah
           Mother of Jehoram / Athaliah, Queen of Judah / Zibiah
           Jehoaddin / Jecoliah / Jerusha / Mother of Ahaz / Abi
           Hephzibah / Meshullemeth / Jedidah / Hamutal
           Zebidah / Nehushta
        Jehosheba

c. 721–650   After the Fall of the Northern Kingdom
        Edna / Sarah's Maid / Susanna

After 500   After the Return from Exile, Reconstruction, Diaspora
        Job's Daughters / Noadiah / Judith / Esther
        Queen Vashti / Arsinoe

After 175   Maccabean Period
        Jewish Mother

◇ WOMANWITNESS: A PSALM ◇

All   Sing
to Her
a new song

Choir 1   of serendipity
and
shalom,

Choir 2   faith
finding
its own way
home,

Choir 1   love
breaking
through the ice
cold wall
of introverted pain,

Choir 2   hope
raised to life
again:

Choir 1   one world
sensitivities,

Choir 2   passion
for possibilities:

All   summer
autumn
winter
spring
sing of woman
witnessing,

Choir 1   making
a difference,

Choir 2   making
a start
in owning the seasons
of the heart.

   By M. T. Winter, Crossroad Pub. Co., © 1992 Medical Mission Sisters

◇ I ◇

Legendary Women

TAMAR

◇ **Scripture Reference**   Gen 38:6–30; 1 Chr 2:3–6

◇ **Biography**

Tamar was the wife of Er, the firstborn son of Judah and his Canaanite wife, Bathshua. When Er died, his brother Onan, obliged to take Tamar as wife, prevented her from becoming pregnant, and soon after he too died. Judah kept her away from his third son, Shelah. After the death of Bathshua, Tamar tricked her father-in-law into sleeping with her and gave birth to twin sons, Perez and Zerah. Perez was an ancestor of David.

◇ **Context**

After Tamar's husband died, it was her brother-in-law Onan's duty to marry her and give her a child in her deceased husband's name. Onan prevented his semen from impregnating Tamar because the child would not be his, and when he too had died, her father-in-law Judah withheld from Tamar his only remaining son. Not only did he deny Tamar her right to a levirate marriage, but he also neglected to perform the ceremony of *halizah*, which would have released Tamar from the levirate bond so she could freely marry another. After Judah's wife died, Tamar, disguised as a prostitute, secretly seduced Judah and secured some personal items as his pledge of future payment. When she became noticeably pregnant, Judah condemned her to death. Just as she was being dragged away she produced his personal pledges, and he accepted responsibility, not only for her condition, but also for the situation that compelled her to

2

go about getting pregnant in that way. Although their stories are very different, there is some similarity between Tamar's situation with Judah and Ruth's approach to Boaz (see p. 52), and the birth of Tamar's twin sons is reminiscent of Rebekah's giving birth to Jacob and Esau.

Tamar's deception and prostitution are part of the genealogical history of David, and her story is replete with patriarchal overtones. Bound by her widowhood to wait for an offer of marriage from her brother-in-law, Tamar devised a way to fulfill an equally important obligation, to perpetuate her dead husband's name. Producing a child overrode all question of morality, for the woman's duty here was to have a baby, or, more specifically, a son. Judah, on the other hand, had complete freedom to seek out and enjoy the pleasures of a prostitute, secretly of course. He had no qualms about condemning a female family member to death because she had slept with a man, even though he, as recently as she, had slept with an unidentified woman, offering her payment in exchange for sex without ever seeing her face. Judah did own up to what he had done and to his failure to provide for Tamar, but the narrative implies that Tamar most likely had to continue to make it on her own.

◇ **Lectionary Reading**

Judah took a wife for Er, his firstborn,
and her name was Tamar.
But Er offended God greatly,
so God put him to death.
Then Judah said to Onan, his son,
"Take your brother's wife,
which is your duty as a brother-in-law,
and produce a child for your brother."
But since the child would not be his,
Onan prevented his semen from entering Tamar
whenever he slept with her
so she could not conceive his brother's child.
What he did was wrong and an angry God
brought about his untimely death.
Then Judah said to his daughter-in-law,
"Remain a widow in your father's house
until my young son Shelah grows up,"
for he feared that Shelah would suffer the same fate
and die like his older brothers.
So Tamar retired to her father's house.
After a length of time had passed,
the wife of Judah died,
and when his time of mourning was over,
he went with his friend Hirah the Adullamite
to his sheepshearers up in Timnah.

When Tamar heard that her father-in-law
was going to Timnah to sheer his sheep,
she took off her widow's garments,
disguised herself with thick robes and a veil,
and went and sat where the road to Enaim
branches off to the road to Timnah.
For Tamar was aware that Shelah had matured
and still she was not his wife.
When Judah approached, he saw her,
but because her face was heavily veiled
he thought she was a prostitute.
He came over to her and said to her,
"Come, let me sleep with you,"
for he failed to recognize
that she was his daughter-in-law.
"What will you give me to sleep with me?"
she asked, and Judah answered,
"I will send you a kid from my flock."
She said, "I will do it if you give me some token
as pledge that you will keep your word."
He said, "What kind of token shall I give you?"
She replied, "Your seal, your cord,
and the staff in your hand."
So he gave these to her as a pledge of his word,
and they went off and slept together,
and at that moment she conceived.
Then Tamar got up and left him,
and when she was home she took off her veil
and returned to her widow's clothes.
Judah kept his word,
and he sent his friend the Adullamite
to give the kid to the prostitute
and recover the tokens he had given as pledge,
but she was nowhere to be found.
When he asked the local men
where he might find the prostitute
who had sat by the side of the road
on the way to Enaim, they replied,
"There has been no prostitute there."
So he returned to Judah and said to him,
"I have not been able to find her,
and all of the men insisted
that there has been no prostitute there."
"Let her keep the tokens I gave her," said Judah,
"and let us keep this to ourselves,
otherwise we will be ridiculed.

I tried to send this kid to her.
It's not my fault that we cannot find her."
About three months later Judah was told,
"Your daughter-in-law is pregnant.
Tamar is a whore."
"Bring her here and burn her!" he replied.
And as they were dragging her out to be burned,
she sent word to her father-in-law,
"It was the owner of these who made me pregnant,"
and she sent him his seal and cord and staff.
Then Judah admitted that these things were his
and that he had had intercourse with her.
"She is more in the right than I am," he said,
"for it was my duty to give her in marriage
to my son Shelah, and I did not."
He did not sleep with her again.
When the time of her delivery arrived,
she was found to have twins in her womb.
While she was in labor,
one of the babies put out a hand
and the midwife tied to it a crimson thread, saying,
"This child came out first."
But he drew back his hand,
and his brother came first.
"What a breach you have opened for yourself!"
said the midwife,
so they named the baby Perez.
A little while later his brother was born
with the crimson thread on his hand,
and so he was named Zerah.

◇

The sons of Judah
and the Canaanite Bathshua were:
Er, Onan, and Shelah.
Now Er, their firstborn, was evil,
and God put him to death.
Their daughter-in-law Tamar
also bore two sons, Perez and Zerah.
Judah had five sons in all.
The sons of Perez were Hezron and Hamul.
The sons of Zerah were Zimri, Ethan, Herman,
Calcol, and Dara, five in all.

◇ **Points for Shared Reflection**

- There was a double standard of morality in ancient Israel and there is a double standard in most societies now. Discuss the different expectations associated with gender.

- Until the present time, men have been fairly free to have sex with a woman without having to bear any burdens. Discuss the impact of AIDS on our changing expectations.

- Comment on Tamar's deception and its place in the ancestry of David. What do her actions have to say about biblical ethics and morality?

- Reflect on Tamar's story from a feminist perspective — her lack of freedom, isolation, desperation, her object status, her roles as wife, daughter-in-law, mother — and the ways she accomplished her own liberation.

◇ **A Psalm of Struggle** (see p. 7)

◇ **Prayer**

We struggle to know You
and name You, Shaddai,
and to live in the truth
of our naming,
despite all efforts
to cut us off,
lock us out,
disengage and disempower us.
We are so bound
to the Essence of You
that nothing at all can separate us
from the Source of Your unfailing love.
Be with us now,
warm and strong,
and stay with us always.
Amen.

◇ A PSALM OF STRUGGLE ◇

Choir 1   There is a struggle
in the womb of life
between the forces of good and evil,
a dualistic tendency
that is at the heart of all tragedy
of war over peace,
sin over grace,
and oppressive domination.

Choir 2   There is a struggle
in the womb of hope
between faith
and the forces of despair.
Genuine commitment huddles there
in an interim of agitation.

Choir 1   There is a struggle
in the womb of love
between simply being
and being good,
between seeing the worst
and setting free the gift
of essential humanhood.

Choir 2   There is a struggle
in the womb of me
between ought
and ought not
constantly,
between dream
with its daughters of intuition
and rational forces
of cold cognition.

Choir 1   There is a struggle
in the womb of word
between what must be said
and what will be heard
in the Spirit-charged intensity
of a changing world
stuck to its roots
in unchanging tradition.

Choir 2 There is a struggle
in wisdom's womb
between substantive speech
and empty shell,
for it knows more than it can tell,
and we are so unreceptive.

Choir 1 There is a struggle
in the womb of the church,
the shrine,
the synagogue,
the sanctuary,
between Spirit-power
and institution,
between promises
and their execution,
between rubric
and reality.

Choir 2 There is a struggle
in the womb of the world
between love and hate
and its representation in
rich and poor,
female and male,
in and out,
the power of choice
and powerlessness,
the bondage of fear
and the freedom to bless.

All We struggle to know You
and name You, Shaddai,
and to understand something of You,
grateful to be committed
and free
to choose You
and to love You.

   By M. T. Winter, Crossroad Pub. Co., © 1992 Medical Mission Sisters

POTIPHAR'S WIFE

◇ **Scripture Reference**   Gen 39:1–23

◇ **Biography**

The woman who was married to Potiphar, the captain of Pharaoh's guard, was an Egyptian woman of substance with a lot of time on her hands. Her unsuccessful seduction of Joseph resulted in his imprisonment and was a turning point in his career.

◇ **Context**

Joseph's brothers, jealous of their father's affection for him and angry at his feelings of superiority, sold Joseph to some Midianite merchants who took him to Egypt and sold him to Potiphar, the captain of Pharaoh's guard. Joseph, a slave in Potiphar's house, quickly rose to a position of prominence. Because of his sharp administrative skills, Potiphar put him in charge of all he possessed. Joseph proved worthy of his trust. Potiphar's estate prospered and Joseph himself flourished, until the incident with Potiphar's wife. History has not been sympathetic to the woman in this story. From the way the narrative unfolds in scripture, it is clear that she was a stepping stone in Joseph's rise to power. She intruded on Joseph's serenity and then she disappeared. Joseph needed a career change, according to God's plan, and he was able to achieve that by way of the prison to which her accusation sent him. Scripture continues with Joseph's story and we never hear of the woman again.

9

Potiphar's wife has been presented to us through centuries of interpretation as a calculating, despicable woman — oversexed, deceitful, a
liar, an adulteress, the stereotypical seductress out to fell the man of God.
This hardly seems fair to the woman. There are two sides to every story.
We have not yet heard from Potiphar's wife. What was it really like for
her? What led her to behave the way she did? What were the circumstances that drove her to pursue Joseph so relentlessly? Was she lonely?
Unhappy? Bored? Did she not have enough to do? Was she one of those
poor little rich girls of antiquity, all dressed up in the best brocades with
nowhere to go, nothing to entertain her, no one with whom to commu-
nicate? She seemed to have no responsibilities. Joseph was in charge of
everything. He even supervised the house. Her husband seemed to be
more preoccupied with Joseph than he was with her. And Joseph was
very attractive. The seduction was followed by false accusation, and the
facts submerge speculation, leaving no pity for Potiphar's wife. The text
implies that she remained with her husband. Perhaps in time he forgave
her. Perhaps in time, so will we.

◇ **Lectionary Reading**

Now Joseph was taken down to Egypt
and Potiphar, an Egyptian,
an officer of Pharaoh
and captain of the guard,
bought him from the Ishmaelites.
He lived in the house of his Egyptian master.
God favored Joseph
and he became a successful man.
When his master saw that God was with Joseph
and that all his efforts prospered,
he was very pleased with him.
He made him his personal attendant
and then put him in charge of his household,
entrusting all his property to him.
Everything flourished under Joseph's care,
for God blessed Potiphar's household
and his possessions and his estate
because Joseph was in charge.
The Egyptian was free of worry
and concerned himself with nothing
beyond the daily food that he ate.
Now Joseph was well-built and handsome,
and after some time
Potiphar's wife was sexually attracted to Joseph
and she set out to seduce him.
"Sleep with me," she whispered to him.

He would not submit to his master's wife
and said these words to her.
"With me in charge of his property,
my master has absolutely no concern
about anything in his house.
He treats me like an equal.
He withholds from me nothing but you, his wife.
How then can I betray him
and sin against my God?"
She kept at Joseph, day after day,
but he would not lie beside her
or consent to be with her.
One day he was working inside the house
and nobody else was present.
She caught hold of his tunic, entreating,
"Come and lie with me."
But he ran from her and in his haste,
left his tunic in her hand.
So she called her servants and said to them,
"See how I have been insulted!
Joseph tried to rape me,
but when I cried out, he ran away
and left this here with me."
Then she held on to his tunic
until her husband had come home.
She told him the same story, saying,
"The Hebrew servant whom you trusted
tried to violate me,
but I cried out and he ran away,
leaving this tunic behind.
See how your servant has treated me!"
When Potiphar heard the words of his wife,
he became enraged, apprehended Joseph,
and threw him into the prison
where those convicted by the king were confined.
And Joseph remained in prison.
But God was there with Joseph
and he became the head guard's favorite.
The official committed to Joseph's care
all those who were imprisoned,
giving him responsibility
for administrating prison affairs.
Because God favored Joseph,
all that he managed prospered.

◇ **Points for Shared Reflection**

- The text insists that God favored Joseph. To what extent does this editorial comment condition our attitude toward Potiphar's wife?

- Desperate women do desperate things. Potiphar's attention had settled on Joseph until his wife intervened. Comment on the part the men played in the indiscretion attributed to Potiphar's wife.

- Have you ever been caught in a compromising situation where everything seemed to suggest you were guilty but you were really innocent? Did anyone believe you? Does anyone believe Joseph? Does anyone believe Potiphar's wife?

- What, if anything, does this particular scripture have to say to us today, or to those instances where women are accused of having seduced men of political, social, and religious prominence?

◇ **A Psalm in Time of Temptation** (see p. 13)

◇ **Prayer**

O God,
Creator of Heaven and Earth,
Holy is Your name.
Holy is Your claim on us.
Holy are Your commandments.
Turn us from our sinful ways.
Turn us to the good.
For Yours is the power
within us,
forever and ever.
Amen.

◇ A PSALM IN TIME OF TEMPTATION ◇

Voice   Remember that I am God.
I brought you out of bondage.
You shall have no other gods.

Chorus   The gods of metal,
the gods of war,
the golden calves of avarice
call out to us
from their pinnacles of power.

All   Deliver us from their seduction, Shaddai.
Keep us from falling under the spell
of temporal deities.

Voice   You shall not quarrel
over My name,
nor name Me to define Me.

Chorus   Father, Mother, Yahweh, Shaddai,
Allah, Elohim, Shekinah:
God is above and beyond all names,
yet mysteriously within them.

All   Deliver us from our theological quarrels
and their seductive influence.
Let us simply praise Your name.

Voice   Remember to keep the sabbath.
Holy is this day.

Chorus   Praise be to God for sabbaticals,
for the soul's solitary sabbath,
for shabbat
and its shalom.

All   Deliver us from our frenetic need
to manipulate the created order.
Help us enter into right relationship
and give us sabbath peace.

Voice   Remember your parents.
Love them.
Just as I, your Mother and Father,
am loving them
and loving you.

Chorus   Mothers and fathers abandon their children
and children abandon their mothers and fathers.
Forgive us, our Mother, our Father.

By M. T. Winter, Crossroad Pub. Co., © 1992 Medical Mission Sisters   *WomanWitness* / 13

All   Deliver us from the need to be delivered
from domestic violence
or misunderstanding.
Bless those who gave us birth.

Voice   You shall not murder anyone.
Hear Me: you shall not kill.

Chorus   Guns, knives, bombs, stones,
words, deeds, silence —
there are all kinds of ways to kill.

All   Deliver us from the many ways
we kill love,
kill relationships,
kill our chances to be a saint.

Voice   You shall not commit adultery.
You shall not sleep with another's spouse.

Chorus   Provocative forces tempt us
with their powers of persuasion.
How can we resist?

All   Deliver us from infatuation,
from the devastating temptation
to violate someone's home.

Voice   You shall not steal.
You shall not take
what does not belong to you.

Chorus   We steal things,
steal time,
steal hearts,
steal away from responsibility:
how easy it is to steal.

All   Deliver us from taking advantage,
from taking over,
taking off,
taking on more than we can handle,
taking it out on someone else,
from taking what does not belong to us.
Taking is really stealing.

Voice   You shall not bear false witness.
You shall not lie about your neighbor.

   By M. T. Winter, Crossroad Pub. Co., © 1992 Medical Mission Sisters

Chorus	Lies and false accusations
	perjure our interactions
	too easily and too often.

| All | Deliver us from deception, |
| | from lies, dishonesty, and deceit. |

| Voice | You shall not covet your neighbor's love. |

| Chorus | If we wish for what we cannot have, |
| | we will not have what we wish for. |

All	Deliver us from illicit desire.
	It will only disturb and destroy us.
	There is nothing at all to gain.

| Voice | You shall not covet your neighbor's treasure. |

| Chorus | If we envy another's goods and goals, |
| | we will not achieve our own. |

All	Deliver us from looking over our shoulder
	at what other people have.
	Help us to be at peace.

Voice	Love God.
	Love one another.
	Do all that God commands.

Chorus	We praise You,
	God of heaven and earth.
	Holy is Your name.

All	Lead us not into temptation,
	but deliver us from evil.
	For Yours is the power and the glory, O God,
	forever and forever.

By M. T. Winter, Crossroad Pub. Co., © 1992 Medical Mission Sisters

SHIPRAH AND PUAH

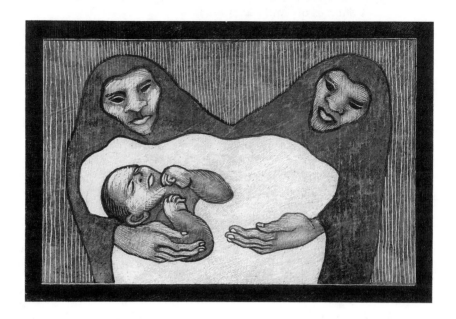

◇ **Scripture Reference**   Ex 1:15–22

◇ **Biography**

Shiprah and Puah were Hebrew midwives in Egypt prior to the Exodus. God-fearing women and mothers themselves, they defied Pharaoh's orders to kill all male babies born to Hebrew women, enabling the Jews to increase in number. They may have delivered Moses.

◇ **Context**

At the height of Pharaoh's persecution of the Hebrews, in order to stem the rapid growth of the people he had enslaved, Pharaoh had ordered that no more male babies were to be allowed to survive. When it became obvious that the order had been ignored, he called the Hebrew midwives together and demanded an explanation. They gave a plausible answer. Hebrew women were capable of delivering on their own and they were hiding their newborn sons. Shiprah and Puah were two of the midwives present. Some commentators assume they were the only midwives, which hardly seems possible given the size of the population and an understanding of the culture, or that they were the only ones present at the audience with Pharaoh, which is one way of interpreting the text. It is also assumed that they were the ones who spoke up, which may be why they were named. Or perhaps they were named because they delivered Moses and let him live. Because of their courage, perhaps both in speaking out as well as in heroic action, God gave families —

16

households — to both Shiprah and Puah, which may mean not only that they were blessed with children of their own but that they became the matriarchs of enduring families in Israel.

◇ **Lectionary Reading**

Pharaoh, king of Egypt,
said to the Hebrew midwives:
"When you are called by the Hebrew women
to assist them in giving birth,
be attentive to the delivery.
If a boy is born, kill him.
If you deliver a girl, let her live."
But the midwives were God-fearing women
and they refused to do as the king commanded,
but let the baby boys live.
Now one of the midwives was named Shiprah
and another was named Puah.
The king summoned the midwives and said,
"Why have you disobeyed my order
and allowed the boys to live?"
And the midwives answered Pharaoh,
"Because the Hebrew women are vigorous,
not like the Egyptian women,
they give birth before the midwife arrives."
So the Hebrew people grew numerous and powerful
and God rewarded the midwives.
Because of their courage and reverence for God,
they were blessed with households of their own.
Then Pharaoh commanded the Egyptians,
"Every boy that is born to a Hebrew woman
must be thrown into the Nile,
but you may let their daughters live."

◇ **Points for Shared Reflection**

- Midwives bring to birth. Shiprah and Puah brought to birth in opposition to the law. What have you midwifed in your public or personal life in opposition to someone or something?

- Reflect on the image of God as a midwife. Can you recall the biblical basis for this image? Is it a meaningful image for you?

- We have traditionally prayed to God to "deliver us from evil." In addition to the liberation or rescue aspects of "deliver," the word also means to bring to birth. Why have we not used this meaning in addressing God? What possibilities does this hold for your own life of prayer?

- In an ironic twist, Pharaoh orders the midwives to let female babies live. In what ways do females ordinarily die? Respond on all levels — physical, spiritual, psychological, social — as well as from your own experience.

◊ **A Psalm of Delivery** (see p. 19)

◊ **Prayer**

Deliver me,
Midwife of my soul,
into those sacred moments
of life
immediately after birth,
when mother and child
are bonded in love
to each other again
and forever.
Hold me close
and sing to me
of the way I was formed in You
and will always be Yours.
Amen.

◇ A PSALM OF DELIVERY ◇

Choir 1   Deliver me, Shaddai,
from the cramped quarters
where my spirit sojourns.

Choir 2   Deliver me into a freedom
where I can be myself and grow.

Choir 1   Deliver me from a dependency
on any but You
Who are my Creator.

Choir 2   Cut the bonds that force me to feed
on another's spirituality.

Choir 1   Deliver me into a brand new day
and into a new beginning,

Choir 2   where heart and mind and soul and spirit
can really start anew.

Choir 1   Deliver me into the wide-open arms
of Your Maternal Presence.

Choir 2   Let me cling to the Source
of my sustenance
until I have had my fill.

Choir 1   Deliver me into a world
that has some answers
to the questions
I have not yet dared to ask.

Choir 2   Deliver me into a household of faith
and an inner security.

Choir 1   Your blood is in my veins, Shaddai,
Your love is the milk
that sustains me.

Choir 2   Your touch is the feel
of the fullness of faith
when the night falls thick around.

Choir 1   I shall not want,
I shall not fear
for I have been within You.

Choir 2   I know You are near,
I feel You here
at home inside of me.

PHARAOH'S DAUGHTER

◇ **Scripture Reference**   Ex 2:1–10

◇ **Biography**

Although Pharaoh, king of Egypt, ordered all Hebrew baby boys to be destroyed at birth, his daughter rescued Moses from his basket in the Nile and raised him in the royal household until he was an adult. This woman, who saw to the survival of the hero of the Exodus, is known to us only as Pharaoh's daughter. Her name, her dynasty, the particular pharaoh who was her father are facts that have been lost to us.

◇ **Context**

Little is known about Pharaoh's daughter beyond the deed that gained her a place in the memory of the people of Israel. She was royalty, a princess, and no doubt had all the material possessions her heart desired. What drew her to adopt the Hebrew baby with all the risk such an act entailed? Did she have no children of her own and did she long for a child? Or was she a mother and therefore acted out of maternal compassion? Was she opposed to her father's edict in general? Did she intervene to save other Hebrew babies? Did she lobby for a change in the law? For a change in her father's attitude? One wonders what became of the law that all the women refused to follow. Pharaoh's daughter is a symbol of one in authority taking initiative to supersede an unjust law. She shows us how those responsible for oppressive structures are the very ones who can turn things around.

◇ **Lectionary Reading**

The Israelites were fruitful and prolific.
They multiplied and grew powerful
and spread over the land of Egypt.
Pharaoh, king of Egypt, said to the Hebrew midwives,
"When you are called by the Hebrew women
to assist them in giving birth,
be attentive to the delivery.
If a boy is born, kill him.
If you deliver a girl, let her live." (Ex 1:7, 15–16)

Now a man from the house of Levi
married a Levite woman
who conceived and bore a son.
When she saw how beautiful her baby was,
she hid him for three months.
When she knew she could hide him no longer,
she procured a papyrus basket,
sealed it with bitumen and pitch,
put her baby in the basket
and set it among the reeds
on the edge of the river Nile.
His sister stood by at a distance
to see what would happen to him.
Pharaoh's daughter came to the river to bathe
while her attendants strolled along its banks.
She saw the basket among the reeds
and sent her maid to fetch it.
She opened the basket and saw the child
and he began to cry.
"This must be one of the Hebrew children," she said,
and she took pity on him.
His sister approached Pharaoh's daughter.
"Shall I find a Hebrew woman
who is able to nurse the child for you?"
"Yes," the woman replied.
So the girl went and got her mother

and brought her to Pharaoh's daughter who said,
"Nurse this child for me
and I will see that you are paid."
So the woman took the child and nursed it.
When the boy grew older,
she brought him to Pharaoh's daughter
who treated him like a son.
She named the young boy Moses,
because "I drew him out of the water."

⬦ **Points for Shared Reflection**

- In various ways women in the text are responsible for the survival of men. Relate this text to your own socio-political or religious situation.

- Have you ever done something forbidden by some law or regulation because you felt you had to do it? Share what you did and why.

- What might happen if women refused to obey all those unjust laws that oppress them? Have you stopped adhering to a particular law or regulation? Which one and why?

- This narrative illustrates how goodness resides in unexpected places, even in the halls of oppression. Do you ever look for good among the oppressors, or the competition, or ones you have personally signed off? Can you name some good you have observed or experienced in one or more of these arenas?

⬦ **A Psalm of Grace in Unexpected Places** (see p. 23)

⬦ **Prayer**

We turn to You,
God Who gives grace in unexpected places,
and You teach us to look
with expectation
for goodness all around.
As we learn to see
through Your eyes,
we are less and less disappointed,
and more and more grateful
that Your grace in us
continues to prevail.
For this we thank You
and praise You.
Amen.

◇ A PSALM OF GRACE IN UNEXPECTED PLACES ◇

Choir 1 Goodness and kindness and grace reside
in unexpected places.

Choir 2 Surely there is one who dares resist
the stereotypes that prevail.

Choir 1 Justice and peace still have a chance
in the chaotic courts of power.

Choir 2 Surely there is one who holds on to hope
when it seems about to fail.

Choir 1 Seeds sprout and sometimes flower
in the wilderness of destruction.

Choir 2 Surely there is one who thrives
though unsupported and alone.

Choir 1 Breasts burst with unused milk
in a world that is weak from famine.

Choir 2 Surely there is one who will feed
just one other child besides her own.

Choir 1 The homeless huddle in doorways
that lead to nowhere, nothing, no one.

Choir 2 Surely there is one who will make
the ones around her feel at home.

Choir 1 Women feel at a loss for life
because their growth is stunted.

Choir 2 Surely there is one who has seen the sun
and the seasons of shalom.

Choir 1 Authority thinks it knows it all
by divine right of succession.

Choir 2 Surely there is one who will one day
call an end to such oppression.

Choir 1 There are many of us who feel
we are afloat on troubled waters.

Choir 2 Survival may depend on
the ingenuity of our daughters.

RAHAB

◇ **Scripture Reference**   Josh 2:1–24; 6:1–2, 15–25

◇ **Biography**

Rahab was a harlot who sheltered two of Joshua's men when they came to spy on Jericho. She defied the king's orders, deceived his soldiers, and helped the Israelites escape to safety. For this act she and her family were spared by Joshua during the destruction of Jericho.

◇ **Context**

Rahab was a prostitute by profession. She had a house in the wall of the city and access to the secrets of the many men who came to sleep with her. What she learned she used to her advantage. When the Israelite spies came to her house, their reputation had preceded them. When the king's soldiers came for the spies, Rahab demonstrated the extent of her resourcefulness in a series of courageous actions. She hid the spies on the roof of her house and told the soldiers they had already gone. She offered the spies a stratagem for survival, extracted a promise of safety for herself and all her family, and helped them escape through a window. Rahab was a remarkable woman. Cunning, quick-witted, assertive, she bargained with spies, lied to soldiers, and took charge of her own life. She professed her faith in Israel's God and put her trust in strangers rather than in her own people and was thereby instrumental in Israel's entering the land of Canaan. She was unmarried and quite capable of looking after herself. She also took charge of seeing to the safety and well-being of all her family members. Matthew lists Rahab in his Davidic genealogy along with Tamar and Ruth, all of whom were foreigners, where she is said to be the mother of Boaz. According to rabbinic tradition, Rahab was an ancestor of eight prophets, including Jeremiah and Huldah. She is one of those biblical women who lied for the faith and for the preservation of the covenant community (see "Women Who Lied for the Faith" by Toni Craven in *Justice and the Holy*, Scholars Press, 1989, pp. 35–49).

◇ **Lectionary Reading**

Joshua son of Nun
secretly sent two spies from Shittim
across the Jordan river, saying,
"Take a look at the land,
especially Jericho."
So they went and spent the night
in the house of a harlot named Rahab.
Word came to the king of Jericho:
"Some Israelite spies are surveying the land."
So the king sent orders to Rahab:
"Bring out the men who have entered your house;
they are spies surveying the land."
But Rahab hid the men and said,
"Indeed they spent some time with me.
I had no idea where they came from.
But when it got dark, the men went out
before they could close the gate to the city.
Where they went from here, I do not know.
Go after them, quickly, you will overtake them."
However, she had hidden them on the roof
among some stalks of flax.
The soldiers set out in swift pursuit,
all the way to the Jordan,
as far as the fords in the river,
and as soon as they had left the city,
the gate was shut behind them.
Before the two Israelites fell asleep on the roof,
Rahab said to them,

"I know that God has given you this land.
Fear has fallen upon us.
We are terrified of you.
For we heard how God went ahead of you
to dry up the waters of the Sea of Reeds
when you came out of Egypt,
and what you did to the kings of the Amorites
who lived beyond the Jordan,
how you utterly destroyed both Sihon and Og.
When word came to us, our hearts melted
and all our courage fled.
Your God is indeed God of heaven and earth.
Now then, since I have been good to you,
swear by your God that you in turn
will be good to me and my family.
Give me a sign of your good faith
that you will spare my father and mother,
sisters and brothers,
and all who belong to them,
and that you will deliver our lives from death."
The two men said to her,
"Our life for yours!
If you do not tell anyone we were here,
we will deal fairly and faithfully with you
when God gives us the land."
Now Rahab's house was at the edge of Jericho
on the outer side of the city wall,
although inside the wall itself.
She helped them descend by rope through a window
and gave them this advice.
"Head for the hills and hide there
until your pursuers have returned.
Stay three days and then go your way."
The men then said to Rahab,
"Do this before we invade the land:
tie a crimson cord in the window
through which you helped us escape;
gather your father and mother
and all your family
and keep them in the house.
If any of you should go outside,
we will be innocent of your death,
but if any are harmed inside this house,
the responsibility is ours.
However, if you reveal any of this,
we will be released from the oath we made."

"So be it," she said, "according to your words."
The Israelites departed,
and Rahab tied a crimson cord in the window
through which they escaped.
The king's soldiers searched the roads,
but clearly the spies had vanished.
When it was safe,
the men came down from the hills,
crossed the river Jordan,
and reported to Joshua son of Nun
everything that had happened.
"Truly God has given the land
into our hands," they told him,
"for all fall in fear before us."

                    ◇

Now Jericho was securely barricaded
against the Israelites.
No one went in and no one came out.
God said to Joshua,
"I will deliver Jericho over to you,
along with its king and soldiers.
All your warriors shall circle the city,
marching around it once, daily,
for six days in a row,
as seven priests carry seven trumpets
of rams' horn before the ark.
On the seventh day
you shall circle the city seven times,
sounding the trumpets as you march."
So on the seventh day the Israelites rose early
and circled the city seven times,
and when the trumpet sounded the seventh time,
Joshua said to the people,
"Sound the battle cry,
for God has said that the city is yours."
Now Joshua had given these orders.
"In the name of God,
Jericho and all that is in it
shall be destroyed.
Only the harlot Rahab
and all who are with her in her house
shall come out of this siege alive,
for she protected our messengers.
Stay away from idolatrous objects.
Do not covet anything that is sure to bring
destruction on Israel's camp.

Silver and gold,
vessels of bronze and vessels of iron
shall go into the sacred treasury,
for they are consecrated to God."
So the trumpet sounded,
the people shouted,
and the walls of Jericho crumbled.
The Israelites stormed into the city
and captured it,
and massacred everyone and everything,
men and women, young and old,
even oxen and sheep and donkeys.
Joshua charged the former spies,
"Go into the harlot's house
and rescue the woman
and all who belong to her,
just as you had promised."
So the two men went and brought Rahab out
with her father and mother,
her sisters and brothers,
and all who belonged to her,
and they set them outside the camp of Israel,
and they burned the city down.
Everything in it was utterly destroyed.
Only the silver and gold,
the bronze and iron,
were salvaged for the sacred treasury.
And Rahab the harlot,
her family and all who belonged to her,
these alone Joshua spared,
for she protected the messengers
Joshua sent to spy on Jericho.

◇ **Points for Shared Reflection**

- Rahab the prostitute figures prominently and positively in the biblical tradition. Do you find that surprising? Why? And why is her story so important?

- What are the qualities exhibited by Rahab that women today would do well to imitate?

- Do you categorically dismiss prostitutes as a class of people? Have you ever been friends with one? What does Rahab's story have to say about the dangers of class prejudice?

- Do you think it is acceptable to lie for religious reasons? Can you give an example of when this might be legitimate?

◇ **A Psalm about One Brave Woman** (see p. 30)

◇ **Prayer**

Who are the brave,
O Strength of Warriors,
except those who grow strong in You,
except those who belong to You
and have learned to lean on Your power.
The mission to which we are called
and commissioned
requires more than we have
within us
and more than we understand.
Strengthen us and inform us
so that we might do
what needs to be done,
today and always.
Amen.

◇ A PSALM ABOUT ONE BRAVE WOMAN ◇

Voice   One brave woman
can change the course of history.

Choir 1   She is unafraid
to wage peace
in place of wars of conquest.

Choir 2   She is swift
to know and name the facts,
to question the way it always is,
to lift herstory from the ancient annals
of anonymity.

All   Make us brave enough, Shaddai,
to challenge our history.

Voice   One brave woman
can change the course of theology.

Choir 1   She sees herself
in the image of God
Whose power pushes the least to life,
Whose mercy measures a just response,
Who loves beyond the limits,
Who is visible and decisive.

Choir 2   She speaks of a God
she knows by name
and faithfully follows
her Spirit's lead
beyond and above all textual claims,
all ritual traditions.

All   Make us brave enough, Shaddai,
to challenge theology.

Voice   One brave woman
can change the course of spirituality.

Choir 1   She knows what prayer
is all about,
she comes at life
from the inside out.

Choir 2   She does not dwell
on introspection
nor try to match some other path
or feel compelled
to seek direction,

    By M. T. Winter, Crossroad Pub. Co., © 1992 Medical Mission Sisters

but tastes what is and what will be
from the Source within,
the Mystery.

All   Make us brave enough, Shaddai,
to challenge spirituality.

Voice   One brave woman
can change our relationship to creation.

Choir 1   In the beginning
one woman rose from sleep
to tend her Garden gifts
in a paradise
not of her making.

Choir 2   Woman knows
how her garden grows,
what it takes to bring to life,
how it hurts to be raped and razed
and forced to submit to domination,
so she will reach down deep inside
to bring about the new creation.

All   Make us brave enough, Shaddai,
to challenge our relationship to creation.

Voice   One brave woman
can change the way we order our world.

Choir 1   She who clothes
her naked baby,
feeds her child from within herself,
makes sheltered space
in her loving arms
for utter helplessness,
cannot pretend
such basic necessities do not extend
to all of God's creation.

Choir 2   Her love would have people
off the street
and given shelter
and something to eat,
for true compassion
knows no defeat
but only a new beginning.

All   Make us brave enough, Shaddai,
to challenge the ways of our world.

DEBORAH

◇ **Scripture Reference** Judg 4:1–22; 5:1–31

◇ **Biography**

Deborah was a judge, a warrior, and a prophet in Israel during the time of the judges. She was also a singer of songs. She lived in the "hill country" of Ephraim and was the wife of Lappidoth. Scripture records her heroic stance against the Canaanite army and attests to her stature among the people.

◇ **Context**

The biblical account of Deborah is remarkable for a number of reasons. Deborah was a judge, a warrior, a prophet, and a leader of song. As a woman, her competency in several of these arenas and her visibility in the public sector offer a new perspective to tradition. Moreover, the ease with which her accomplishments are recounted suggest that women may have been more active in these contexts than the literature implies. The period of the judges in ancient Israel extended from the death of Joshua after the Israelites had settled in the land of Canaan to the institution of a monarchy with the anointing of Saul as king. The term "judges" is not to be interpreted in a legal sense but rather as a designation for heroes and a heroine upon whom the spirit of God rested and whose temporary rule was not necessarily supported by all the tribes of the federation.

Deborah combined three important offices. She exercised legal functions, she was a military leader, and she was a channel for prophetic oracles. Deborah was unique among the judges, not only because she was a woman, but also because she was the only judge who actually exercised a judicial function (4:5). She was a national leader, "judging Israel" (4:4), a "mother in Israel" (5:7). She promoted a war of liberation, the only war against Canaanite oppression described in the Book of Judges and possibly Israel's last campaign against the Canaanites. It was not a war of isolated tribes but a war of national deliverance carried out by volunteers. The victory was woman's victory, brought about by Deborah and Jael, the woman who killed the Canaanite commander.

The song of Deborah is among the earliest of Hebrew heroic poems, and although it is attributed to both Deborah and Barak, the presence of many female images has led scholars to acknowledge that the author was a woman. It is a victory song similar to Psalm 68, which it seems to have influenced, and is related in style, spirit, and content to Miriam's "Song of the Sea" in Exodus (chap. 15), which has been attributed to Moses.

Deborah seems to have been a woman of wealth, enabling her to dispense justice apparently without remuneration. In a complete reversal of the norm, her husband is named without a single descriptive word about him. This has led to speculation that *'eshet lappidot* may not mean "wife of Lappidoth" but rather "spirited woman."

◇ **Lectionary Reading**

The Israelites again sinned before God,
so God gave the Canaanite king, Jabin,
dominion over them.
Sisera commanded his army.
He lived in Harosheth-ha-goiim.
He had nine hundred chariots of iron,
and for twenty years
he had cruelly oppressed the Israelites
who cried out to God for deliverance.
At that time Deborah, a prophet,
was judge in Israel.
She was the wife of Lappidoth.
She used to sit under the palm of Deborah
between Ramah and Bethel

in the hill country of Ephraim,
and the people would come to her for judgment.
She summoned Barak son of Abinoam
from Kedesh in Naphtali and said,
"The God of Israel commands you,
'Go, take ten thousand men
from the tribes of Naphtali and Zebulun
and position yourself at Mount Tabor.
I will draw out Sisera, general of Jabin's army,
and force him to face you by the Wadi Kishon
with his chariots and his troops,
and I will hand him over to you.'"
Barak said to Deborah,
"If you go with me, I will go;
if you do not go with me, I will not go."
And she said, "Indeed, I will go with you,
but what lies ahead of you will not lead to your glory,
for God will deliver Sisera
into the hands of a woman."
Then Deborah went with Barak to Kedesh
where Barak summoned Zebulun and Naphtali.
Ten thousand warriors joined him,
and Deborah marched with him.
When Sisera heard that Barak son of Abinoam
had gone up to Mount Tabor,
he called out all his chariots,
nine hundred chariots of iron,
and all the troops who were with him.
Then Deborah said to Barak,
"This is the day God will deliver Sisera into your hands.
Go forward! God goes before you!"
So Barak took ten thousand warriors
and moved out from Mount Tabor.
Sisera, his chariots, and all of his army
were thrown into a panic.
Sisera left his chariot and fled,
while Barak pursued the rest of the forces
to Harosheth-ha-goiim,
where all of Sisera's army was slain.
Not a single man escaped.
Now Sisera had fled on foot
and he sought asylum in the tent of Jael
the wife of Heber the Kenite,
for there was peace between King Jabin of Hazor
and Heber the Kenite's clan.
Jael came out to meet Sisera and said,

"Stay here with me, my lord,
you are safe. Do not fear.
Stay here with me."
So he stayed with her in her tent
and she covered him with a rug.
"I am thirsty," he said,
"please give me some water."
So she opened a skin of milk,
gave him a drink,
then covered him up again.
"Stand at the entrance to the tent," he said,
"and if someone should ask,
'Is anyone here?'
say, 'No.'"
Then he fell asleep,
for he was utterly exhausted.
Jael took a tent peg
and a hammer,
went softly to the side of Sisera
and drove the tent peg into his temple,
right through to the ground.
When Barak came in search of Sisera,
Jael went out to meet him and said,
"Come and I will show you
the man whom you are seeking."
Inside her tent he saw Sisera, dead,
with a tent peg through his temple.
Then Deborah sang this song that day,
accompanied by Barak.

DEBORAH'S PSALM

The shofar sounded the call to arms,
but the soldiers delayed too long;
so the people willingly offered themselves
and sang the warrior's song.

Why so slow, O clans of Reuben?
Did you linger among your herds
to hear the sounds of the shepherd's pipe
or to wage a war with words?

Gilead stayed beyond the Jordan,
Dan remained at sea,
and Asher sat in its harbors,
safe in its own security,
but Zebulun confronted death,
and so did Naphtali.

Word went out: war is at hand,
destruction is drawing near;
and yet, from the might of Israel,
not a single shield or spear.

Loud the hoofs of the horses
of the galloping, galloping steeds;
yet where were Israel's mighty ones,
and all their valiant deeds?

The people themselves marched down to the gates.
They came from near and far —
peasants from Ephraim and Benjamin,
princes from Issachar.

Faithful to Deborah and to Barak,
the peasants, with staff and rod,
marched against the militia,
marched for freedom, marched for God.

Earth trembled, heaven shook,
and clouds overflowed; they tell
how mountains melted as people marched
in defense of Israel.

They fought in the region of Taanach,
by the waters of Megiddo,
and received no spoils; the stars of heaven
insist that this is so.

The torrent of Kishon
swept the fallen away into the night,
while the peasants sang of victory
and marched with all their might.

For Deborah arose, a leader arose
as mother in Israel.
Sing of women warriors,
of Deborah and Jael.

Awake, Deborah! Awake! Hear us!
Awake and sing a song!
Arise and lead the captives away,
for the weak overtake the strong.

Sing of it, you passers-by
in carpeted caravans,
and you who walk along the way —
sing a song of the clans.

Sing to the sound of musicians,
sing at every village well
of the triumph of simple people
in liberating Israel.

Travelers had kept to the byways,
caravans had ceased to buy and sell
in the days of the peasant army,
in the days of the brave Jael.

Blessed be Jael among women,
among tent-dwelling women most blessed,
for Sisera sought sanctuary;
she offered eternal rest.

He asked for water, she gave him milk,
brought cream in an ornate bowl,
then seized the worker's mallet,
pulled a tent peg from a pole
and struck Sisera, pierced his temple
with a smashing blow to his head,
and he fell,
fell at her feet,
lay at her feet where he fell,
dead.

Sisera's mother sat at the window
wondering, day after day,
"Why is his chariot so slow? Tell me,
why do his horses delay?"

The woman answers herself.
She says: "The long delay is for
dividing the booty among the victors,
dividing the spoils of war.
A girl or two for every man,
a garment or two for my son,
an embroidered scarf, two scarves for me!
Something for everyone."

Deborah sang this song that day,
telling how Israel
was defended by its people
who fought valiantly, and well,
was liberated, by the grace of God,
through Deborah and Jael.

◇ **Points for Shared Reflection**

- Deborah was a judge who dispensed justice and gave good counsel. Name instances in which women today are called upon to do the same. Tell the story of one recent heroine who functioned in this way.

- Deborah was a warrior who exercised military leadership and traveled with the troops. How do you feel about women in military service today, and why?

- Deborah was a prophet who spoke the word that God revealed to her. Name some prophetic roles to which women are called today, to which you are called today. Are you able to function in the arena to which you are called? If not, why not?

- Deborah exercised a ministry of music. Describe the ways in which music ministers to you. If you are a musician, describe how music is or can be your ministry to others.

◇ **A Psalm for the Gift of Counsel** (see p. 39)

◇ **Prayer**

Make us wise in Your ways,
O One Who judges all with justice.
May we guide
and give good counsel
to those who present themselves to us
on their journey home to You,
and give voice to the vision
Your word evokes
and Your love verifies.
Praise be to You
forever and ever.
Amen.

◇ A PSALM FOR THE GIFT OF COUNSEL ◇

Leader   We celebrate the witness of women,
women who gave good counsel,
women who give good counsel
in public life,
institutional life,
in politics,
academics,
medicine,
religion,
and corporate industry.

All   We pray for the gift of counsel
to be given to ourselves.

Choir 1   We praise You, God,
for the witness of women today
and throughout the ages.

Choir 2   We sing of Deborah
and all other women
who gave and give good counsel,

Choir 1   women judges and women on juries,

Choir 2   women lawyers and women employers,

Choir 1   women in congress, governors, mayors,
and all civic leaders today,

Choir 2   women who are socially responsible,
women who are corporately accountable,

Choir 1   women scholars, instructors, coaches, advisors,
and all who are engaged in research,

Choir 2   women bishops, preachers, priests, teachers,
ministers, counselors, caregivers,

Choir 1   women physicians, musicians, analysts, panelists,
journalists, and media people,

Choir 2   women executives, administrators, producers, directors,
inspectors, and supervisory personnel.

All   May all in the public sector
be blessed with the gift of counsel.
May we too give good counsel
in the roles of our public lives.

By M. T. Winter, Crossroad Pub. Co., © 1992 Medical Mission Sisters   *WomanWitness* / **39**

Leader	We celebrate the witness of women,
	women who gave good counsel,
	women who give good counsel
	in personal life,
	in domestic life.

| All | We pray for the gift of counsel |
| | to be given to ourselves. |

Choir 1	We praise You, God,
	for the witness of women
	who gave and give good counsel.

Choir 2	We celebrate
	all those domestic roles
	that support, affirm, and nourish,
	in which advice and counsel flourish,
	on which our world depends.

Choir 1	We celebrate mothers
	and significant others
	concerned with raising children.

Choir 2	We celebrate wives
	who guide men's lives
	and all who partner another.

Choir 1	We celebrate all within the web
	of family relationship:
	great grandmother, grandmother, mother-in-law,
	sister, cousin, sister-in-law
	aunt, niece, daughter-in-law,
	daughter, granddaughter,
	godmother, goddaughter,
	nanny, nurse, and friend.

| Choir 2 | We celebrate all who assess and advise |
| | with wise acuity. |

All	May all in domestic circles
	be blessed with the gift of counsel.
	May we too give good counsel
	in the roles of our personal lives.

    By M. T. Winter, Crossroad Pub. Co., © 1992 Medical Mission Sisters

JAEL

◇ **Scripture Reference**   Judg 4:1–3, 14–22; 5:1, 6, 24–27

◇ **Biography**

Jael, wife of Heber the Kenite, is remembered for an act of heroism during the time of the judges. She enticed Sisera the general of the Canaanite army to seek refuge in her tent, then drove a tent peg through his skull. Her deed was celebrated throughout Israel.

◇ **Context**

The Kenites were a semi-nomadic tribe with longstanding ties to the Israelites and, at the same time, on good terms with the Canaanites. Jael's husband was descended from Jethro, the father-in-law of Moses, but his clan seems to have been allied to Jabin, Israel's enemy, which is why Sisera felt free to seek refuge there. Politically, Jael's action implies a switch of loyalties back to Israel. The narrative itself catches us by surprise. It begins with some typically female actions. Jael offers asylum

41

to an ally who is cornered and in danger of death, the commander of the Canaanite forces with whom she and her husband have no quarrel. She makes him welcome and comfortable. She is hospitable, encouraging, consoling, reassuring. She gives him nourishment. She insists that he get some rest. When he falls asleep exhausted, she goes over to his bed, and nails him. With a tent peg. Right through the skull. One interpretation of this event, taken from the text of the song, suggests that Jael, whose name means "mountain goat," was a Bedouin woman who offered the fugitive a bowl of milk, a sign of nomadic hospitality, then struck Sisera down as he bent over the bowl to drink. The prose passage identifies Jael as the wife of Heber the Kenite and sketches a different scenario. According to a talmudic tractate, Jael's action teaches us that a transgression performed with good intent is more meritorious than a commandment performed with no intent. If it were not for her action, the children of the matriarchs would have been destroyed.

◇ **Lectionary Reading**

The Israelites again
sinned before God,
so God gave the Canaanite king, Jabin,
dominion over them.
Sisera commanded his army.
He had nine hundred chariots of iron,
and for twenty years
he had cruelly oppressed the Israelites
who cried out to God for deliverance.
Then Deborah said to Barak,
"This is the day on which God has given Sisera into your hands.
Go forward! God goes before you!"
So Barak took ten thousand warriors
and moved out from Mount Tabor.
Sisera, his chariots, and all of his army
were thrown into a panic.
Sisera left his chariot and fled,
while Barak pursued the rest of the forces
to Harosheth-ha-goiim,
where all of Sisera's army was slain.
Not a single man escaped.
Now Sisera had fled on foot
and he sought asylum in the tent of Jael
the wife of Heber the Kenite,
for there was peace between King Jabin of Hazor
and Heber the Kenite's clan.
Jael came out to meet Sisera and said,
"Stay here with me, my lord,

you are safe. Do not fear.
Stay here with me."
So he stayed with her in her tent
and she covered him with a rug.
"I am thirsty," he said,
"please give me some water."
So she opened a skin of milk,
gave him a drink,
then covered him up again.
"Stand at the entrance to the tent," he said,
"and if someone should ask,
'Is anyone here?'
say, 'No.' "
Then he fell asleep,
for he was utterly exhausted.
Jael took a tent peg
and a hammer,
went softly to the side of Sisera
and drove the tent peg into his temple,
right through to the ground.
When Barak came in search of Sisera,
Jael went out to meet him and said,
"Come and I will show you
the man whom you are seeking."
Inside her tent he saw Sisera, dead,
with a tent peg through his temple.

        ◇

Then Deborah sang this song that day,
accompanied by Barak:

Blessed be Jael among women,
among tent-dwelling women most blessed,
for Sisera sought sanctuary;
she offered eternal rest.
He asked for water, she gave him milk,
brought cream in an ornate bowl,
then seized the worker's mallet,
pulled a tent peg from a pole
and struck Sisera, pierced his temple
with a smashing blow to his head
and he fell, fell at her feet,
lay at her feet where he fell, dead.

◇ **Points for Shared Reflection**

- We are more accustomed to hearing about violence done to women than by women. How do you feel about Jael's action?

- Would such an action ever be permissible for women today? If so, when and why?

- Jael took action against someone with whom her husband was politically allied. In what ways do you differ politically from your husband or your partner, your family or your best friend?

- Discuss the rabbinic teaching: a transgression performed with good intent is more meritorious than a commandment performed with no intent. Do you agree or disagree?

◇ **A Psalm of Heroic Action** (see p. 45)

◇ **Prayer**

Holy are You,
Heroine of all who hope
and all who suffer.
Powerful is the two-edged sword
embedded in Your sacred word,
setting captives free.
Fear-ridden souls find courage
and rise to heroic action
in the strength
that flows abundantly
from promise and prophecy.
Be with us here,
be with us now
as we do what we can
and more than we dare
to lift the load of oppression
that is breaking the back
of so many faithful followers
of Your way.
This we pray.
Amen.

◇ A PSALM OF HEROIC ACTION ◇

Choir 1 Here's to the woman warrior
who liberates those held captive
by the threat of evil forces.

Choir 2 Here's to the one with courage enough
to garner the strength of angels
in a desire to overcome.

Choir 1 Woe to the one who stereotypes
the elusive female gender.

Choir 2 Woe to the world that turns its back
on a smoldering female force.

Choir 1 Holy the hand that holds the sword
of justice and liberation.

Choir 2 Holy the heart that takes its stand
in the midst of the oppressed.

Choir 1 Beware, you who go down in tents
to the battlefields of annihilation.

Choir 2 Beware, you who go into tents
to seduce the children of light.

Choir 1 Blessed are you who try to prevent
the destruction of cherished values
and the loss of liberty.

Choir 2 Blessed are you who see and act
without any hesitation
to redress unmerited injury.

Choir 1 Praise to the slayers of demons.
May the tears of all the victims
purge culpability for the dead.

Choir 2 Praise to all our heroines.
May the milk of life revitalize
the blood that has been shed.

By M. T. Winter, Crossroad Pub. Co., © 1992 Medical Mission Sisters

DELILAH

◇ **Scripture Reference**   Judg 16:4–31

◇ **Biography**

Delilah was Samson's lover and the cause of his undoing. His legendary strength was hardly a match for her persuasive wiles. She was from the Sorek Valley just west of Jerusalem and was probably a Philistine.

◇ **Context**

The story of Delilah is interwoven with the story of Samson, an early Israelite hero whom tradition honors as a judge. He was a man of Herculean strength whose exploits arose more from personal vendettas than from any national concern. Samson and Delilah are legendary. She has been depicted as the woman who seduced the man of God, accepted money from his enemies to extract from him the secret of his physical prowess, then weakened him and betrayed him to imprisonment and death. The story may well be told another way. Samson was no gentle giant. Before he met Delilah, he had already wreaked havoc on the Philistine community, killing vast numbers in irrational outbursts driven by an insatiable need for revenge. We do not really know how Samson got involved with Delilah, if he came to her or if she had first come to him. We do not really know how she felt about him. The text says that he loved her. She may not have intended to set him up for death; she may have wanted only to subdue him, to make him human like everyone else, to remove a threat of violence from the local community, to make a little money to support herself. It seems unlikely she had a family of her own. Delilah is intriguing. After the episode with Samson, she is never heard from again.

◇ **Lectionary Reading**

Samson fell in love with a woman
from the valley of Sorek.
Her name was Delilah.
Philistine leaders approached her and said,
"Find out the source of his strength
so that we might overpower him
and subdue him.
Coax his secret from him
and each of us will give you
eleven hundred pieces of silver."
So Delilah said to Samson,
"Please tell me the secret of your strength.
How might someone overpower you
so that you might be subdued?"
Samson answered her,
"Bind me with seven new bowstrings,
ones that are not yet dry,
and I shall be like anyone else."
The Philistines gave Delilah
seven new bowstrings not yet dry,
and she went and bound Samson with them.
But Samson snapped the bowstrings
like fire snaps a strand of fiber,
and his secret remained unknown.
Then Delilah said to Samson,
"You have mocked me,
for you have lied to me.
Please tell me how you might be subdued."
Samson said to her,
"Bind me with new ropes
that have never been used,
and I shall be like anyone else."

So Delilah bound Samson with new ropes, saying,
"Samson, the Philistines are at the door!"
They were actually hiding in another room.
He snapped the ropes from his arms like thread,
and his secret remained unknown.
Then Delilah said to Samson,
"Still you mock me and tell me lies.
How is it then that you might be subdued?"
And Samson said to Delilah,
"Weave a web of seven locks of my hair
and fasten it tight with a pin,
and I shall be like anyone else."
So while he slept,
Delilah wove a web of his hair,
fastened the seven locks with a pin,
then wakened him, shouting,
"Samson, the Philistines are at the door!"
He awoke from his sleep,
removed the pin, loosened his locks,
and his secret remained unknown.
Then Delilah said to Samson,
"How can you say, 'I love you,'
when your heart is hidden from me?
Three times now you have mocked me
by not revealing the source of your strength."
She nagged him and pestered him, day after day,
until finally, weary to death of her words,
he shared his secret with her, saying,
"A razor has never touched my head,
for I am a nazirite,
consecrated to God from my mother's womb.
If my head were shaved,
my strength would leave me,
and I would be like anyone else."
Delilah knew this time he had told the truth,
so she sent for the Philistine leaders and said,
"He has shared with me the secret of his strength."
They gave her the money they had promised her.
Delilah lulled Samson to sleep on her lap,
then she called someone to shave his locks.
They cut off the source of Samson's strength
and Samson's body weakened
and he became like everyone else.
Then Delilah said,
"Samson, the Philistines are here!"
He awoke and proceeded to shake himself free,

but the strength of God had left him.
So the Philistines seized him,
gouged out his eyes,
shackled him with chains of bronze,
and imprisoned him in Gaza,
where he worked at the prison mill.
But the hair of his head
began to grow again
after it had been shaved.
Now the Philistine leaders
gathered together
to offer sacrifice and to rejoice.
"Our god Dagon has delivered Samson our enemy
into our hand," they said.
When the people saw him,
they praised their god.
"The ravager of our country,
the one who has killed so many of us,
has been delivered into our hand."
When their hearts were merry, they said,
"Call Samson, and let him entertain us."
So they had Samson perform for them.
They stood him between two pillars.
"Let me feel the pillars on which the house rests,
so that I might lean against them,"
Samson said to his attendant.
Now the house was filled with men and women,
and all the leaders of the Philistines were there.
On the roof about three thousand persons
watched Samson perform.
Then Samson called upon God and said,
"O God, remember me,
and strengthen me one more time,
so that I may perform one act of revenge
to repay the Philistines for my two eyes."
Then Samson grasped the middle pillars
on which the whole house rested,
and he leaned his weight against them,
his right hand on the one pillar
and his left hand on the other.
Then Samson said,
"Let me die with the Philistines."
He stretched and strained with all his strength
and the house came crumbling down.
It fell on the leaders and all the people
who had assembled there.

So those Samson killed at his death
were more than he killed in his lifetime.
Then his family came and took him away
and they buried him with his father.
He had judged Israel twenty years.

◇ **Points for Shared Reflection**

- Delilah sought to know the source of Samson's strength and, in the process, probably discovered the source of her own. What is the source of your strength?

- Delilah sought ways in which brute force might be subdued. Name the demon in your life that needs to be subdued. What must you do to restrain it?

- Women usually lift up the men in their lives. Delilah brought her man down. What are the ways in which you empower and disempower the men in your public and personal life?

- Delilah and Samson had a communications problem, not unusual between women and men. What is your communications problem with one or more of the men in your life and what is needed to overcome it?

◇ **A Psalm about Sharing Secrets** (see p. 51)

◇ **Prayer**

You are the secret of my strength
and the source of my achievement,
O Power Beyond and Within Me,
and nothing on earth
or apart from earth
can take You away from me.
Promise me now
that You will maintain
and sustain me
in Your inspiration,
so that all that I speak,
all that I write
flows out of the word
that is You,
living and loving,
now and forever.
Amen.

◇ A PSALM ABOUT SHARING SECRETS ◇

Choir 1 Tell me the secret of your strength,
O trees of the field and forest.

Choir 2 How deep are the roots you are grounded by?
How do you keep from going dry?
How long will it take till you touch the sky?

All God of trees
and God of me,
sink my roots deep down in Your Being,
sustain me by grace
and give me a vision
that far exceeds my petulant grasp,
so I may be more like You.

Choir 1 Tell me the secret of your strength,
O waters of creation.

Choir 2 How long is your river? How deep is your ocean?
Why is your brook in perpetual motion?
Where is the wellspring of your devotion?

All God of the springs
and God of me,
wash me in Your living waters,
slake my thirst
and cleanse my wounds
and refresh my arid spirit,
so that I may be more like You.

Choir 1 Tell me the secret of your strength,
O wind and airborne currents.

Choir 2 How does the breath of being form?
What is the source of a tropical storm?
Why are you cold and why are you warm?

All God of the winds
and God of me,
blow through me now
with Your sacred breath
and let Your grace resound in my being,
so that I may be more like You.

Choir 1 Share the secret of Your strength,
Creator of all beings.

Choir 2 You are the secret of my strength.
Make me more like you.

By M. T. Winter, Crossroad Pub. Co., © 1992 Medical Mission Sisters

RUTH AND NAOMI

◇ **Scripture Reference**   The Book of Ruth

◇ **Biography**

During the time of the judges, Naomi with her husband, Elimelech, and her two sons, Mahlon and Chilion, emigrated from Bethlehem in Judah to Moab in a period of famine. Elimelech died and the sons took Moabite wives. Mahlon married Ruth and Chilion married Orpah. Ten years later the sons died, leaving both of their widows childless. When Naomi set out to return to her country, Ruth accompanied her to Bethlehem where she married Boaz, her husband's relative, and gave birth to Obed, the grandfather of David.

◇ **Context**

The Book of Ruth is an artfully constructed historical short story that links the time of the judges to the beginning of the monarchy. It is the story of Ruth, the great grandmother of David, and it is essentially a story of relationship and loving kindness. The Syriac spelling of Ruth's name suggests "friend, companion" and a Hebrew derivation comes from the root word to "be satisfied," "refreshed." The story reflects an openness to the wider world and an acceptance of other cultures, for Ruth was a Moabite who married into a family from Judah, then chose to leave the family, culture, and religion of her birth to remain with her mother-in-law, who loved her as a daughter. Ruth's devotion to Naomi was rewarded with a rich new life according to the rabbinic teaching: "how great is the reward that accrues to those who perform kindly deeds" (Midrash Rabbah, Ruth II.14). Despite her alien origins, Ruth was accepted in Israel and married into the ancestry of David. She is listed in the Matthean genealogy of Jesus (1:5). Naomi, the image of the ideal mother-in-law, cared passionately about the women who married her sons and wanted only what was best for them. For this she too was richly rewarded. She was provided for by a loving daughter-in-law whose son was like a son of her own. The women of Bethlehem rejoiced with Naomi, saying Ruth was of more value to her than seven sons.

◇ **Lectionary Reading**

In the days when the judges ruled,
there was a famine in the land.
A certain man of Bethlehem in Judah
went to live in the land of Moab
with his wife and his two sons.
The man's name was Elimelech
and his wife's name was Naomi.
The names of his sons were Mahlon and Chilion.
Elimelech died in Moab,
and his sons took Moabite wives.
One of the wives was named Orpah;
the name of the other was Ruth.
They had lived there together about ten years
when Mahlon and Chilion died,
leaving Naomi without a husband and sons.
She prepared to return
with her daughters-in-law
to the country from which she had come,
for word was about in Moab
that the famine had come to an end.
They began the journey together,
and on the way to the land of Judah,
Naomi said to her daughters-in-law:
"Go back now to your mother's house,
and may God deal kindly with you,
as you have dealt with my sons and me.

May God grant you security
with a husband of your own."
Then she kissed them and they wept,
and the women said to her,
"We will go with you to your people."
But Naomi said, "Turn back, my daughters.
Why will you go with me?
Do you think I still have sons in my womb
that might become your husbands?
Turn back, my daughters, and go your way.
I am too old to marry again.
Even if I thought there was such a hope,
would you wait until my sons were grown?
Would you then refrain from marrying?
No, my daughters, life has been bitter,
for me more than for you,
because God's hand has turned against me."
The three women wept again.
Then Orpah kissed her mother-in-law
and returned to her own people.
Ruth, however, held on to her,
committing herself to Naomi.
"Do not insist that I leave you
or cease from following you.
Wherever you go, I will go.
Wherever you live, I will live.
Your people will be my people.
Your God will be my God.
Wherever you die, I will die,
and there I too will be buried.
Death shall not part me from you."
When Naomi saw how determined she was,
she said no more to her.
Together they traveled to Bethlehem
and they set the whole town talking.
"Is this Naomi?" the women said,
and Naomi responded to them:
"Call me not Naomi, which means Pleasant,
but call me Mara, which means Bitter,
for God has dealt bitterly with me.
I went away full and I return home empty.
So why call me Naomi
when God has dealt so harshly with me
and brought such calamity upon me?"
So Naomi and Ruth, her daughter-in-law,
came back from the country of Moab

and settled down in Bethlehem
at barley harvest time.

Naomi had a relative on her husband's side,
a prominent man named Boaz,
a man of considerable wealth.
Ruth said to Naomi,
"Let me go to the field and glean the grain
in the footsteps of one who will favor me."
Naomi said, "Go, my daughter."
So Ruth gleaned behind the reapers,
and it just so happened
that she came to that part of the field
that belonged to Boaz
and Boaz just happened to be there.
He said to his reapers, "God be with you,"
and they answered, "May God bless you."
He said to his servant in charge of the reapers,
"To whom does this woman belong?"
He answered,
"She is the Moabite
who returned here with Naomi.
She said to me,
'Please, let me glean among the sheaves,
let me follow behind the reapers.'
And she has been working tirelessly
since very early this morning
and has taken no time to rest."
Then Boaz said to Ruth,
"Listen to me, my daughter.
Do not go to glean in another field.
Stay here among my women.
Wherever the reapers are at work in the field,
follow close behind them.
I have instructed my men not to bother you.
And if you are thirsty, go to the pitchers
and drink what the men have drawn."
Then Ruth bowed with her face to the ground,
and said, "Who am I, a foreigner,
that you should favor me?"
And Boaz answered her,
"All you have done for your mother-in-law
since your husband's death
has been told to me,
how you left your mother and father,
how you left the land of your birth

to come to a land you do not know.
May God richly reward you,
the God of Israel to whom you have come
to find shelter beneath Her wings."
Then Ruth responded,
"May I continue to find favor with you, my lord,
for you have comforted me
and you speak kindly to your servant,
even though I am not one of yours."
At mealtime Boaz said to Ruth,
"Come, eat some bread,
have a bit of wine."
So she sat beside the reapers,
and he filled her dish with roasted grain
and she ate till she could eat no more.
When she left to glean,
Boaz gave this instruction to his men,
"Let her glean among the standing sheaves,
and do not try to stop her,
and drop some stalks from the bundled sheaves
and leave them for her to glean."
Ruth gleaned the field until evening.
When she beat out and gathered what she had gleaned,
she had quite a bit of barley.
She shared it with her mother-in-law,
who said, on seeing how much she had,
"Where did you glean today?
Blessed is the man who took notice of you."
Ruth told her all that had happened and said,
"The name of the man is Boaz."
Then Naomi said to her daughter-in-law,
"Blessed be God, whose kindness
has not forsaken the living or the dead.
The man you met is a relative,
one of our nearest of kin."
Then Ruth said to Naomi,
"He even said,
'Stay with my servants
until all my harvest is done.'"
Naomi advised her daughter-in-law,
"Stay with his women, my daughter.
There is danger of being molested
if you move to another field."
So Ruth remained close to the women of Boaz,
gleaning beside them daily,
until the barley harvest and wheat harvest

finally came to an end.
And she lived with her mother-in-law.

Naomi said to her daughter-in-law,
"It is my duty to see that your future is secure.
Now here is our relative Boaz
with whose women you have been working.
He will be winnowing barley tonight
and will sleep on the threshing floor.
Go now and wash and anoint yourself
and dress in your nicest clothes,
but conceal yourself from Boaz
until he finishes eating and drinking.
Note where he lies when he falls asleep,
then go, uncover his feet, and lie down.
He will tell you what to do."
"I will do whatever you tell me," she said.
So Ruth went down to the threshing floor,
just as Naomi had instructed.
When Boaz had finished his food and drink
and was thoroughly contented,
he fell asleep beside a heap of grain.
Quietly, Ruth uncovered his feet
and lay there as instructed.
At midnight Boaz awoke, startled to see a woman
lying there at his feet.
"Who are you?" he asked.
And she answered, "I am Ruth.
Spread your cloak over your servant,
for you are next-of-kin."
Then Boaz said to Ruth the Moabite,
"May you be blessed by God, my daughter.
For this last act of kindness
is even greater than the first.
You have not looked for younger men,
whether they were rich or poor.
Do not be afraid, I will do for you
everything you ask,
for all the people with me know
what a wonderful woman you are.
Although I am a relative,
there is one more closely related than I.
Stay tonight, and in the morning,
should he come forth to claim you,
let him exercise his right,
but if he is unwilling,

then as God lives, as next of kin,
I will take you home with me.
Lie down now until morning."
So Ruth lay at his feet until morning,
but arose to leave while it was still dark
so that she would not be recognized,
and none would know
that she, a woman, had spent the night
asleep on the threshing floor.
As she was leaving, Boaz said,
"Hold out the cloak you are wearing."
She did and he filled it full of barley,
helped her place it on her back,
and watched as she headed home.
Naomi asked her daughter-in-law,
"How did it go last night?"
Then she told her what Boaz had said and done
and showed her the cloak full of barley.
"Be patient, my daughter," Naomi said,
"he will settle the matter today."

Boaz went down to the city gate,
and as soon as he was settled there,
the next-of-kin of whom he had spoken to Ruth
came passing by.
He said,
"Come here, my friend, sit down with me,"
and summoned ten elders to sit with them.
"Naomi has returned from Moab,
and she is selling the parcel of land
that belonged to our kinsman Elimelech.
You are the next-of-kin.
Buy it in the presence of those sitting here,
these elders of our people.
If you will redeem it, then redeem it.
If not, please let me know,
for I am the next one after you
to exercise that right."
So he said, "I will redeem it."
Then Boaz added, "By the way,
when you acquire the field from Naomi,
you also acquire the Moabite, Ruth,
who is the dead man's widow,
and along with her the responsibility
to continue the dead man's name,
ensuring his line of inheritance."

At this, the next-of-kin replied,
"I cannot do this without jeopardizing
my own inheritance.
Take my right of redemption
and exercise it for yourself."
Now the custom then in Israel
was for a man to remove a sandal
and hand it to the other to signify
the transaction was confirmed.
The next-of-kin took his sandal
as Boaz said to the elders
and all the people who were gathered around,
"Today you are all witnesses
that I have acquired from the hand of Naomi
all that belonged to Elimelech
and all that belonged to Chilion and Mahlon.
I have also acquired Ruth the Moabite, wife of Mahlon,
to be my wife,
in order to maintain the dead man's name
and continue his inheritance.
To this you are witnesses today."
Then all said, "We are witnesses.
May God make the woman who enters your house
like her sisters, Rachel and Leah.
May you have children
and through those children,
bestow a name in Bethlehem."
So Boaz took Ruth to be his wife,
and he made love to her,
and she conceived and gave birth to a son.
Then the women said to Naomi,
"Blessed be God who has not left you today
without any next-of-kin.
May the child be renowned in Israel!
May he be to you restoration of life
and nourishment in your old age.
For your daughter-in-law who loves you,
who is more to you than seven sons,
is the mother of this child."
Then Naomi took the boy and nursed him,
and the women of the neighborhood named him, saying,
"A son has been born to Naomi."
And they named the baby Obed.
He was the father of Jesse,
who was father of David the king.

◇ **Points for Shared Reflection**

- Discuss the relationship of Ruth and Naomi. Is this typical of a woman and her mother-in-law? If relevant, speak from experience.

- Recall what it felt like to leave home, either for school, a job, to get married, or just to get out on your own. What advice would you give young women facing that same challenge today?

- Have you ever left your country or entered into another culture? What did it feel like? How did you cope?

- If you were Ruth, what would you have done?

◇ **A Covenant Psalm** (see p. 61)

◇ **Prayer**

Wherever I go,
Eternally Present One,
You go before me,
behind me,
within me,
and I find strength in the knowledge
that I will never be alone.
Like a pillar of fire
that lights my way
or a pillar of cloud,
day after day
I depend on You
for all that I need
for comfort
and survival.
Be with me tangibly,
speak to me audibly,
show Your love visibly,
so that now and forever
Your people will be my people
and You will always be my God.
Amen.

◇ A COVENANT PSALM ◇

All   Wherever you go, I will go.
I will live and love beside you.
Your family will be my family,
and together we will go with God.

Voice   Blessed be God Who helps us transcend
the strong birth ties that bind us,
Who ties the cord that connects us in faith
to a new security.

All   Wherever you stay, I will stay,
content and secure around you.
Your hopes will be the source of my hope
and together we will hope in God.

Voice   Blessed be God Who unites two streams
to form one current together,
enriching the lives of all on whom
their fullness overflows.

All   Wherever you are, I will be,
living and loving inside you.
Your dreams will be my energy
and our future will be with God.

Voice   Blessed be God who sinks deep roots in us
as the new creation,
taking the best of what has been
for the seeds of what will be.

All   Wherever You go, we will go,
wherever You are, there we will be.
Your love is all-encompassing,
and that is enough for me.

By M. T. Winter, Crossroad Pub. Co., © 1992 Medical Mission Sisters

BATHSHEBA

◇ **Scripture Reference**   2 Sam 11:1–18, 25–27; 12:1–25;
1 Kings 1:1, 11–40; 2:13–25; 1 Chr 3:5

◇ **Biography**

Bathsheba, daughter of Eliam, wife of Uriah the Hittite, was a beautiful woman who caught King David's eye. He got her pregnant, had her husband killed in battle, then took her as his wife. Their child died soon after birth as a consequence of divine retribution. Bathsheba then gave birth to Solomon, who would succeed to his father's throne and be famous for his wealth and his wisdom and for building the temple in Jerusalem to house the ark of God. Bathsheba gave David three other children: Shimea, Shobab, and Nathan, and she lived to see her son Solomon succeed David as king.

◊ Context

The tradition of interpretation surrounding the story of David and Bathsheba, one of the more popular narratives in the annals of the kings of
Israel, presents Bathsheba as she appeared to men — to David and the
biblical writers and to generations of preachers, teachers, and scholars
down to the present day. David, specially chosen servant of God, illus-
trious king of Israel, key figure in the genealogy of Jesus, got into trouble
with a woman and it was all her fault. He happened to be walking on
his palace roof and he happened to see Bathsheba bathing, and she was
very beautiful. He wanted her. He sent for her. He got her pregnant. And
he went to a lot of trouble to cover up the fact. He recalled her husband
from the front so that he might sleep with his wife and consider the child
his own. But when Uriah abstained from sex as an act of solidarity with
the troops at war, David saw to it that he was returned to the war zone
and killed in the line of fire. He married Bathsheba, was chastised by the
prophet Nathan, and their male baby died as his punishment for their
sin. David quickly impregnated Bathsheba again and palace life went on.

Now what kind of woman would seduce a king, a religious one at that,
commit adultery while her husband was off fighting wars, and marry so
soon into her widowhood? If we let Bathsheba respond, we hear a different story. She happened to be bathing one day, and it just so happened
that she was beautiful. Suddenly the king's messengers barged in unan-
nounced to escort her to the palace, where the king himself raped her.
She let him have it when she knew she was pregnant, never dreaming
he would do what he did. He killed her gentle, loving husband, and she
was left with no choice but to marry the one who had abused her, the
murderer of her husband. But why did God punish her? None of this
was her fault. Why did her baby have to die? Bathsheba, who was a
queen and a queen mother, probably grew into her roles, but they may
not have been all that satisfying. She had to share her husband with
many other women, and palace life was full of violence and political intrigue. Facts reflect the nuance of the interpreter. There are dimensions
to Bathsheba's story that the facts have yet to reveal.

◊ Lectionary Reading

It was spring, that time of year
when kings go out to battle;
and David sent Joab, his officers and army
to massacre the Ammonites
and to put Rabbah under siege,
but David remained in Jerusalem.
It happened late one afternoon
that David was walking on the palace roof
when he saw a woman bathing.
The woman was very beautiful.

When David inquired about her,
he was told, "She is Bathsheba,
daughter of Eliam and wife of Uriah the Hittite."
David sent for the woman.
She came and he made love to her
before she went back home.
Bathsheba, who had just finished her period
and had been purifying herself
when she was seen from the palace roof,
soon discovered she was pregnant,
and she let David know.
David sent word to Joab, "Send me Uriah the Hittite."
When Uriah arrived, David inquired about Joab and the war.
Then David said to Uriah,
"Go down to your house and wash your feet."
Uriah left, and behind him followed
a present from the king.
But Uriah did not go home that night.
Instead, he slept at the entrance
to the king's house, with the servants.
When David heard he had not gone home,
he sent again for Uriah.
"You have just returned from a journey," he said.
"Why did you not go home?"
Uriah said to David,
"The ark and Israel and Judah
are housed right now in tents,
and Joab and all the army
are encamped in an open field.
Shall I retire to my own house,
to eat and drink and make love to my wife?
No, as you live and your soul lives,
I tell you that I will not!"
Then David said to Uriah,
"Remain behind here another day,
and tomorrow I will send you back."
So Uriah remained in Jerusalem.
He ate and drank in the palace,
and David made him drunk;
still he did not go down to his house at night,
but slept among the servants.
In the morning, David wrote to Joab
and gave the letter to Uriah
to deliver to him by hand.
This is what David wrote:
"Put Uriah on the front line.

When the fighting is fierce, let him die."
As Joab was besieging the city,
he assigned Uriah to the front line
where the valiant warriors were.
Some of David's servants died.
Uriah was killed as well.
Joab sent word to David of the outcome of the battle
and the news that Uriah was dead.
Then David said to the messenger,
"Go and say to Joab,
'Do not let this trouble you,
for the sword kills now one and now another;
press your attack on the city.'
Go and encourage him."
When Bathsheba heard that Uriah was dead,
she lamented for her husband.
When the time of mourning was over,
David sent for her and made her his wife
and she gave birth to a son.
But the deed that David had done to Uriah
was really displeasing to God.

◊

So God sent Nathan to David.
He came and said to him,
"There were two men in a certain city,
one rich and the other poor.
The rich man had many flocks and herds,
the poor man had but one ewe lamb
which he had raised with his children;
it used to eat of his meager fare
and drink from his cup and lie in his lap;
it was like a daughter to him.
Now the rich man had a visitor one day,
and loathe to reach into his own herd,
he took the poor man's one ewe lamb
and made a meal for him."
David's anger flared up against the man
and he said to Nathan,
"As God lives, the man who has done this thing
truly deserves to die.
He shall restore the lamb fourfold
for doing such a thing
and because he had no pity."
Nathan said, "You are the man!
Thus says the God of Israel:
I anointed you king over Israel

and I saved you from the wrath of Saul.
I gave you your master's house and wives
and the house of Israel and Judah,
and if that had been too little,
I would have added that much more.
Why have you despised God's word
and done such evil in God's sight?
You have slain Uriah the Hittite
and you have taken his wife as your own.
Because you have killed him with the sword,
the sword shall hover over your house,
and I will raise up trouble against you
within these very walls.
I will take your wives before your eyes
and give them to your neighbor.
He will lie with them in the light of day,
doing that which you did in secret,
but this I will do before all Israel
in the bright light of the sun."
Then David said to Nathan,
"I have sinned against our God."
And Nathan said to David,
"Now God has cast away your sin;
you shall not die, but the child
who has been born to you will die,
because you have scorned God by this deed."
Then Nathan returned to his home.
And David's child by Uriah's wife
suddenly became very ill.
David pleaded with God for the child;
he fasted and lay all night on the ground.
The elders stood beside him, urging him to rise;
but he would not, nor would he eat with them.
On the seventh day the child died,
and his servants were afraid to tell him.
"If he would not listen while the child was alive,
what now that the child is dead?
He may even try to harm himself."
When David saw them whispering,
he knew that his child was dead.
"Is the child dead?" David asked them.
"He is dead," his servants replied.
Then David got up, went and bathed
and anointed himself, and changed his clothes
and went before God to worship,
and then he returned to his own house,

asked for food, and ate.
Bewildered, his servants said to him,
"How are you behaving?
You fasted and wept when the child was alive
and you eat now that it is dead."
And David explained to his servants,
"While the child was alive, I fasted and wept,
saying, 'Who knows? God may be gracious.
Maybe the child will live.'
But now he is dead, why should I fast?
Can I bring him back again?
More likely it is I who will join him,
but he will not return to me."
Then David consoled Bathsheba, his wife,
and he made love to her,
and she in time gave birth to a son
and David named him Solomon.
God loved him and made this known to them
through the word of Nathan the prophet
who named him Jedidiah,
which means, Beloved of God.

⋄

These children were born to Bathsheba and David:
Shimea, Shobab, Nathan, and Solomon,
four children by Bathsheba
were born to David in Jerusalem.

⋄

King David was old and advanced in years
when Nathan said to Bathsheba,
"Adonijah son of Haggith has been made king
and David does not know it.
Now let me give you some advice
so you may save the life of Solomon your son
and your own life as well.
Go in at once to David and say,
'Did you not swear to your servant, saying:
Solomon your son shall succeed me as king
and shall sit upon my throne?
Why then is Adonijah king?'
Then while you are there still speaking with the king,
I will come in and confirm your words."
So Bathsheba went to the king in his room.
Now the king was very old;
Abishag was attending to him.
Bathsheba bowed to the king and he said,
"What is it you wish?"

She repeated Nathan's words,
adding some more of her own.
"Adonijah has prepared a lavish feast
and invited all but Solomon.
The eyes of all are on you, my lord.
Tell them who will succeed you.
Otherwise on the day you die,
my son and I will be outcasts."
Then Nathan came in, bowed to the ground,
and repeated the words of Bathsheba, adding,
"Everyone including the priest Abiathar
is saying, 'Long live King Adonijah!'
But they did not invite me, or Zadok the priest,
or Solomon, or Benaiah.
Has all this been done by you, my lord,
and have you neglected to tell us
who will follow you to the throne?"
Then King David answered,
"Bring Bathsheba to me."
She came into his presence,
and the king swore an oath, saying,
"As God lives who has saved me from all adversity,
as I swore to you by the God of Israel,
'Your son Solomon shall succeed me as king,
and he shall sit on my throne after me,'
so will I do this day."
Then Bathsheba bowed to the ground and said,
"May King David live forever!"
David said, "Summon before me
Zadok the priest, Nathan the prophet,
and Benaiah son of Jehoida."
When they had arrived, he said to them,
"Take my servants with you,
have Solomon ride on my own mule,
and bring him down to Gihon.
There let the priest and the prophet
anoint him king over Israel;
then blow the trumpet and say to all,
'Long live King Solomon!'
Let him enter and sit upon my throne.
He shall be king in my place,
for I have appointed him ruler over Israel and over Judah."
Benaiah answered the king,
"Amen! May God so ordain it.
As God has been with my lord the king,
may God also be with Solomon,

and make his throne even greater
than the throne of King David my lord."
So Zadok the priest, Nathan the prophet,
and Benaiah son of Jehoida,
and the Cherethites and the Pelethites,
led Solomon down to Gihon astride King David's mule.
And there they anointed Solomon,
then blew the trumpet as the people shouted,
"Long live King Solomon!"
And all the people followed him,
playing the pipes with gladness
and making a joyful noise.

◇

Adonijah, son of Haggith,
came to Bathsheba, Solomon's mother.
She asked, "Do you come peaceably?"
He said, "I come in peace. May I have a word with you?"
She said to him, "You may."
He said, "You know that the kingdom was mine.
All Israel thought I would reign.
The kingdom has now been turned around.
It has become my brother's,
because it was his from God.
I have one request to make of you.
Please do not refuse it."
"What is it?" Bathsheba asked him.
He said, "Please ask King Solomon —
he will not refuse you —
to give me Abishag as my wife."
"Very well," said Bathsheba, "I will speak on your behalf."
So Bathsheba went to Solomon.
The king stood up to meet her,
bowed down to her, then sat on his throne
and had a throne brought for his mother,
who sat at his right hand.
She said, "I have one small request to make.
Please do not refuse me."
Her son, the king, responded,
"Make your request, my mother, for I will not refuse you."
She said, "Give Abishag the Shunammite
to Adonijah as his wife."
King Solomon answered his mother,
"Why ask for Abishag the Shunammite?
Why not ask for the kingdom as well!
Adonijah is my elder brother;
Abiathar the priest and Joab

are completely committed to him."
Then Solomon swore an oath, saying,
"May God do to me and more besides,
for Adonijah has devised this scheme
at the risk of his own life!
By the God who placed me on this throne
and made me a house as promised,
today Adonijah dies!"
So Solomon dispatched Benaiah
who struck Adonijah dead.

◇ **Points for Shared Reflection**

- In your opinion, was Bathsheba an innocent victim or a willing participant in her first encounter with David?

- Comment on society's tendency, then and now, to blame and therefore further victimize the woman in incidents involving rape and incest. Or do your disagree? If so, why?

- Women often have to adjust to abusive situations and make the best of it. Has this been your experience or the experience of a family member or a friend?

- David saw what he wanted and took it and suffered the consequences. How prevalent is this attitude in today's world? In your own world? What have been some of the consequences?

◇ **Bathsheba's Psalm** (see p. 71)

◇ **Prayer**

O Holy One of God,
we turn to You,
the source of every blessing,
and pray that You will be with us
when we fall beneath the cloud of suspicion,
when we are taken against our will,
when the life within us is stripped away
and we are forced to begin again.
We turn to You
and we learn from You
that there is strength in Your blessing,
strength to endure
and to overcome
and always to start anew.
Thank You, Shekinah-Shaddai.
We praise You. We love You.
Amen.

◇ BATHSHEBA'S PSALM ◇

Voice   Look upon me, Shekinah-Shaddai,
and know that I am faithful.
Never has my affection strayed
in search of other gods.

All   Shekinah-Shaddai,
be with us all
who struggle to be faithful.

Voice   Reach out to me, Shekinah-Shaddai,
and hide me in Your shadow.
Shield the naked soul of me
from disapproving eyes.

All   May those of us
who are vulnerable
not regret our transparency.

Voice   Come to my aid, O Holy One,
for violence overpowers me,
desecrates my integrity,
blames me for its sin.

All   Be with those
who have been violated
and victimized by sin.

Voice   Be gentle with me, O Holy One;
help me to make right choices,
to live within the boundaries imposed,
to adjust myself to Your will.

All   Help us to live
with the consequences of evil
in our world.

Voice   Indeed, though I walk
in the valley
of the shadow of suspicion,
I fear no reprisals,
for You are my surety.

All   Ewe lamb of God,
peace be with you,
and may She strengthen us.
Gentle God, please strengthen us.

QUEEN OF SHEBA

◇ **Scripture Reference**   1 Kings 10:1–13; 2 Chr 9:1–12

◇ **Biography**

The queen of Sheba was a contemporary of Solomon in the tenth century B.C.E. She visited Solomon to test his wisdom, which had become legendary. Although she herself was a wealthy woman, Solomon's wealth and his wisdom astonished her. The precise location of her country is not evident from biblical sources.

◇ **Context**

Countless generations have been intrigued by the oriental queen who crossed a desert to visit King Solomon at the height of his reign. Her precise identity and nationality are unknown, yet she is claimed by both Arabs and Ethiopians and much mythology surrounds her. In Arab legends she is Queen Belkis of Saba in southwest Arabia (now Yemen), who married Solomon and is buried in a splendid tomb he built for her in Palmyra on the northern edge of the Syrian desert. Her story appears in the Qur'an in sura 27:22–44, where she is described as "ruling over a people who prostrate themselves to the sun." Ethiopian kings traced their lineage back to a union between the Queen of Sheba, whom they called Makeda, and Solomon. The story is told in *Kebra-Nagasht*, an ancient Abyssinian book whose title means "The Glory of Kings." Queen Makeda, meaning "woman of fire," slept with Solomon the night before she left Jerusalem to return to her own capital, Aksum, in northern

Ethiopia. On the way home she gave birth to a son whom she named Menelik. Ethiopian kings, claiming descent from Prince Menelik, have always been known as the "Elect of God" and the "Lion of Judah."

It is said that the Queen and Solomon posed riddles to test one another's wisdom. An example from a Jewish legend reads, "The Queen said, 'Seven depart. Nine enter. Two pour. One drinks.' Solomon replied, 'Seven days represents the period of a woman's menstruation; nine months the period of her pregnancy; two pouring is a reference to her breasts; and one drinking, a reference to her baby.' " It is hard to uncover the real queen who is buried beneath so much legend. It is just as hard to determine the nature of her relationship with Solomon. Given the size of Solomon's harem, his attraction to foreign women, and the queen's own magnetic persona, it is fair to suspect that this king and queen shared more than clever words. The Queen of Sheba was a woman of power and influence, prosperity and prestige, who showed the women of biblical tradition another way of being female.

◇ **Lectionary Reading**

When the queen of Sheba
heard of the fame of Solomon,
she decided to test him
with difficult questions.
She arrived in Jerusalem
with a retinue of riches:
camels with spices,
caches of gold
and quantities of precious stones.
In the presence of Solomon,
she spoke her mind.
Solomon answered all her questions.
No point was too obscure for him.
When the queen of Sheba
saw the wisdom of Solomon,
the palace he had built,
the food that he ate,
the organization of his staff
and the way they were dressed,
his cup-bearers
and the holocausts he offered
in the house of his God,
how he accommodated his officials,
it took her breath away.
"So it really is true,
all that I heard in my land
of your accomplishments and your wisdom,"

she said to Solomon,
"but I did not believe the things I heard
until I had seen with my own eyes.
Not even half of the story has been told.
Your wisdom and prosperity
surpass all reports.
How happy are your wives!
Happy are these your servants
who wait on you and hear your wisdom!
Blessed be your God who has delighted in you
and enthroned you in Israel.
Because of God's everlasting love for Israel,
God made you king to establish justice
and execute the law."
Then she gave the king of Israel
one hundred twenty talents of gold
and quantities of spices
and precious stones,
such a wealth of spices
as had not been seen
and would not be seen again
were given by the queen of Sheba
to Solomon the king.
And the ships that carried gold from Ophir
in the fleet of Hiram
brought more precious stones
and almug wood,
great quantities of wood
which Solomon used for the temple supports
and for lyres and harps for the singers,
and also for beams for his own palace.
King Solomon fulfilled for the queen of Sheba
every desire that she expressed
in addition to what he gave her
out of his personal treasury.
Then she left, she and her servants,
to return to her own country.

◇ **Points for Shared Reflection**

- What do you remember hearing about the Queen of Sheba when you were growing up? Is your image of her positive or negative, and why?

- The queen tested Solomon's wisdom with words. Can real wisdom be put into words? What is your definition of wisdom?

- Staying strictly with the biblical text, what message have we to learn from the story of the Queen of Sheba?

- The narrative is filled with extravagance. Is there a material, physical, or spiritual extravagance in your life that you are sometimes led to question?

◇ **A Psalm Celebrating a Royal Priesthood** (see p. 76)

◇ **Prayer**

We come together, Shekinah-Shaddai,
around Your throne of grace and glory,
for we are ministers of Your mercy,
priests of Your compassion,
proclaimers of Your liberating word
to all who are oppressed.
Empower us to carry out the call
to which we have been ordained
from the time we were in our mother's womb.
We are more than ready now.
Amen.

Voice Women surrounded the throne of blessing,
lifted their hands to the All-Holy One,
lifted their face to Her and cried:

All We are Your chosen people,
we are a holy nation,
we are a royal priesthood,
we are a cherished gender.

Voice Women ascended to the Torah,
took the scroll into their hands,
prayed to the Holy One of Blessing,
proclaimed Her living word and cried:

All We are Your chosen people,
we are a holy nation,
we are a royal priesthood,
we are a cherished gender.

Voice Women circled the table of grace,
took the cup
and a loaf of bread,
blessed, broke, ate, and cried:

All We are Your chosen people,
we are a holy nation,
we are a royal priesthood,
we are a cherished gender.

Voice Women went out among the oppressed,
preached a word of freedom,
broke the bread of justice,
poured the tears of all the poor
into their blessing cup and cried:

All We are Your chosen people,
we are a holy nation,
we are a royal priesthood,
we are a cherished gender.

    By M. T. Winter, Crossroad Pub. Co., © 1992 Medical Mission Sisters

JEZEBEL

◇ **Scripture Reference** 1 Kings 16:29–34; 18:1–20, 38–40;
19:1–3; 21:1–25; 22:51–53;
2 Kings 9:1–13, 21–37

◇ **Biography**

Jezebel, daughter of Ethbaal, king of Tyre and Sidon, was the wife of
Ahab, king of Israel in Samaria around 850 B.C.E. She was cunning,
influential, and, according to the biblical texts, wielded power ruthlessly.
A devotee of Baal and Asherah, she supported their prophets and at one
point mandated the wholesale slaughter of the prophets of Israel. Elijah
foretold the details of her death. She was thrown from the palace window
and her body was devoured by dogs.

◇ **Context**

Jezebel. Her very name is an epithet for evil woman. How evil was she
really? Her narrative, a composite of several sources focusing on the

prophets Elijah and Elisha, is negative and condemnatory, and because it lacks salient information about the nature of her reign, we do not have a balanced picture of either Jezebel or her accomplishments. Before her marriage to Ahab, Jezebel was a princess in Tyre whose father King Ethbaal, according to Josephus, had been a priest of the goddess Ashtoreth before usurping the throne. Unlike other wives and queen mothers in Israel, she was a queen in her own right. She had both power and influence in the royal palace and abroad. She carried out a pogrom against the Hebrew prophets, she saw to the execution of Nabor through official channels under her direction, and when she threatened the prophet Elijah, he fled from her in fear. She was given the title *gebira*, "Lady," held by only two other royal women, both queen mothers from Judah. She was a worshiper of Baal and Asherah and patroness of their cults and prophets. While the numbers themselves may be exaggerated, it is said that nine hundred of these prophets ate at Jezebel's table, suggesting a degree of palatial wealth and quarters of her own. She was the reigning monarch following the death of Ahab and her two sons, and the only way Jehu could secure the throne for himself was to see that she was destroyed.

Jezebel may have been an unsavory character, but she did have a distinction accorded few other woman in biblical history. She was princess, queen, queen mother, interim ruler of Israel, and grand patroness of the cult and prophets of Baal. Jewish scholar Athalya Brenner suggests that she may also have been a Baal priestess from her younger days in Tyre, which would explain her religious fanaticism, her special status in her husband's court, and her own leadership skills. The roles of priestess and patroness of Baal would have provided a legitimate basis for her authority and power (see *The Israelite Woman*, JSOT Press, 1985, p. 24). This may have been the reason why the authors of the Book of Kings minimized Jezebel's role. She was also a foreigner and a woman, a very powerful woman, and this could only have hurt her memory.

◊ **Lectionary Reading**

In the thirty-eighth year of King Asa of Judah,
Ahab son of Omri became king of Israel
and reigned from Samaria for twenty-two years.
Ahab son of Omri was evil in God's eyes,
more than any who had gone before him.
Following in the footsteps of Jeroboam son of Nebat,
Ahab married Jezebel, daughter of Ethbaal, king of the Sidonians,
and proceeded to serve Baal and to worship him.
He erected an altar for Baal
in the house he built for Baal in Samaria.
He also put up a sacred pole
and committed other offenses,

provoking the anger of the God of Israel
more than any other king who preceded him.
It was at this time that Hiel of Bethel rebuilt Jericho.
Foundations were laid at the cost of his firstborn, Abiram,
and the gates at the cost of his youngest son, Segub,
according to the word of God
spoken through Joshua son of Nun.

◇

The word of God came to Elijah
in the third year of the drought, saying,
"Present yourself to Ahab. I will send rain on the earth."
The famine was severe in Samaria.
So Elijah set out for the palace of Ahab
and on the way met Obadiah.
Now Obadiah was in charge of the palace.
At the time when Jezebel was butchering the prophets,
he hid a hundred prophets, fifty to a cave,
and provided them with bread and water,
because of his reverence for God.
Ahab had sent Obadiah in search of grass
for the horses and mules, to keep them alive,
for the drought was hard on the animals.
He told him to check in the wadis
and near all the springs of water.
Dividing the land between them,
Ahab headed off in one direction and Obadiah in another.
That's when he met Elijah.
He recognized him and bowed to the ground.
"So it is you, my lord Elijah," he said.
"It is I," Elijah responded.
"Go tell Ahab that Elijah is here."
And Obadiah said, "What have I done to offend you,
that you should give Ahab cause to kill me?
As God lives, no nation, no kingdom
has evaded his determination to seek you and to find you;
if they would say of you, 'He is not here,'
he would demand an oath of the kingdom or nation
that in truth they had not found you.
So now you stand there and say to me,
'Tell Ahab that Elijah is here,'
when I know very well that as soon as I leave,
God's spirit will carry you I know not where,
so when I tell Ahab and he cannot find you,
he will strike me down and kill me.
I have revered God from my youth.
Have you not heard how I hid God's prophets,

a hundred of them, fifty to a cave,
when Jezebel was slaughtering the prophets?
Yet here you are now, saying to me,
'Tell Ahab Elijah is here!'
Believe me, he is sure to kill me."
Elijah said, "As God lives, the God whom I serve,
I will present myself to him today."
So Obadiah went to Ahab and told him,
and Ahab went to meet Elijah.
When Ahab saw Elijah, he said to him,
"So there you are, you scourge of Israel!"
"It is not I who am scourge of Israel," said Elijah,
"it is you, yes, you and your family,
because you have forsaken the laws of God
and have turned to the worship of Baal.
Give orders at once for the people to assemble
with you and me at Mount Carmel,
and with the four hundred fifty prophets of Baal
and the four hundred prophets of Asherah
who eat at Jezebel's table."
So Ahab sent word to the Israelites
and called the prophets to Mount Carmel.
Then the fire of God fell from heaven
and consumed the burnt offering of Elijah,
devouring the wood, the stones, the dust,
and even the trench full of water.
When the people saw it, they fell to the ground, saying,
"Mighty indeed is God; mighty indeed is God."
Then Elijah said to the people,
"Seize the prophets of Baal; let not a single one escape."
They seized them
and Elijah brought them down to the Wadi Kishon
and killed them.

◇

Ahab told Jezebel what Elijah had done,
how he had killed all the prophets with a sword.
Then Jezebel sent a messenger to Elijah, saying,
"So may the gods do to me, and more,
if your fate is not like the fate of these
by this same time tomorrow."
Elijah was afraid and fled for his life
to Beer-sheba, which belongs to Judah,
and he left his servant there.

◇

Later the following events took place.
Now Naboth had a vineyard in Jezreel

beside the palace of Ahab of Samaria.
Ahab said to Naboth one day,
"Give me your vineyard for a vegetable garden,
because it is near my house.
I will give you a better vineyard in exchange,
or if your prefer, money of equal value."
But Nahob said to Ahab, "God forbid
that I should give my ancestral inheritance to you."
Ahab went home resentful and sullen
because of what Naboth had said.
He lay on his bed, his face turned away,
and stubbornly refused to eat.
His wife Jezebel said to him,
"Why are you so depressed?
What happened to keep you from eating?"
And Ahab said to her,
"I spoke to Naboth the Jezreelite
and asked him for his vineyard
but he would not sell it to me."
Jezebel said to him, "Are you not the king?
Get up and eat and try to cheer up.
I will get Naboth's vineyard for you."
So she wrote letters in Ahab's name
and sealed them with his seal,
sending them to the elders and nobles
who resided in Naboth's city.
"Proclaim a fast and seat Naboth
at the head of the assembly," Jezebel wrote.
"Seat two scoundrels opposite him
and have them make some accusation, saying,
'You have cursed God and the king.'
Then take him out and stone him."
The elders and nobles of Naboth's city
did as Jezebel had directed,
and Naboth was stoned to death.
Then they sent word to Jezebel, saying,
"Naboth has been stoned. He is dead."
As soon as Jezebel heard the news,
she hurried to Ahab and said,
"Take possession of Naboth's vineyard
which he refused to give you for money.
Naboth now is dead."
Then God's word came to Elijah the Tishbite.
"Go down to King Ahab of Israel, who rules in Samaria.
He is now in Naboth's vineyard.
He has taken possession of it.

Say to him, 'Thus says God:
You have committed murder.
Will you confiscate this as well?'
Say to him, 'Thus says God:
There where dogs licked the blood of Naboth,
they shall lick your blood as well.' "
Ahab said to Elijah,
"So you have found me out, my enemy!"
"I have found you out," he responded.
"Because you have done what is evil in God's eyes,
I will bring disaster upon you.
I will sweep away all your descendants,
wipe out every male in your household,
and I will make your house like the house of Jeroboam
and like the house of Baasha,
because you have provoked me to anger
and have caused Israel to sin.
With regard to Jezebel, God said,
'Dogs shall eat Jezebel within Jezreel.'
Those of Ahab's family who die in the city
shall be eaten by the dogs.
Whoever dies in the open country
will be eaten by the birds."
There was no one like Ahab, no one at all,
more evil in the eyes of God.
He chased after idols
and behaved outrageously,
urged on by Jezebel, his wife.

◇

Ahaziah son of Ahab
began to reign over Israel in Samaria
in the seventeenth year
of the reign of King Jehoshaphat of Judah.
He reigned two years over Israel.
He did what was evil in the eyes of God
and walked in the ways of his father and mother
and the path of Jeroboam,
serving and worshiping Baal.
He provoked God to anger,
just as his father had done.

◇

Then the prophet Elisha
called a member of the company of prophets and said,
"Take this flask of oil
and look for Jehu son of Jehoshaphat in Ramoth-gilead.
Get him to leave his companions,

take him into an inner chamber,
pour this flask of oil on his head and say,
'Thus says God: I anoint you king of Israel.'
Then open the door and flee."
So the young prophet did as Elisha commanded.
The chiefs of the army were in council when he announced,
"I have a message for your commander, Jehu."
So Jehu got up and stepped inside
and the prophet said to him,
"Thus says the God of Israel:
I anoint you king over the people of God, king over Israel."
And he poured oil on his head.
"You shall demolish the house of Ahab,
so that I may avenge on Jezebel
the blood of my servants the prophets
and the blood of all the servants of God.
The house of Ahab shall perish.
Every male will be destroyed.
Dogs will eat Jezebel in Jezreel,
and no one will bury her."
Then he opened the door and fled.
When Jehu returned to the officers, they inquired,
"Is everything all right?
What did that madman want?"
He said, "You know the type, how they babble on."
"Liar!" They answered. "What did he say?"
So he said, "This is what he told me:
'Thus says God, I anoint you king over Israel.' "
Then they hurriedly spread their cloaks on the steps
and blew the trumpet, proclaiming, "Jehu is king."
Then Jehu moved against Jehoram.
King Jehoram of Israel and King Ahaziah of Judah
set out in their chariots toward Jehu,
and they met at the property of Naboth the Jezreelite.
When Jehoram saw Jehu, he said, "Is it peace?"
Jehu answered, "How can there be peace
as long as the many whoredoms and sorceries
of your mother Jezebel continue?"
Then Jehoram reeled around and fled, shouting,
"Treason, Ahaziah!"
Jehu drew his bow, and with all his strength
he shot Jehoram between the shoulders,
and the arrow pierced his heart.
Jehu said to Bidkar his aide,
"Lift him out of his chariot,
and throw him on the plot of ground

belonging to Naboth the Jezreelite.
For remember, when we rode side by side
behind his father Ahab,
God uttered this oracle against him:
'For the blood of Naboth
and for the blood of his children,
I swear I will repay you
on this very plot of ground.'
So pick him up and throw him there
in accordance with the word of God."
When King Ahaziah saw this,
he fled toward Bethlehem,
but Jehu pursued him, shouting,
"Shoot him as well," and they shot him,
and he drove on to Megiddo and died.
His officers brought him to Jerusalem
and buried him with his ancestors.
When Jehu came to Jezreel,
Jezebel heard of it.
She put makeup on her eyes,
adorned her head,
and stood looking out the window.
As Jehu entered the gate, she said,
"Is it peace, murderer of your master?"
He looked up to the window and called aloud,
"Who is with me up there? Who is on my side?"
Several eunuchs looked down at him.
"Throw her out of the window," he said.
So they threw her down
and some of her blood spattered on the wall
and on the horses which trampled on her.
Then he went in and ate and drank and said,
"See to that cursed woman and bury her,
for she is a king's daughter."
But when they went to bury her,
they found nothing of her except her skull
and her feet and the palms of her hands.
When they came and told Jehu of this, he said,
"This is the word of God
spoken through Elijah the Tishbite,
'In the territory of Jezreel
dogs shall eat the flesh of Jezebel,
and the corpse of Jezebel shall be like dung
on the field in Jezreel,
so that none can say, ever again,
This is Jezebel.'"

◇ **Points for Shared Reflection**

- Can you recall an incident in your personal life or professional life when you wielded power ruthlessly? Would you be willing to share the details?

- Can someone who completely rejects your views really describe or represent you fairly?

- Have you ever experienced someone's uncompromising condemnation of your religious beliefs and practices? How did you feel? How did you react?

- Can you name a prophet or a prophetic word you may have figuratively killed because some proposed change in ritual, theology, or religious rules came about before you were prepared to receive it?

◇ **A Psalm about Power** (see p. 86)

◇ **Prayer**

O Sacred Power,
empowering all
who are powerless
and overpowered
by all the forces
rising up
to take control
of the universe
by taking control of us,
give us the means
to change our status
and forgive us
our triumphal traits,
for we know
that Yours is the glory
and power
forever and ever.
Amen.

◇ A PSALM ABOUT POWER ◇

Voice 1   Women, what is power?

All   Power is not power over.
Power is not being overpowered.

Voice 2   Women, how do you exercise power?

All   By taking control of ourselves.
By refusing to be controlled by others.

Voice 3   Women, where do you get your power?

All   From the One Who is All-Powerful.
We name Her Power!
We claim Her power.
Praise to Her Who empowers us.

Voice 1   Women, what is power?

All   Power is power with.
Power is sharing power with others.

Voice 2   Women, how do you exercise power?

All   By giving control to others.
By not controlling others ourselves.

Voice 3   Women, where do you get your power?

All   From the One Who is All-Powerful.
We name Her Power!
We claim Her power.
Praise to Her Who empowers us.

Voice 1   Women, what is power?

All   Power is in and through.
It is in ourselves and through the Spirit.

Voice 2   Women, how do you exercise power?

All   By being in control of ourselves.
By living and working through the Spirit.

Voice 3   Women, where do you get your power?

All   From the One Who is All-Powerful.
We name Her Power!
We claim Her power.
Praise to Her Who empowers us.

   By M. T. Winter, Crossroad Pub. Co., © 1992 Medical Mission Sisters

Voice 1	Women, what is power?
All	Power is empowering. Power is not empiring.
Voice 2	Women, how do you exercise power?
All	By empowering others to empower others. By creating empowering circles. By resisting empire building.
Voice 3	Women, where do you get your power?
All	From the One Who is All-Powerful. We name Her Power! We claim Her power. Praise to Her Who empowers us.
Voices	Women, when will you claim your power?
All	We are naming it and claiming it by naming Her and claiming Her Who is Power and Who is empowering. We the powerless have the power to liberate and transform ourselves and to do the same for others. Praise to Her Who empowers us.

By M. T. Winter, Crossroad Pub. Co., © 1992 Medical Mission Sisters

ATHALIAH

◇ **Scripture Reference**   2 Kings 8:16–18, 25–26; 10:13; 11:1–21;
2 Chr 21: 4–6; 22:1–3, 9–12; 23:12–15, 20–21;
24:1–2, 7

◇ **Biography**

Athaliah was the only ruling queen of Judah. She was either the daughter or the sister of Ahab king of Israel and the wife of Jehoram king of Judah. She secured the throne after the death of her son Ahaziah by ordering the slaughter of all male heirs. After six years the boy Joash, her grandson, who had escaped the purge, was crowned by Jehoiada the priest and Athaliah was put to death.

◇ **Context**

It is often hard to get a clear storyline in scripture because biblical writers had other agendas. The narrative of Athaliah is one such story. Issues of legitimacy, religious and otherwise, may well have distorted the few available facts concerning her rise to power. Athaliah was reared in the palace of Ahab under the influence of Jezebel during one of the more ruthless reigns in history, according to the writers, and it is suggested that Athaliah was a lot like them. During her son Ahaziah's brief kingship, she functioned as his counselor, whether informally or in some official capacity it is impossible to say. Chronicles states that there was no one to rule following the king's untimely death, so Athaliah seized the chance to be queen of Judah. She must have had some basis for making such a move, and in order to secure her position, she eliminated all possible heirs, which was a common practice among male monarchs. Her husband had killed his six brothers, and even Solomon had destroyed his brother Adonijah when he perceived him as a threat to his reign. Unknown to Athaliah, her little grandson escaped the massacre and was hidden in the temple by the priest's wife. Six years later the priest Jehoiada crowned the boy Joash king. Athaliah's strong objections indicate she was convinced her authority was legitimate. Her death unleashed a sweeping purge of the Baal sanctuary in Jerusalem, which had enjoyed the queen's protection.

Athaliah was the only woman to claim the throne of Judah. Her six-year reign interrupted the Davidic dynasty whose continuity had been assured by God. This in itself would have been enough to turn the chroniclers against her. One wonders if she was really as ruthless and unpopular as the text suggests. She must have had some measure of support, both political and military, judging from the length of her reign and the number of troops Jehoiada required to ensure a transfer of power. The biblical narrator does not accord her the traditional formulas that indicate the legitimacy of a monarch. This may have been for a variety of reasons. Surely among them were the facts that she was a foreigner in Jerusalem, a worshiper of Baal, and a woman.

◇ **Lectionary Reading**

In the fifth year of King Joram, son of Ahab of Israel,
Jehoram son of King Jehoshaphat of Judah began to reign.
He put all of his brothers to death,
and also executed some of Israel's leaders.
He was thirty-two years old when he became king
and he reigned eight years in Jerusalem.
He walked in the way of the kings of Israel,
as the house of Ahab had done,
for the daughter of Ahab was his wife.

◇

In the twelfth year of King Joram of Israel,
Ahaziah son of King Jehoram of Judah began to reign.
He was twenty-two years old,
and he reigned one year in Jerusalem.
His mother's name was Athaliah;
she was a granddaughter of King Omri of Israel.
Ahaziah son of Jehoram
reigned one year as king of Judah.
Ahaziah walked in the ways of Ahab,
for his mother was his counselor
and advised him in doing wrong.

Ahaziah did what was evil in God's eyes,
just as Ahab had done.

◇

Jehu met relatives of King Ahaziah of Judah and said,
"Who are you?" They answered,
"We are relatives of Ahaziah.
We have come down to visit the royal princes
and the sons of the queen mother."

◇

Ahaziah was captured in Samaria
and put to death by Jehu.
And the house of Ahaziah
had no one able to rule the kingdom.
When Athaliah, mother of King Ahaziah of Judah,
saw that her son was dead,
she set out to destroy all the royal family.
But Jehosheba, Ahaziah's sister,
took Joash, Ahaziah's son,
and with the boy's nursemaid
hid him in a bedroom
when the purge began
so the child would not be killed.
For six years Joash hid in the temple
while Athaliah reigned over Judah.
In the seventh year,
Jehoiada the priest called together
the captains of the guards
and showed them the king's son
who had been hiding in the temple.
They made a covenant, swore an oath,
and drew up a battle plan
to be carried out at the change of guard
just before the sabbath:
one division to guard the palace,
two divisions to surround and protect the king
and to kill any who would approach him.
The captains carried out their orders.
Each brought men who were scheduled
to go off duty on the sabbath,
as well as men scheduled
to come on duty on the sabbath.
They came to the priest Jehoiada
who gave the captains spears and shields
that had once belonged to David
and were now kept in the temple.
The guards stood, weapons in hand,

from the south side of the temple
to the north side of the temple;
they surrounded the altar and the house of God
to guard the king on every side.
Then Jehoiada presented the king's son,
put a crown on him, gave him the covenant,
proclaimed him king and anointed him,
as everyone clapped and shouted,
"Long live the king!"
When Athaliah heard the outburst
from the guards and all the people,
she went to the temple and there was the king,
standing by the pillar, according to custom,
with the captains and the trumpeters,
and with all the people rejoicing
and the trumpets all resounding.
Athaliah tore her clothes and shouted,
"Treason! Treason!"
Then the priest Jehoiada
commanded the captains in charge of the army:
"Bring her out between the ranks
and kill any who follow her."
They seized her and led her away.
When they reached the gate where the horses enter,
Athaliah was put to death.
Jehoiada made a covenant
between God and the king
and all the people of Judah,
that they would be God's people.
Then the people went out to the house of Baal.
They destroyed the sanctuary,
the altars and the images,
and they killed Mattan, the priest of Baal,
as he stood before the altars.
Jehoiada posted guards around the temple
and brought the king from the house of God
into the king's palace.
Joash took his seat on the throne of the kings,
and all the people rejoiced.
The city was quiet after Athaliah was killed.
Joash the king was seven years old
when he began to reign.

◇

Joash was seven years old
when he became king of Judah
and he reigned forty years in Jerusalem.

His mother's name was Zibiah of Beer-sheba.
Joash did what was right in God's eyes
all the days of the priest Jehoiada.
Now the children of Athaliah who had done such evil
broke into the temple
and used all the dedicated things of God's house
for the worship of Baal.

◇ **Points for Shared Discussion**

- Why did the biblical writers denounce Athaliah? What can we learn from her?

- Sometimes when women make it in a man's world, they end up taking on the patriarchal characteristics of ruthless, insensitive domination. Have you seen evidence of this?

- What constitutes legitimate authority? When, if ever, is it legitimate to overthrow authority by violent means?

- How do you justify all the violence in the biblical narratives? What is your position on non-violence? How and when does it operate in your life?

◇ **A Psalm of Non-Violence** (see p. 93)

◇ **Prayer**

O Love Inviolate,
power and purpose
pervade Your interaction
with the world You have created.
You wield Your power with wisdom,
yet the violence that surrounds Your ways
exceeds our understanding.
We know in our hearts
we are called to be
non-violent, peace-loving people.
Please give us a clear direction
on how to orient ourselves
in a world so prone to war.
Be gentle, Shaddai,
non-violent,
in Your dealings with Your people
now and always.
Amen.

◇ A PSALM OF NON-VIOLENCE ◇

Voice The violence of a summer storm
smashes against my serenity
and makes me anxious.

All Gentle my soul, Shekinah-Shalom.
Let there be no violence in me.

Voice Thunder throws itself against the landscape
with such a force,
it breaks the silence in me.

All Gentle my spirit, Shekinah-Shalom.
Let there be no violence in me.

Voice Wind whips with typhoon force
across theological absolutes
and renders me defenseless.

All Gentle my mind, Shekinah-Shalom.
Let there be no violence in me.

Voice Waves leap from turbulent depths
to question the ebb and flow
of my most sensitive convictions.

All Gentle my heart, Shekinah-Shalom.
Let there be no violence in me.

Voice The eagle's talons pierce its prey
as shrill shrieks reach
protected portions of my memory
and wounds reopen.

All Gentle my memories, Shekinah-Shalom.
Let there be no violence in me.

Voice Leopards leap and rip to shreds
the vulnerable,
non-violent ways
we keep our boundaries sacrosanct.

All Gentle my response, Shekinah-Shalom.
Let there be no violence in me.

Voice Famine eats at human hope,
forcing us all to face the hunger
latent deep within us.

By M. T. Winter, Crossroad Pub. Co., © 1992 Medical Mission Sisters

All	Gentle my need, Shekinah-Shalom.
	Let there be no violence in me.

Voice War wields its guns and clubs
across a peace-loving planet;
its violent shot across my bow
solicits my surrender.

All Gentle my nerves, Shekinah-Shalom.
Let there be no violence in me.

Voice Those who abuse their privileged role
to batter into submission
the life and spirit entrusted to them
give rise to fears
that the child in us
will also be busted beyond repair.

All Gentle my fears, Shekinah-Shalom.
Let there be no violence in me.

Voice Humans rape and violate
the last shreds of integrity,
unleashing unknown angers in me,
forcing my shame to surface.

All Gentle my anger, Shekinah-Shalom.
Let there be no violence in me.

Voice Ritual runs its rites roughshod
over the suppliant worshiper
and my heart grieves
for all the credos
lost beyond recall.

All Gentle my pain, Shekinah-Shalom.
Let there be no violence in me.

Voice Words tear the veil away,
exposing frail humanity
in me and my companions.

All Gentle my truth, Shekinah-Shalom.
Let there be no violence in me.

   By M. T. Winter, Crossroad Pub. Co., © 1992 Medical Mission Sisters

ESTHER

◊ **Scripture Reference**   The Book of Esther

◊ **Biography**

Esther, daughter of Abihail, was raised by her relative Mordecai after her parents died. She was a Jew in the city of Susa in the kingdom of Media and Persia, and because of her beauty she was conscripted into the royal harem. She was crowned queen after she won the heart of King Ahasuerus, and she used her position to intercede for the lives of her people. Because of Queen Esther the Jews who were about to be destroyed won the right to defend themselves by killing those who would have killed them. Their victory gave rise to the feast of Purim. Its authorization as an annual holiday is attributed to Esther and Mordecai.

◊ **Context**

The ten chapters of the Book of Esther, which probably date from the fourth century B.C.E., serve as a festal legend for Purim, an annual cele-bration of the deliverance of Jews in Persia from persecution and death. While neither the events nor the central figures can be verified, there may well be a historical basis to the story and to the existence of its heroine. The book itself has been described as a historical novella dealing with human needs. It is included in the Hebrew canon and is consequently part of the Christian canon even though it has no overt religious mes-sage and it does not mention God. Because of this its canonical status has been challenged by both Jews and Christians, and various additions to the book have surfaced to form part of the present Apocrypha. The name Esther is derived from the Persian *stara* ("star") and from the Babylonian goddess Ishtar. Esther's Jewish name in the book and in tradition is Hadassah. In the broad outline of her story, the beauty of a poor orphan girl, a commoner, caught the fancy of a king and she was made a queen. She was of an alien culture, which she concealed from the king, and when the very existence of her people was threatened, she intervened to save them, and herself, from extinction. She moved from naive, unassuming passivity to cunning, daring, courageous action. The risking of her own life was rewarded with the fulfillment of her wish and the salvation of her people.

From that day forward, the orphan was raised to the status of national heroine and her memory has been perpetuated in a holiday celebrated each year. This is the stuff of which fairy tales are made. In between these lines, however, her experiences were more mundane. She was crowned queen, but she was royalty in name only. She had no authority, no power, no privilege. Like everyone else she risked death to come into the king's presence unsummoned, and she shared his bed with hundreds of other women. Valued on the basis of her looks, she learned to use that to her advantage. Reduced to using her sexual savvy to get what she wanted, she made her moves with discretion and maintained her integrity. There is much about Esther, both the reality and the ideal, that appeals directly to women. There are many in the universal sisterhood who can say, "I have been there," or "That's where I want to be." Because Esther's story is so long — it fills an entire book in the Bible — it has seldom been read in liturgical settings, but perhaps now that will change.

◇ **Lectionary Reading**

In the days of Ahasuerus,
who sat on the royal throne
in the citadel of Susa
and ruled one hundred twenty-seven provinces
from India to Ethiopia,
the king gave a banquet
for his officials and his officers,
his ministers and his governors,
to display the wealth of his kingdom
and the splendor of his majesty.
The banquet lasted seven days.
It was opulent and lavish.
Queen Vashti also gave a banquet
for the women of the palace.
On the seventh day, when Ahasuerus
had had more than his share of wine,
he commanded his seven eunuchs

to bring Queen Vashti before the king,
commanded she wear the royal crown,
so that all might admire her beauty.
Queen Vashti refused the king's commands
conveyed to her by the eunuchs.
Her defiance enraged the king
and his anger burned within him.
He consulted the sages who knew the laws.
What should he do with Queen Vashti
who had rebelled against the king?
Memucan, his Persian official, said,
"Not only has she insulted the king,
she offended the people as well.
Soon all women will hear of her deed
and will look with contempt on their husbands.
They will say, 'The king commanded her
and Queen Vashti did not come.'
This very day all noble women
will defy the king's officials,
citing the queen's behavior.
There will be no end to contempt and wrath.
Send out a royal order —
write it among the laws —
word it so that it may never be altered:
Vashti will never again be allowed
to come before King Ahasuerus,
and the king will give her royal position
to another who is better than she.
Proclaim this decree throughout your kingdom,
vast though it may be,
so women will honor their husbands,
all women honor all husbands,
whatever their state in life."
The king was pleased with this advice
and wrote to all the provinces
in their local scripts and dialects,
bluntly declaring that every man
should be master in his own house.

When the king's anger had abated,
he remembered Vashti and what she had done
and what was decreed against her.
The king's servants said to him,
"Let beautiful young virgins be brought for the king,
taken from all the provinces
to the harem in the citadel

and given cosmetic treatments
in the custody of the eunuch Hegai.
And let the girl who pleases the king
be queen instead of Vashti."
The king thought this was a good idea,
so they did as they had said.
Now there was a Jew in the citadel of Susa
whose name was Mordecai.
He had raised his cousin Esther
and had adopted her as his daughter
after her parents died.
The girl was beautiful.
She was among those lovely young women
taken into custody under edict of the king.
Every day Mordecai came near the harem
to learn how Esther was.
Now Esther had not revealed her background.
Mordecai had told her not to.
The head eunuch Hegai favored Esther.
He planned her cosmetics and diet,
gave seven palace maids to her,
and then advanced her and her maids
to the best place in the harem.
After twelve months under custody for cosmetic preparation,
each girl in turn went in to the king
and returned the following morning,
but to a different harem,
the one for concubines
under custody of Shaashgaz, the king's eunuch.
She did not return to the king again
unless she was summoned by name.
Now Esther was admired by everyone.
When it was time for Esther's turn,
she won the heart of Ahasuerus
who loved her very much,
more than all the other women.
He set the crown on Esther's head
and made her queen instead of Vashti.
Then he gave a royal banquet —
he called it "Esther's banquet" —
declared a royal holiday
and showered his court with gifts.
Now Mordecai was at the king's gate
when the virgins were being gathered,
and he overheard two of the king's eunuchs
planning the king's assassination.

Mordecai told Queen Esther,
she told Ahasuerus,
mentioning Mordecai's name;
and when the affair was investigated
and proved indeed to be so,
the villains were hung on the gallows.
The incident was recorded in the annals of the king.

Ahasuerus promoted a man named Haman
and set him over all.
The king's servants bowed down to him,
and they also paid him homage
as was commanded by the king.
Mordecai did not bow to him
and did not pay him homage.
The king's servants challenged him.
"Why do you disobey the king?"
Day after day they taunted him,
and they even challenged Haman,
for Mordecai had revealed to them
the fact that he was a Jew.
Haman himself was furious
because Mordecai would not bow before him
and would not pay him homage.
Secretly Haman plotted revenge.
He had a plan to destroy the Jews:
he would wipe out Mordecai's people
throughout the kingdom of Ahasuerus.
Then Haman said to the king,
"There is a group of people
dispersed throughout the provinces
who are different from all the rest;
they do not keep the king's laws,
they are separate from other people.
Why do you tolerate this?
If you will decree their destruction,
I will see that it gets done.
I will pay ten thousand talents of silver
into the king's own treasury
for those who will do the deed."
The king agreed to the plan of Haman,
the enemy of the Jews.
"Keep your money," the king told Haman,
"take my men and do with them
whatever seems right to you."
Decrees were sent to the provinces

in every language and every script,
written by King Ahasuerus
and sealed with his signet ring.
The letters sent by couriers
gave orders to destroy, kill, annihilate
all Jews, young and old,
even women and children,
on the thirteenth day of the twelfth month,
which is the month of Adar,
and to plunder all their goods.
The king and Haman sat down to drink,
but Susa was thrown into chaos.

When Mordecai learned what had been done,
he tore his clothes, wore sackcloth and ashes,
and went through the city, wailing
with a loud and bitter cry.
In every province the cry was heard
of mourning among the Jews.
They fasted, wept, lamented,
and most wore sackcloth and ashes.
When Esther's maids and eunuchs told her,
the queen was deeply distressed.
She sent her eunuch to Mordecai
to find out what was going on.
Mordecai told him that Haman was plotting
the destruction of the Jews.
He gave him a copy of the written decree
that had been issued there in Susa
so that he might take it to Esther
and charge her to go before the king
to intercede for her people.
The eunuch told Esther what Mordecai had said,
and Esther sent word to Mordecai,
"All the king's servants and all the king's people
know that if anyone, woman or man,
should go to the king without being called,
they would be executed. That is the law.
There is but one exception:
if the king should hold out his golden scepter to someone,
that person would live.
For thirty days I have not been called
to come in to the king."
Then Mordecai sent word to Esther,
"You may be in the palace,
but you are still a Jew.

What makes you think that you will escape?
If you keep silent at such a time,
deliverance will come from another quarter,
but you and your family will perish.
Who knows the mind of God?
Perhaps you have come to your royal role
for just such a time as this."
Then Esther sent word to Mordecai,
"Gather all the Jews in Susa, and fast on my behalf.
Do not eat or drink for three days and three nights.
My maids and I will also fast,
and then I will go to the king.
Even though it is against the law.
And even if I perish."

After she had fasted
and three full days had passed,
Esther put on her royal robes
and went to the king's palace.
She stood waiting in the inner court
opposite the king's hall.
When the king saw Esther standing in the court,
he held out his golden scepter.
Esther approached and touched the scepter.
The king then said to her,
"What is it, Queen Esther?
What is your request?
I promise it shall be given to you,
even to half my kingdom."
"If it pleases the king," Esther said,
"come to the banquet I have prepared
and bring Haman with you."
The king acted quickly to fulfill her desire.
At the banquet he said to Esther,
"What is your petition? It shall be granted you.
Even to half my kingdom, your request shall be fulfilled."
"This is my petition," said Esther.
"If I have won the king's favor,
and if it pleases the king,
come with Haman again tomorrow
to the banquet I will prepare.
Then I will do as the king has said."
Haman was happy that day,
but when he saw Mordecai at the king's gate,
saw that he did not bow to him
nor did he tremble before him,

he was infuriated, but he restrained himself.
At home he called his wife Zeresh
and a gathering of friends,
and he boasted of his riches
and the number of his sons,
his promotions and his advancements,
and announced to everyone,
"Even Queen Esther invited me
to her banquet with the king.
Yet tell me, what good is all of this
when I see that Jew Mordecai
sitting at the king's gate."
Then his wife Zeresh and his friends replied,
"Build a gallows and tell the king
to have Mordecai hung on it.
Then go to the banquet in good spirits
and make merry with the king."
This advice pleased Haman,
and he had the gallows made.

That night the king was unable to sleep,
so he sent for the book of records
and they read this to the king.
It was written there how Mordecai
had reported the two assassins
and saved the life of the king.
The king asked his attendants,
"What honor was given Mordecai?"
"Nothing has been done for him," they said.
"Who is in the court?" he asked.
Now Haman had just entered the outer court.
He wanted to speak to the king
about having Mordecai put to death
on the gallows he had prepared.
"Haman is there," the servants said.
The king said, "Let him come in."
"What shall be done for the man
the king would honor?" asked the king.
"He must be thinking of me," thought Haman,
so this was his reply.
"For the man whom the king would honor,
let royal robes be brought to him,
and a horse which the king has ridden,
and a royal crown for his head.
Let the one to be honored be robed
by the king's most notable official,

who will then lead the man on horseback
through the city's public square, proclaiming,
'Thus shall it be done for the man
whom the king wishes to honor.' "
Then the king said to Haman, "Quickly,
take the robes and the horse, just as you said,
and honor the Jew Mordecai
who sits at the king's gate."
So Haman did as the king commanded,
parading Mordecai in public, proclaiming,
'Thus shall it be done for the man
whom the king wishes to honor.' "
Then Mordecai returned to the king's gate,
while Haman went home humiliated
and deeply distressed.
He reported to his wife and friends
who offered advice to him.
"If Mordecai is a Jew,
then you will not prevail against him.
It is you who will surely fall."
While they were speaking, eunuchs arrived
and hurried Haman off to the banquet
that Esther had prepared.

The king and Haman were at Esther's feast.
On the second day, while drinking wine,
the king said again to Esther,
"What is your petition?
Even if half my kingdom,
your request shall be fulfilled."
Then Queen Esther answered,
"If I have won favor with you,
and if it pleases the king,
let my life be spared —
and spare the life of my people —
that is my petition; that is my request.
For we have been sold, I and my people,
to be killed, destroyed, annihilated.
If we had only been sold as slaves,
I would have held my peace;
but no enemy can compensate
this damage to the king."
Then Ahasuerus said to Esther,
"Who is he, and where is he,
who presumed to do this thing?"
Esther said, "He is Haman,

a wicked enemy in our midst."
The king rose up in wrath and went out
into the palace garden,
while Haman, terrified, remained with Esther
to plead with her for his life,
for he knew beyond a doubt
that King Ahasuerus would destroy him.
When the king returned,
Haman was by the couch where Esther was reclining.
Seeing him there, he shouted,
"Will he even assault the queen in my house
and right here in my presence?"
One of the eunuchs said to the king,
"The gallows that Haman made for Mordecai,
the man whose action saved the king,
stands at Haman's house."
The king said, "Hang him there."
So they hung Haman on the gallows he built
for Mordecai the Jew.
And the king's anger abated.

Mordecai came before the king,
for Esther had told of his relationship to her,
and the king took off his signet ring
and gave it to Mordecai.
On that day he gave Queen Esther
the house that belonged to Haman,
and Esther in turn set Mordecai over the house of Haman.
Then Esther spoke again to the king.
She fell at his feet, weeping and pleading
that he stop the evil plot that Haman
had devised against the Jews.
The king held out the golden scepter
and Esther rose before him, saying,
"If it pleases the king, let an order be sent
to revoke the letters of Haman."
King Ahasuerus said to Queen Esther
and to Mordecai the Jew,
"You may write as you please with regard to the Jews
and seal it with my ring."
So an edict was sent by Mordecai,
in the name of the king and sealed with his ring,
allowing the Jews everywhere
to assemble and defend their lives,
to kill, destroy, annihilate
any armed force that attacked their person

or plundered what they possessed
on the thirteenth day of the twelfth month,
which is the month of Adar.
Couriers mounted swift royal steeds,
urged on by the king's command,
and carried the letters everywhere,
announcing that Jews had the right
to take revenge on their enemies
on a single day that year.
The decree was also posted in the citadel of Susa.
Mordecai went out in royal robes, a golden crown,
and a mantle of linen and purple,
and the city of Susa rejoiced.
There was light and gladness, honor and joy
for Jews throughout the kingdom.
In every city of every province,
wherever the edict was posted,
the Jews felt joy and gladness,
and they held a festival
and announced a holiday.
Many people professed to be Jews,
because they were afraid,
because the fear of Jewish revenge
had suddenly fallen upon them.

On the thirteenth day of the twelfth month,
which is the month of Adar,
the Jews struck down their enemies
and all who hated them.
In the citadel of Susa,
they killed five hundred people
and the ten sons of Haman,
but they did not touch their goods.
The king said to Queen Esther,
"What now is your petition?
It shall be granted you."
"If it pleases the king," said Esther,
"let the Jews who are in Susa
do tomorrow what they did today,
and let them hang the sons of Haman
on the gallows their father built."
And so the king commanded.
On the fourteenth day in Susa,
they killed three hundred persons
and hung the sons of Haman,
but they did not touch their goods.

The other Jews in the provinces
also defeated their enemies;
seventy-five thousand people died,
but they did not touch their goods.
In the provinces they accomplished this
on the thirteenth day of the month of Adar.
On the fourteenth day, they rested,
and held that day a holiday of feasting and of gladness.
But the Jews who were in Susa rested on the fifteenth day
with a feast of joy and gladness.
Therefore the Jews of the villages
hold holiday on the fourteenth day,
sending gifts of food to each other.
Esther and Mordecai recorded all these things
and established the Jewish holiday
as the day on which the Jews
had gained relief from their enemies.
Two full days, year after year,
would be days of feasting and gladness,
of sending gifts of food to each other
and presents to the poor,
for what had been a month of mourning
had become a time of gladness.
So the Jews adopted as custom keeping an annual holiday,
as Esther and Mordecai had established.
These days are called Purim,
for Haman in casting Pur — "the lot" —
to decimate all the Jews,
caused instead his own destruction.
These days shall be remembered.
Queen Esther and Mordecai
enjoined them on the Jews.

The honors accorded Mordecai,
all his acts of power and authority,
the status to which the king had advanced him,
all is written in the annals of the kings of Media and Persia.
For Mordecai was second in rank only to King Ahasuerus.
He was powerful and popular among the Jewish people,
always seeking to do them good,
interceding for their welfare,
and championing their cause.

Queen Esther confirmed by written authority
this second letter about Purim.
It was her command that fixed for Jews
these practices of Purim.

◇ **Points for Shared Reflection**

- Have you as a woman ever felt that you had been given a position in name only, without the authority, privileges, resources, or respect ordinarily accorded that status?

- From time immemorial, women have had to get by on the basis of their bodies, either by their looks or by their sexual favors. Has this changed much in our changing world or are things still pretty much the same?

- Do you think there is anything worth dying for today? Would you be willing to risk your life on behalf of a person or a people or a cause? Please elaborate on your response.

- Today, women in professional positions or in public office are expected to be advocates for all women, and many feel personally responsible for fostering the advancement of their gender. Has this ever been true for you?

◇ **A Psalm in Praise of Heroines** (see p. 108)

◇ **Prayer**
O Heroine of heroines,
Your wisdom is reflected
in the stories of our sisters,
and Your power is made manifest
in the outlines of their lives.
You were there when they stood for justice
and You rode with them into battle
against all the evil forces
that surrounded and still surround.
Be with us now as we too face
the hour of our decision.
Make us strong, secure, confident
that You will achieve what we must do.
We praise Your name,
and we thank You
in the name of all women.
Amen.

◊ A PSALM IN PRAISE OF HEROINES ◊

Leader   Remember Eve, our matriarch,
and mother of all the living.

All   We praise you, Eve,
and all women
who have had to make difficult choices
in seductive environments.

Leader   Remember Hagar, matriarch
of a portion of God's people.

All   We praise you, Hagar,
and all women
who bravely bear the burden
of being labeled second-class.

Leader   Remember Shiprah and Puah,
midwives in the land of bondage.

All   We praise you, Shiprah and Puah,
and all women
who risk their lives to bring forth life
when the laws are stacked against them.

Leader   Remember Miriam,
prophetic leader of the Exodus.

All   We praise you, Miriam,
and all women
who have challenged male authority
and been cursed with banishment.

Leader   Remember Mahlah, Noah, Hoglah, Milcah, and Tirzah,
feminists in the promised land.

All   We praise you,
Mahlah, Noah, Hoglah, Milcah, and Tirzah,
and all women
who have pushed religious authority to consider
gender equality.

Leader   Remember Jael,
liberator of her people.

All   We praise you, Jael,
and all women
who have single-handedly saved us
from destruction of any kind.

 By M. T. Winter, Crossroad Pub. Co., © 1992 Medical Mission Sisters

Leader	Remember the heroine of Thebez, who spontaneously saved her people.

All	We praise you, heroine of Thebez, and all women who waste no time in solving problems, who learn through experience.

Leader	Remember the Shunammite woman, the prophet Elisha's friend.

All	We praise you, Shunammite woman, and all women who refuse to be dismissed.

Leader	Remember Rizpah, a mother who had to deal with kings.

All	We praise you, Rizpah, and all women who stand firm and refuse to cover up a patriarchal sin.

Leader	Remember Judith, a widow and savior of her people.

All	We praise you, Judith, and all women who make the impossible possible and do it with finesse.

Leader	Remember Queen Vashti, who resisted pressure from the throne.

All	We praise you, Queen Vashti, and all women who resist the pressure to parade and perform before the eyes of men.

Leader	Remember Esther, our sister Hadassah, and the courage of her deed.

All	We praise you, Esther, our sister Hadassah, and all women who use their status to foster life, who have intervened to counteract genocidal extermination.

Leader/All	We remember all our heroines, named and unnamed, known and unknown. We thank you and we praise you.

By M. T. Winter, Crossroad Pub. Co., © 1992 Medical Mission Sisters

JUDITH

◇ **Scripture Reference**   The Book of Judith

◇ **Biography**

Judith daughter of Merari, wife of Manasseh, was a beautiful, wealthy, courageous woman who lived in the town of Bethulia and liberated her people from an Assyrian siege by seducing Holofernes, general of the Assyrian army, and chopping off his head.

◇ **Context**

Many are of the opinion that the Book of Judith and its heroine are fictitious. Originally written in Hebrew and included in the Septuagint, this historical narrative or novel is part of the Roman Catholic and Greek church canons and the Apocrypha of other Christian churches. From a literary perspective, it is one of the most finished works of Second Temple times, and from a religious perspective, it is significant for its *halakhah* and for the faith it reflects. Historically, the point in time, political regime, territorial setting, and chief characters of its storyline cannot be verified. Determined to punish vassal nations for not contributing troops to support him in his war, the king in question sent out a massive contingent to retaliate. Surprisingly, their forward movement was halted by a tiny Jewish town guarding the mountain pass into Jerusalem. After a devastating siege of thirty-four days, when their cisterns were dry and their food about finished, the people of the town pushed their leaders to promise surrender at the end of five days. Challenging that decision, Judith was told by the male leadership to pray for rain, but she had other plans. Deeply religious, she made all the appropriate ritual preparations. Stunningly beautiful, she fulfilled stereotypical expectations by preparing her body, augmenting her beauty, and setting out for a soiree of seduction. Atypically, she slaughtered the abuser of nations, dropped his head into her food bag, slipped through enemy lines unmolested, and returned to her beleaguered town to energize its resistance and spur her people on to victory. Their liberation lifted Judith to heroic stature. After a jubilant celebration, she was content to continue in her widowhood for the remainder of her days.

The question is, was there a Judith? It seems more appropriate to ask, why wouldn't there be? Her story is well within the realm of possibility, particularly in light of the many extreme persecutions to which the Jewish people have been subjected. Judith's story could well be a fictional reconstruction based on solid historical fact, a popular genre even in our times. Then why would a world, hungry for heroines, be so quick to dismiss her? Maybe because we fear she already exists in spirit in far too many women, and maybe because the violence of her act triggers a primal terror in males, that to succumb to a woman is to be vulnerable to death. If Judith is conceivable, then she is open to imitation, and that is really terrifying. Judith's story comprises sixteen chapters of scripture. It is well worth taking the time to read it. The full story follows. For an abbreviated version, turn to the narrative for Judith's maid on p. 343.

◇ Lectionary Reading

In those days Nebuchadnezzar
ruled over the Assyrians in the great city of Nineveh.
Arphaxad ruled the Medes in the city of Ecbatana.
In the twelfth year of the reign of King Nebuchadnezzar,
he waged war against King Arphaxad,
and all the people from the hill country
to the Tigris and the Euphrates rallied to his aid.
Then he sent messengers to Persia,
to Lebanon and Damascus,
to those among the nations of Carmel and Gilead,
the Upper Galilee and Samaria,
and way beyond the Jordan
as far as Jerusalem and Bethany and Kadesh
and the territory of Goshen,
to Egypt and Ethiopia,
but the whole region ignored him
and refused to join him in war,
for they were not afraid of him.
Nebuchadnezzar king of Assyria
was furious with the region

and swore by his throne and his kingdom
that he would take revenge,
that all the inhabitants of Moab and Ammon,
of Egypt and all Judea,
all who lived between the two seas
he would slaughter with his sword.
In the seventeenth year
Nebuchadnezzar defeated Arphaxad in battle,
captured Ecbatana,
plundered all its markets,
turned its glory to disgrace.
Then he returned to Nineveh
and he and his forces rested and feasted
for one hundred twenty days.

In the eighteenth year
there was talk in the palace
that Nebuchadnezzar would carry out his revenge.
He summoned all his ministers
and set before them his secret plan,
and together they decided
that every country that did not come to his aid
would be destroyed.
Nebuchadnezzar called Holofernes,
the general of his army,
second only to himself, and said,
"Take one hundred twenty thousand soldiers
and twelve thousand cavalry
and march against these people.
Tell them that I am coming
and that my troops will cover the earth,
that their wounded will fill the ravines and gullies,
that the river will swell with their dead,
and that I will lead away captives
to the day of their punishment,
and I will show no mercy,
but will slaughter and plunder all.
By the power of my kingdom
I will accomplish what I have said."
Holofernes picked his divisions
and mustered a massive army,
adding camels and mules and donkeys and oxen,
silver and gold from the palace,
and sheep and goats for food.
Then he set out with his army,
with his chariots and his cavalry,

accompanied by an enormous crowd —
a multitude that could not be counted —
thick as a swarm of locusts,
like dust that covers the earth.
In advance of King Nebuchadnezzar,
they marched three days from Nineveh
and camped in an open plain.
By means of forays into the hills
they ravaged all around them,
through fortified towns and the desert
they fought as far as the sea,
sacking, burning, killing, pillaging
tents, towns, sheepfolds, harvests,
down into the plains of Damascus,
all were put to the sword.
The fear and dread of the Assyrians
fell upon all the people who lived along the sea.

Couriers were sent to sue for peace.
This is what they said.
"We, your servants,
O Great King Nebuchadnezzar,
lie prostrate before you.
Do with us what you will.
Our buildings, our land,
our wheat fields and flocks and encampments
lie before you;
do with them as you please.
Our towns and their inhabitants
you may take and make your slaves."
When Holofernes heard this,
he went and stationed garrisons
in all the fortified towns.
The people of town and countryside
welcomed him with garlands and tambourines and dancing.
He demolished all their sacred shrines
and destroyed their gods, for all were expected
to worship Nebuchadnezzar as god.
Then Holofernes came to Esdraelon
by the great ridge of Judea,
and that is where he camped.

When the Israelites in Judea
heard of all that Holofernes had done,
how he had plundered towns and temples,
they were exceedingly terrified,
for themselves and for Jerusalem

and for the temple of their God.
They had just returned from exile,
and the temple, altar, and sacred vessels
had been consecrated again.
So they notified every district,
they fortified hilltop villages,
they set in stores of food in preparation for all-out war.
The high priest, Joakim, in Jerusalem said,
seize the mountain passes whereby Judea might be invaded
and station garrisons there.
So the Israelites saw that this was done,
and everyone fervently cried to God
and humbled themselves with fasting,
wore sackcloth and ashes,
pleaded with God to protect their towns,
their infants, and their wives,
and prayed that the sacred sanctuary
would not be desecrated or profaned.

It was reported to Holofernes
that Israel was prepared for war.
They had closed the mountain passes,
fortified the hilltops,
and barricaded the plains.
In anger he asked the Canaanites
about who these people were,
in what their power consisted,
who was their king,
who led their army,
could they give an estimate of their strength,
and why did they alone, of all the lands,
so staunchly resist surrender?
Then the leader of the Ammonites
recounted to Holofernes
the history of Israel,
from the time they settled in Canaan
to their Exodus from Egypt
and their conquest of the land.
He said their God was with them
as long as they did no evil,
told how they were completely defeated
and led off into captivity
as punishment for their sins.
But now they have returned
from all those places where they were scattered
and have reoccupied Jerusalem

where their sanctuary is.
Then Achior the Ammonite concluded,
"So then, my lord, if they have sinned,
we can go forth and defeat them,
but if they have not, then pass them by,
for their God will surely defend them
and make of us a laughingstock
throughout the rest of the world."
Bystanders who overheard his words
said he should be cut to pieces.
"We are not afraid of the Israelites,
for they are a powerless people," they said.
"Go ahead, Holofernes, let's make war,
and our armies will swallow them up."

When the din had settled,
Holofernes spoke before all the foreign contingents:
"Who are you, Achior, to prophesy
that their God will defend them against us?
What god is there but Nebuchadnezzar?
His forces will overwhelm them.
Their mountains will run with blood.
Their fields will be full of their dead.
Not even their footprints will survive our attack.
The people will utterly perish.
As for you, Achior, at my return
you shall fall among their wounded.
My slaves will put you in one of their towns.
You will perish along with them."
They took Achior to Bethulia,
to the springs below the town,
and they had to dodge a shower of stones
before they returned to camp.
The Israelites came for Achior.
They took him into Bethulia,
set him before the magistrates,
assembled all the elders
and proceeded to question him.
He told them of all that had been said
at the council of Holofernes,
how he boasted of conquering Israel.
Then the townspeople worshiped God, saying,
"O God of heaven, see their arrogance,
and have pity on our people.
Look kindly today on the faces of those
who are consecrated to you."

They reassured Achior, praised him highly,
then one of the magistrates took him home,
and all that night, the people of Israel
called on God for help.

The next day Holofernes moved against Bethulia.
He ordered his army to seize the passes
and make war on the Israelites.
The warriors and all the fighting forces,
in number a very great multitude,
encamped in the valley near Bethulia,
and when the Israelites saw their strength,
they were greatly terrified.
And yet they seized their weapons
and remained on guard all night.
On the second day,
Holofernes reconnoitered the town's approaches,
seized the springs that supplied their water
and put them under guard.
The auxiliary leaders and chieftains said,
"If you do not fight against them,
not a man of your army will fall.
Remain in camp, restrain your forces,
and maintain possession of the spring of water
that flows from the foot of the mountain,
for this is their water supply.
Let their thirst destroy them,
and they will surrender the town.
Keep watch from nearby mountaintops
to see that no one leaves.
They will waste away with famine
long before they feel the sword;
they will be strewn in the city streets,
and you will have won the war."
Holofernes agreed and moved ahead.
They held the spring, took charge of the hills,
and the rest of the Assyrian army,
a vast and sprawling multitude,
remained there in the plain,
and they covered the face of the land.
The Israelites were surrounded.
There was no way of escape.
Their courage failed and they cried to God.
Thirty-four days from the start of the siege,
the water containers of Bethulia were empty,
the cisterns were going dry,

all their water was rationed,
there was never enough to drink.
Children were listless,
women and men, fainting from thirst,
fell in the streets of the town.
They no longer had any strength.
Then all the people cried out in despair
and said before the elders,
"We should have made peace with Assyria.
Now we have no one to help us.
God has sold us into their hands.
Surrender the town to Holofernes.
It is better to be captured and made their slaves
than to watch our babies, our children, our wives
die before our eyes.
The God of our ancestors is punishing us
for our sins and the sins of the past."
Loud cries and lamentation
were interrupted by their leader, Uzziah.
"Courage, my brothers and sisters!
Hold out for five days more.
By then our God will show mercy,
for God will not forsake us.
If these days pass and no help comes,
I will do just as you say."
He dismissed the people to their various posts
and went up on the walls and towers.
He sent the women and children home.
There was misery throughout the town.

Now in those days Judith of Bethulia
suffered all these things.
She was the daughter of Merari
son of Ox
son of Joseph
son of Oziel
son of Elkiah
son of Ananias
son of Gideon
son of Raphain
son of Ahitub
son of Elijah
son of Hilkiah
son of Eliab
son of Nathanel
son of Salamiel

son of Sarasadai
son of Israel.
Her husband Manasseh of her tribe and family
had died three years earlier.
Overcome by the heat at harvest time,
he collapsed there in Bethulia
and they buried him among his own.
Judith remained as a widow
in a tent on the roof of her house.
She wore sackcloth and widow's clothing,
and fasted, except on the sabbath,
the new moon, and festivals.
She was beautiful in appearance,
really lovely to behold.
Her husband had left her silver and gold,
slaves, fields, and livestock,
and she managed this large estate.
No one spoke ill of Judith.
She was devoted to God.
When Judith heard the harsh words of the people
who were desperate for water,
and Uzziah's oath to surrender in five days
if God did not come through,
she sent her maid to summon Uzziah
and the elders of the town,
and they came to her and she said,
"Rulers of Bethulia, what you said today is not right.
Who are you to put God to the test?
Do not anger God.
If God does not help us within five days,
God can help us another time,
or even choose to destroy us.
Do not try to bind God's purposes,
for God will not be threatened
or won over by our pleading.
While we wait for our deliverance,
let us call on God to help us.
God will answer when God wills.
Never in our generation
has any tribe or family or town of ours
worshiped gods that were made with hands,
as was done in days gone by.
That is why our ancestors suffered defeat.
If we are captured, our sanctuary will suffer desecration
and we will pay for it with our blood.
The slaughter of our families,

the captivity of the land,
the desolation of our inheritance —
all this will be brought upon our heads
wherever we serve as slaves.
Our slavery will not bring us respite,
but will be to our disgrace.
Let us therefore set an example,
because others depend on us,
and the survival of the sanctuary —
the temple and the altar —
is a burden that is ours.
Give thanks to God who is testing us,
just as God tested our ancestors,
for trials and tribulations accompany those
who are close to God."
Then Uzziah said to Judith,
"All that you say is true.
None can deny your words,
for your wisdom and understanding
have been apparent throughout your life.
But the people were so thirsty,
they compelled us to make that promise
and now we cannot break our oath.
Since you are a God-fearing woman,
pray to God for us,
for rain to fill our cisterns
so that we will no longer thirst."
Then Judith said to them, "Listen to me,
for I have come up with a plan.
What I will do will be spoken of throughout all generations.
Stand tonight at the gate of the town
so that I might go out with my maid.
Within those days which you have promised,
God will deliver us by my hand.
Do not ask what I am doing.
I can only tell you when I am through."
Uzziah and the rulers said,
"Go in peace, and may God go before you."

At the very time when the evening incense
was being offered in Jerusalem,
Judith, in sackcloth and ashes,
cried out aloud to God:
"O God of my ancestor Simeon,
to whom you gave an avenging sword
for the evils accorded your people;

they called on you for help, O God,
hear me too, a widow.
You have been maker of miracles
for those who have gone before
and for those who have followed after.
Well, here now are the Assyrians
who boast in horse and rider,
trust shield and spear, unaware
that you are the God who crushes war.
Break their strength by your power
and pour your wrath upon their heads
and give to me, a widow,
the strength to do what I plan,
so that by the hand of a woman,
their arrogance may be destroyed.
For your strength does not depend on numbers,
nor your power on any power of ours.
You are the God of the lowly,
helper of the oppressed,
strength of those who are weak and fearful,
protector of the forsaken,
savior of those without hope.
God of our ancestors,
God of our heritage,
have pity and hear my prayer.
Make my words of deceit destroy
the ones who conspire against your covenant
and against your sacred house."

When Judith's prayer was ended,
she rose and called her maid —
the one in charge of all she possessed —
and went into the house where she lived on sabbaths
and other festal days.
She took off her widow's garments,
bathed her body with water,
anointed herself with precious ointment,
combed her hair, put on a tiara,
dressed herself in festive attire
and put sandals on her feet.
She took anklets, bracelets, rings, earrings,
and all her other jewelry
and made herself very beautiful
to entice the eyes of all the men
who might chance to look on her.
She gave her maid a skin of wine,

a flask of oil,
and a bag of roasted grain,
dried fig cakes, fine bread,
and her dishes wrapped in a cloth.
They went to the gate of Bethulia
and found Uzziah standing there with the elders of the town.
When they saw her transformed appearance,
they were astounded at her beauty and said,
"May the God of our ancestors favor you
and fulfill your expectations,
that the people of Israel may glory
and Jerusalem may be exalted."
And she bowed down to God.
"Open the gate of the town," she said,
"that I may go out and accomplish
the things you said to me."
So they opened the gate as she requested
and Judith went out with her maid.
They watched her go down the mountain
and enter into the valley
and there they lost sight of her.
As the women were walking through the valley,
they were taken into custody.
The Assyrian patrol asked them,
"Where are you coming from?
Where are you going?
To what people do you belong?"
"I am a daughter of the Hebrews," said Judith,
"but I am fleeing from them,
for they are about to be handed over to you
to be devoured.
I am on my way to Holofernes,
commander of your army,
to give him a true report.
I will show him a way he can enter in
to capture all of the region
without losing one of his men."
When the men heard her words and saw her face —
she was oh, so beautiful —
they said to her, "You have saved your life
by coming over to us.
Go at once to the commander's tent.
Some of us will escort you
and hand you over to him.
When you stand before him, have no fear,
just tell him what you have said,

and he will be good to you."
They chose from their number a hundred men
to accompany her and her maid,
and they brought them to Holofernes' tent.
What excitement there was throughout the camp,
for word of her arrival had been passed from tent to tent.
The troops gathered around her
as she stood outside Holofernes' tent,
waiting for word to enter.
They marveled at her beauty
and admired the Israelites, saying,
"Who can despise these people
who have women such as this?
Yet we must not let a man escape
who might yet beguile the world."
Then Judith was led into the tent.
Holofernes was resting on his canopied bed
of purple and gold and emeralds
and other precious gems.
He got up and came to meet her,
preceded by silver lamps.
Holofernes and all his servants
marveled at her beauty.
She bowed to the ground before him,
but his slaves lifted her up.

Holofernes said to Judith,
"Take courage, woman, do not be afraid,
I have never hurt anyone who chose to serve
Nebuchadnezzar, king of the earth.
Even now, if your people had not slighted me,
I would not be aligned against them.
They have brought this on themselves.
Tell me now why you have fled from them
and why you came over to us.
Take courage! You have come to safety.
I assure you, you will live,
and no one here will hurt you,
but all will treat you well."
Then Judith gave this answer,
"Accept the words of your servant.
I speak nothing false this night.
We have all heard of your wisdom and skill,
how you alone are best in the kingdom,
the most informed, the most astute.
By the life of Nebuchadnezzar, king of all the earth,

you direct every living being.
Humans serve him because of you.
Animals live because of you.
Therefore, lord and master,
do not disregard what Achior said,
for our nation cannot be punished,
nor can the sword prevail against us,
unless the people turn to sin
and turn away from God.
So now I have come to inform you
that God will soon be angry.
What they are about to do is wrong.
Their food supply is exhausted,
their water has given out,
so they plan to kill their livestock
and eat forbidden meat,
they plan to consume the first fruits of grain
and the tithes of wine and oil
which they had consecrated to God.
On the very day they do this thing,
they will be handed over to you.
When I learned of this, I fled to you.
God has sent me to accomplish with you
things that will astonish the world
wherever people hear of them.
So I will remain with you, my lord,
but every night your servant
will go out into the valley to pray.
God will tell me when they have sinned,
then I will come and tell this to you
so that your strength may prevail.
Then I will lead you through Judea
until you come to Jerusalem,
and there I will set your throne.
This, my lord, was foretold to me
and I was sent to tell it to you."
Her words pleased Holofernes.
All marveled at her wisdom and said,
"No woman on earth speaks as wisely
or looks as beautiful as she."
Then Holofernes said to Judith,
"God has done well to send you to us.
You are not only beautiful,
but you are also wise.
If indeed you do as you have said,
then your God shall be my God,

and you shall live in the palace of King Nebuchadnezzar
and be acclaimed throughout the world."

Holofernes ordered a table set
with some of his own delicacies and his silver dinnerware.
Judith said, "I cannot partake of this
or it will be an offense.
I have brought enough things with me."
"If your supply runs out," Holofernes said,
"can we get you more of the same?"
Judith replied, "As you live, my lord,
before your servant consumes these supplies,
God will accomplish by my hand
all that God has determined."
His servants took her to her tent,
and at midnight, she rose and sent word to Holofernes,
"Give orders to allow me to go out and pray."
So Holofernes gave the order
and the guards did not hinder her.
For three days she remained in camp.
She went out each night to the valley of Bethulia
and bathed at the spring to purify herself,
prayed to God to direct her,
then returned and stayed inside her tent
and ate her food toward evening.
On the fourth day Holofernes
held a banquet for his personal attendants.
He did not invite his officers.
He said to the eunuch in charge of his affairs,
"Go and persuade the Hebrew woman
to eat and drink with us.
It would be a disgrace to be near such a woman
and not have intercourse with her.
If we do not seduce her, she will laugh at us."
The eunuch said to Judith,
"Come to my lord, enjoy his presence,
and become like one of the Assyrian women
who serve in the royal palace."
"Who am I to refuse my lord?" said Judith.
"Whatever pleases him, I will do, and it will be a joy."
So she dressed in all her finery.
Her maid went ahead and spread on the ground
the lambskins for reclining.
Judith came into the tent and lay down,
and Holofernes was wild with passion,
for he had waited for this opportunity

from the day he laid eyes on her.
"Have a drink. Be merry!" he said.
"I will gladly drink, my lord," said Judith,
"for this is the greatest day of my life,"
and she ate and drank what her maid had prepared.
Holofernes was so delighted with her,
he drank an enormous amount of wine,
more than he had drunk on any one day
since the day that he was born.

When evening came, his servants withdrew.
The night had been long and they were weary,
so they all went off to bed.
Judith was left with Holofernes
sprawled in a drunken stupor across his canopied bed.
Her maid waited outside the tent,
for Judith had said they would go to pray
as on every other night.
Judith stood beside the bed and prayed within her heart,
"O God of power, guide my hands for the glory of Jerusalem.
Now is the time to destroy the enemies
who have risen up against us
and safeguard your heritage."
She took the sword from the bedpost
where it hung by Holofernes' head
and grabbed hold of his hair, praying,
"Give me strength, O God of Israel!"
She struck his neck, twice, with all her might,
and with that, cut off his head.
She pushed the body off the bed
and rolled it in the canopy.
The head of Holofernes
she put into the bag with her food.
Then she and her maid went out to pray
as they had been accustomed.
They passed through the camp,
circled the valley,
went up the side of the mountain,
and came to Bethulia's gate.
Judith called out to the sentries,
"Open the gate! Our God is with us,
overpowering our enemies yesterday and today."
When the people of Bethulia heard her voice,
they summoned the elders of the town
and all ran to the gate,
astounded that she had returned.

"Praise God," she said, "whose mercy abounds,
for God has destroyed our enemies
this very night
by my hand."
She pulled the head from the bag and said,
"Here is the head of Holofernes,
commander of the Assyrian army.
He died by the hand of a woman!
It is God who has protected me,
for although my face seduced him,
my body committed no sin."
The people were all astonished
and they worshiped God with one accord.
"Blessed are you, O God of Israel,
who has this day humiliated the enemies of your people."
Then Uzziah said to Judith,
"Daughter, you are blessed by the Most High God
above all other women on earth.
Blessed be God who has guided you
to cut off the enemy's head.
Your praise will remain in the hearts of all
who remember the power of God.
God grant you perpetual honor
and reward you with many blessings,
because you risked your life this night
to avert the ruin of our nation.
Straight was your path before God."
And the people said, "Amen!"

Judith said, "Listen to me, my friends.
Take this head and hang it on the parapet of the wall.
At daybreak, take up your weapons
as if you were going down to the plain
to attack the Assyrian outpost.
Sentries will arouse their officers
who will rush to Holofernes,
and when they do not find him,
they will panic and try to flee.
Then all of you pursue them
and cut them down in their tracks.
But first bring Achior the Ammonite here
to see his executioner.
When Achior saw the head of Holofernes,
he fell over in a faint.
When he came to, he threw himself at Judith's feet,
did homage to her, and said,

"You are blessed in every tent of Judah!
Everywhere your name will cause alarm.
Now tell me how you did this."
In the presence of all the people,
Judith told him what she had done
from the moment she left Bethulia
to the moment of her return,
and when she had finished, the people cheered,
and Achior became a believer.
At dawn they hung the head of Holofernes
on Bethulia's city wall,
then took their weapons and went in groups
to every mountain pass.
The Assyrian generals went to Holofernes
for instructions and a call to battle.
"Wake up, wake up, the slaves are coming."
They thought he was sleeping with Judith.
When no one answered,
they entered and saw Holofernes on the floor,
a corpse without a head.
They shouted and wept and tore their clothes,
then rushed to Judith's tent
and saw that she was gone.
"We have been tricked!" they shouted.
"One Hebrew woman has brought disgrace
on the house of King Nebuchadnezzar."
The cries and shouts of the Assyrian army
rose up throughout the camp.

The men in the tents trembled with fear
and stumbled over each other
as they fled from the valley
by every path that led across the plain.
Israelite soldiers chased after them,
and with the help of other nations,
slaughtered the Assyrian forces
in their disorganized retreat.
In Gilead and Galilee,
beyond the borders of Damascus,
they plundered camps, acquired riches,
confiscated booty wherever troops were found.
Joakim the high priest and the elders of Jerusalem
came to visit Judith in order to wish her well.
They blessed her with one accord, saying,
"You are the glory of Jerusalem!
You are the boast of Israel!

You are the pride of our people!
You have done all this with your own hand.
How good you have been for Israel!
God is well pleased with you.
May you be blessed forever!"
And the people said, "Amen."
The people gave Judith the tent of Holofernes
and all his silver dinnerware,
his furniture, his beds, his bowls
which they had taken from the camp.
She loaded her mules, hitched up her carts,
and piled them high with the spoils of war
and took them to her home.
The women of Israel came to see her.
Some performed a dance in her honor.
All the women blessed her.
She gave the women olive branches
and they crowned themselves with ivy wreaths.
Then Judith danced before the people,
led the women in a victory dance
while all the men,
bearing arms, wearing garlands,
joyfully followed after,
singing hymns of praise.
Then Judith sang this song of praise:

JUDITH'S PSALM

Sing a song with tambourines,
sing to God with cymbals,
sing a new psalm to an age-old name.

Praise to the God who crushes wars,
who encamps among the people,
who delivered me from the enemy's hands.

Assyrians came from the mountainous north,
marching with myriad warriors;
their numbers clogged the wadis,
their cavalry covered the hills.
They boasted of burning our territory,
of putting our men to the sword,
of dashing our infants against the rocks,
seizing our children as booty,
taking our virgins as spoil.

They have been foiled by the hand of a woman!
Praise to Almighty God!

Neither man nor giant nor son of a Titan
caused the tyrant's destruction,
but Judith, daughter of Merari,
for Judith's beauty undid him.

She put away her widow's clothes
that she might exalt the oppressed,
anointed her face with fragrant perfume,
crowned her cascading hair.
Her sandal caught his lascivious eye,
her beauty bewitched his bloodthirsty mind,
her sword severed his neck!

Persians and Medes could not compete
with her boldness and her daring.

The oppressed shouted, the weak cried out,
the terrorized enemy turned away
as sons of slave girls pierced them through
and they perished before God's army.

I will sing to my God a new song.
Great and glorious are you, O God,
strong, invincible, wonderful.
You spoke and we, your creatures, were made.
You sent forth your spirit who formed us all.
Now none can resist your voice.
Mountains are shaken to their foundation,
rocks melt before your glance.
Woe to all who slay your people.
God will send fire upon their flesh.
They will weep in pain forever,
but those who fear you feel your mercy
and forever sing your praise.

◇

When they arrived at Jerusalem they worshiped God,
offered burnt offerings, freewill offerings,
and very many gifts.
Judith dedicated to God
the possessions of Holofernes that the people had given her,
as well as his canopy.
For three months the feast continued in the city of Jerusalem,
then Judith returned to her estate in Bethulia.
For the rest of her life she was honored throughout all Israel.
Many desired to marry her but she never wed again.
She grew more and more famous
and she grew old,
to the age of one hundred and five.

She set her maid free and died in Bethulia;
they buried her in the cave of her husband Manasseh.
No one spread terror in Israel
during the lifetime of Judith
or for a long time after.

◇ **Points for Shared Reflection**

- Do you think Judith really existed. If so, why? If not, why not? What aspects of her story are believable? What aspects are not believable?
- What characteristics of Judith's person and experience should women seek to emulate? To which of these are you particularly drawn?
- Judith's narrative is filled with violence and war. What is your opinion of armed resistance in general? Of Bethulia's armed resistance in particular? Of Judith's act of violence? Of her deception? What other alternatives did they have?
- What contemporary heroines does Judith's story bring to mind?

◇ **A Psalm of Resistance** (see p. 131)

◇ **Prayer**

I cannot resist Your goodness, O God,
or Your grace at work within me,
for Your way with me is so wonderful,
Your Presence so profound.
Help me resist temptation,
the kind that is so insidious
it makes an attractive package
of the evils all around me,
trying to trap me, against my will,
into falling prey to its charm.
Be strength in me,
and resistance
against every kind of seduction,
and draw me wholly into Yourself
forever and ever.
Amen.

◇ A PSALM OF RESISTANCE ◇

Voice I have tried to resist all evil, O God.
Help me to remain steadfast
as I lean upon the promises
of Your ever-present word.

Chorus Evil is all around us.
Destructive forces surround us.
Where shall we go?
To whom shall we turn?
Who will protect our souls?

All At times I feel I am under siege
from the pressure to capitulate
to sin and its enticements.
Let me resist all compromise
and let me not be held hostage
to destructive tendencies.

Voice Who am I to root out crime
and say to the wicked, be gone?
I am but a child, Shaddai,
newly weaned from my mother's arms.

Chorus A little child shall lead us
whose faith has already freed us.
Here we stand
by the grace of God,
and we shall overcome.

All I am overwhelmed by social sin.
Injustices render me powerless.
I am tempted to give up.
Help me resist such temptations, O God,
and deliver me from all such evil.

Voice In the face of my fear,
I feel the force of my faith
as a shield around me,
and I know You are with me,
Most Holy One,
protecting me from harm.

Chorus Safe among the stranger,
safe in the midst of danger,
by God's design
you have nothing but fear of fear
to overcome.

All	Hunger, homelessness, poverty
	are the sins of this generation.
	The consequences of addiction
	are the evils that destroy.
	Help us resist their settling into our lives
	on a permanent basis.
	Help us cast out these demons.
	Let them not control our lives.

Voice What will we say
to those amassed on the margins
of privilege and power?

Chorus Rise up, all you who are oppressed.
Resist the enticing securities
doled out by the status quo.

All Generations give birth
to generations who remain
mired in systemic deprivation.

Voice We praise you, Shaddai,
for preferring to be
on the side of the disadvantaged.

Chorus Open our eyes.
Help us to see
the wounded all around us.

All We stand
in solidarity
with all who resist courageously
the injustice in their lives.

Voice Thank You, Shaddai,
for sending me forth
and for bringing me back undefeated.

Chorus We trust in the One
Who gives new life
to all who have been mistreated.

All Empower us
and remain with us
until Your plan has been completed.

 By M. T. Winter, Crossroad Pub. Co., © 1992 Medical Mission Sisters

◇ II ◇
Mothers

JOCHEBED

◇ **Scripture Reference**   Ex 2:1–10; 6:20; Num 26:59

◇ **Biography**

Jochebed, a daughter of Levi, was the mother of Miriam, Aaron, and Moses. She was born in Egypt where she married Amram. The Exodus genealogy says Amram was her brother's son. Jochebed and her husband were both of the priestly tradition by birth.

◇ **Context**

Jochebed was pregnant a third time and she gave birth to a beautiful little boy. What a joy for a Jewish mother, and what an overwhelming sorrow, for Pharaoh had decreed the death of all baby boys born to Jewish women. She knew that she should kill her child, but she just could not do it. So she came up with a plan, she and her daughter, and the two of them by the grace of God became the saviors of the savior of their people. Behind the great man Moses were two very great, very courageous women. Very clever women too. For Jochebed not only saw to her son's survival; she also arranged to be the one to nurse him and she was paid to do it. The daughter of the one who enslaved the Hebrew people paid a Hebrew woman money to nurse her own child, the child who, some years later, would lead the enslaved to freedom. The daughter of the one who decreed the child's death enabled that child to live. At the heart of the story of Jochebed is the story of woman-power.

◊ **Lectionary Reading**

Now a man from the house of Levi
married a Levite woman
who conceived and bore a son.
When she saw how beautiful her baby was,
she hid him for three months.
When she knew she could hide him no longer,
she procured a papyrus basket,
sealed it with bitumen and pitch,
put her baby in the basket
and set it among the reeds
on the edge of the river Nile.
His sister stood by at a distance
to see what would happen to him.
Pharaoh's daughter came to the river to bathe
while her attendants strolled along its banks.
She saw the basket among the reeds
and sent her maid to fetch it.
She opened the basket and saw the child
and he began to cry.
"This must be one of the Hebrew children," she said,
and she took pity on him.
His sister approached Pharaoh's daughter.
"Shall I find a Hebrew woman
who is able to nurse the child for you?"
"Yes," the woman replied.
So the girl went and got her mother
and brought her to Pharaoh's daughter who said,
"Nurse this child for me
and I will see that you are paid."
So the woman took the child and nursed it.
When the boy grew older,
she brought him to Pharaoh's daughter
who treated him like a son.
She named the young boy Moses,
because "I drew him out of the water."
◊

Amram married Jochebed,
his father's sister.
She was the daughter of Levi
who was born to Levi in Egypt,
and she was the mother of Aaron, Moses,
and their sister Miriam.

◇ **Points for Shared Reflection**

- The narrative is filled with women — a mother, a sister, a daughter and her companions — who come together in solidarity to save a little child. Can you think of a similar situation in contemporary times?

- In Jochebed's story, a man makes the laws that enslave and slay and women overturn them through love, wit, and heroic action. Has this ever been true in your experience?

- Jochebed took an enormous risk in trusting the maternal instincts of Pharaoh's daughter. Has there ever been a time when you took such a risk and placed your trust in a stranger?

- Jochebed put all her hopes in one basket. Years later, the Hebrew people put all their hope for liberation in her son Moses. Assuming God works through human agency, in what/whom do you place your hope?

◇ **A Psalm of Trust** (see p. 137)

◇ **Prayer**

I cling to You,
Receiver of My Trust,
for none other
can I turn to
as I look for consolation
in my desperate hour of need.
I place all my hope
into Your hands
and await what lies before me,
trusting in miracles,
trusting in Your holy power
and in Your providence.
I will not be disappointed,
now or ever.
Amen.

◇ A PSALM OF TRUST ◇

Choir 1   I place my trust in You, O God.
Like a little child
fresh from the womb
with the feel of the breast upon me,
I lift my soul
to the satiating,
scintillating taste
of Your blessedness.

Choir 2   I place all my hope in You
as I set sail upon the water,
rocking, so gently rocking
in the currents of compassion
and the wellsprings
of Your love.

Choir 1   Cradle me close
as I weave among
the threatening throngs around me
who are watching,
waiting to trip me up
or put me down
should You depart from me.

Choir 2   Bend down to me
and lift me
from the confines of this moment
into the fullness of Your freedom
and its possibility,
for I am adrift
and way off course
unless You turn to me.

Choir 1   Like a child secure
at its mother's breast,
like a leaf upon still water,
I rest in You
untroubled
as I wait upon Your will.

Choir 2   Like a mother
warm in her child's embrace,
I cling to Your grace within me,
drinking deep of Your love
until my spirit
has its fill.

By M. T. Winter, Crossroad Pub. Co., © 1992 Medical Mission Sisters

SHELOMITH

◇ **Scripture Reference** Lev 24:10–23

◇ **Biography**

Shelomith, a daughter of Dibri and therefore a member of the tribe of Dan, was the wife of an Egyptian. She emerges from a passage of scripture simply as a mother whose son was stoned to death because he had blasphemed. This incident occurred in the Israelite camp during their journey to the promised land.

◇ **Context**

Who is Shelomith? There is nothing about her in the text. She never enters the picture. We meet her only in the person of her son. She is mentioned solely to establish the genealogy of her son, and this is done in order to provide a basis for an interpretation of the law. Her son blasphemes and he is put to death. The point made here is that the same law applies to everyone, the alien and the citizen as well. Shelomith's son was an Israelite even though his father was Egyptian, because his mother was of the tribe of Dan. This pericope about law, lineage, and about a mother's son raises for us the issue of the invisible woman. She haunts us in her absence, for we know she is there in the background, hearing the accusation, listening to the condemnation, feeling the sound of the stones on her own body as life ebbs from the life she bore.

A man whose mother was an Israelite
and whose father was an Egyptian
came out of his tent
and fought with an Israelite
in the middle of the camp.
In the course of their quarrel
he uttered a curse,
blaspheming the name of God.
They brought the man before Moses.
Now his mother's name was Shelomith
and she was a daughter of Dibri,
a member of the tribe of Dan.
They took her son into custody
until a decision was revealed to them.
Then God spoke to Moses, saying,
"Take the blasphemer outside the camp;
let all who heard him lay hands on his head,
and let the whole congregation stone him.
And say this to the people of Israel,
'Whoever curses God shall bear the sin.
Whoever blasphemes God's name
shall be put to death —
this applies to both aliens and citizens —
and the whole congregation shall stone the blasphemer.
Whoever kills a human being
shall also be put to death.
Whoever kills an animal,
shall make restitution for it, life for life.
Anyone who maims another
shall suffer the same injury in return:
fracture for fracture, eye for eye, tooth for tooth —
the injury inflicted is the injury received.
The same law applies to both alien and citizen,
for I am God of all.' "
Thus Moses spoke to the people of Israel;
and they took the blasphemer out of the camp
and the people stoned him to death.
The people of Israel did that day
as God had commanded Moses.

- The woman in this narrative is invisible yet painfully present to the situation. Mention one or more instances in which women today are or have been invisible yet very much a part of what was happening.

- Have you ever felt invisible? What was the situation? Why did it occur? How did you feel?

- Shelomith's son was stoned to death by her friends and her associates. Describe some of her feelings. What is your feeling about capital punishment? When if ever is it justified? If you approve, would you agree that the principle applies also to your own father or brother or son?

- We often throw stones at each other. We kill an idea, a dream, a moment of enthusiasm. Can you remember a time when you did such a thing? Is it too late to say you're sorry?

◇ **A Psalm about Throwing Stones** (see p. 141)

◇ **Prayer**
O Maker of Stars
and sticks and stones,
make us all more sensitive
to the ways we use creation
to abuse You and ourselves.
You Who can turn
our hearts of stone
into havens of tenderness,
help us to treat all
with respect:
people, ideas, creation, stones,
for all come from You
and return to You
through Your Spirit
Who is life.
Amen.

◇ A PSALM ABOUT THROWING STONES ◇

Choir 1   There are so many ways,
so many occasions,
so many reasons we can construct
for putting a person to death.

Choir 2   Sometimes we mean it literally.
A killer kills
and we go crazy,
eager to kill in return.

Choir 1   There are so many ways
to stop another's energy
in its tracks.
Many of us throw stones.

Choir 2   What a painful way
to lose one's life:
to be put to death by stoning.

Choir 1   To lose hope,
to lose ambition,
to lose an opportunity to grow
are ways we die by stoning.

Choir 2   A well-aimed barb,
ruthless critique,
ridicule, rumor,
disparaging words,
even a stony silence
are ways of throwing stones.

Choir 1   Sticks and stones
we can handle;
it is words that usually hurt us,
striking our vulnerable places
with a devastating force.

Choir 2   All of us live
in glass houses,
so why do we
so foolishly fling
so much of our negative energy
ultimately
against ourselves?

By M. T. Winter, Crossroad Pub. Co., © 1992 Medical Mission Sisters

Choir 1   Stones mark
the place where saints
once wrestled the word of God.

Choir 2   Stones should be used
as cornerstones,
not as a chastening rod.

Choir 1   Milestones mark
the miles and years
and measure our coming and going.

Choir 2   Stones are for collecting
and loving.
Stones are not for throwing.

   By M. T. Winter, Crossroad Pub. Co., © 1992 Medical Mission Sisters

SAMSON'S MOTHER

◇ **Scripture Reference**   Judg 13:2–25; 14:1–9; 16:30–31

◇ **Biography**

The mother of Samson was the wife of Manoah of Zorah, a Danite. She had been childless all her married life when an angel of God appeared to her to announce the birth of a son. She raised her child as a nazirite as the angel had commanded and helped arrange his marriage to a Philistine woman even though she disapproved. Samson's mother was a woman of faith who trusted in her God.

◇ **Context**

Samson was the miracle baby of the wife of Manoah of Zorah who, like Sarah before her and Hanna and Elizabeth who were to come after, had waited for a child. After years of infertility, Samson's birth was announced to her by a heavenly visitor. She was told that her son was to be consecrated to God from the moment of his birth. One expects the birth of an angel from a prelude such as this. Samson was no angel. He was certainly of heroic stature. For twenty years he was a judge in Israel, and before he died a violent death, he had achieved lasting fame. But the child of this gentle, faith-filled woman was a force to be reckoned with. Vicious, vindictive, ill-tempered, at the slightest provocation the one dedicated to God from birth would lash out, maim, and kill. The text indicates that at such times a superior force overtook him and concludes that his acts of violence had been ordained by God.

It has been said that Samson was sent by God to harass the Philistines and that the various episodes in his life support this interpretation. Despite this biblical bias, one is tempted to see a man out of control. Was he insufficiently disciplined as a boy because he belonged to God? Samson had a weakness for Philistine women and eventually a sexual liaison brought the giant down. He died in a violent act of revenge against his enemies while uttering the name of God. We must try to understand this mother in light of her relationship to her son. What must she have thought of this boy, so long awaited, divinely consecrated, yet so atypically a man of God? Although Samson was a historical figure, most of what has been said about him has probably originated in folk tales of the daring adventures of a superhuman hero against an oppressive foreign power.

◇ **Lectionary Reading**

There was a man of Zorah of the tribe of Dan
whose name was Manoah.
Now Manoah's wife was barren.
She had never borne a child.
An angel of God appeared to her and said,
"Although you are barren and have borne no children,
you shall conceive and bear a son.
Take care not to drink wine or any strong drink,
or to eat anything unclean,
for you shall conceive and bear a son
who shall be given to God from birth.
No razor is to touch the hair of his head,
for the boy shall be a nazirite.
It is he who shall begin to deliver Israel
from the hand of the Philistines."
Then the woman went and told her husband,
"A messenger of God visited me who looked just like an angel.
I did not ask where the messenger was from,
nor did the messenger give a name.
The messenger said to me,
'You shall conceive and bear a son.
Drink no wine, no alcoholic drink,

and be sure to eat nothing unclean,
for the boy shall be a nazirite, consecrated to God,
from his birth to the day of his death.' "
Then Manoah prayed to God, saying,
"O God, I pray, let the messenger you sent
come again and teach us what to do with the boy to be born."
God heard Manoah.
The angel appeared to the woman again
when she was in the field,
but her husband was not with her.
So she ran to her husband and told him,
"The messenger who came the other day
has appeared to me again."
Manoah got up and followed his wife
and when he saw the messenger, he said,
"Are you the one who spoke to this woman?"
"Yes, I am the one."
Then Manoah said, "When your words are fulfilled,
how is the boy to order his life? How should he behave?"
God's messenger said to Manoah,
"Let the woman take seriously all that I told her.
She may not eat anything that comes from the vine.
She shall not drink wine or any strong drink,
or eat anything that is unclean.
She must observe all that I commanded her."
Manoah said to the messenger of God,
"Honor us then by staying a while
and sharing a meal with us."
Now Manoah did not know
that the messenger was an angel.
The angel said to Manoah,
"If I stay, I will not eat your food;
but if you wish, prepare a burnt offering
and offer it to God."
Manoah said to the angel,
"What is your name, so that we may honor you
when your words are fulfilled?"
But the angel of God responded,
"Why do you ask my name? It is a mystery."
So Manoah took a kid from his flock
and a handful of grain
and offered it to the God who works wonders.
When the flame ascended from the altar toward heaven,
the angel of God ascended in the flame
while Manoah and his wife looked on.
Then they fell to the ground and worshiped.

God's angel did not appear again
to Manoah or his wife.
Realizing it was the angel of God,
Manoah said to his wife,
"We are sure to die, for we have seen God."
But his wife said,
"If God had meant to kill us,
God would not have accepted a burnt offering
and a grain offering from our hands,
or shown us all these things,
or announced these things to us."
So the woman bore a son
and named him Samson.
The boy grew and was blessed by God.

◇

Samson went down to Timnah one day
where he saw a Philistine woman,
and he went and told his father and mother,
"I saw a Philistine woman at Timnah.
Get her for me as my wife."
But his father and mother said to him,
"Is there not a woman among your clan
or among all of our own people,
that you must go and take a wife
from the uncircumcised Philistines?"
Samson said to his father,
"Get her for me. She pleases me."
His father and mother were unaware
that this situation was the will of God
who was seeking an excuse
to assault the Philistines
who had Israel in their power.
So Samson went to Timnah
with his father and his mother.
When he came to the vineyards of Timnah,
a young lion attacked him.
Filled with the Spirit, he seized the lion
and tore it to pieces with his bare hands,
but he did not tell his father or his mother.
He talked with the woman,
she pleased him,
so he returned to her to marry her.
On his way to the woman,
he saw there on the side of the road
the carcass of the lion he had torn apart.
A swarm of bees was in the body of the lion,

so he scraped out some honey into his hands
and ate it along the way.
He gave some to his father and mother,
but he did not tell them he took the honey
from the carcass of a lion.

◇

Samson killed at his death more people
than he had killed during his entire life.
Then his brothers and all his family came
and they took him and buried him
between Zorah and Eshtaol
in the tomb of his father Manoah.
He had judged Israel twenty years.

◇ **Points for Shared Reflection**

- Can you recall an occasion when religious authorities excused some wanton destruction as being the will of God?

- What do you do with a son or a daughter who is totally out of control?

- Samson's mother was a woman of faith who seemed to dote on her son. Were her loyalties justified?

- Mothers have expectations that can affect the life of their child. Did your mother allow or encourage you to take charge of your own life?

◇ **A Psalm for Giving Birth** (see p. 148)

◇ **Prayer**

Mother of all who walk the earth,
of all who are pregnant
and bring to birth
physical or spiritual children,
hear our prayer
as we labor to bring forth now
the new creation.
May the fruit of our wombs
and minds and spirits
fulfill our expectations
and grow to enrich the community
of all nations,
bound or free,
in the name of Life.
Amen.

◇ A PSALM FOR GIVING BIRTH ◇

Choir 1   Let me give birth to truth, Shaddai,
and let it grow beyond me
and be fruitful
and multiply.

Choir 2   Let me give birth to hope, Shaddai,
though fragile as a stalk of winter wheat
in a summer storm.

Choir 1   Let me give birth to belief, Shaddai,
the kind that clings tenaciously
to the last shred of credible cause.

Choir 2   Let me give birth to dreams, Shaddai,
cartwheeling, heart-reeling flights
of free-falling fantasy,
no holds barred.

Choir 1   Let me give birth to a theme of peace
in an irresistible song.

Choir 2   Let me give birth to justice
and let it redress all conceivable wrong.

Choir 1   Let me give birth to freedom for all,
wherever their roots are planted.

Choir 2   Let me give birth to just one wish
with Your promise that it will be granted.

Choir 1   Let me give birth to love, Shaddai,
in the most unexpected places.

Choir 2   Give birth to me and see that I
stay faithful to Your graces.

 By M. T. Winter, Crossroad Pub. Co., © 1992 Medical Mission Sisters

MICAH'S MOTHER

◇ **Scripture Reference**   Judg 17:1–6

◇ **Biography**

Micah's mother, an Ephraimite, was responsible for establishing a religious shrine in her son Micah's house. For her the making of a molten idol was compatible with belief in Israel's God. We know nothing else about her.

◇ **Context**

The narrative is situated in a chapter that had been appended to the Book of Judges by the redactor. It was one of two Micah stories that had probably circulated separately and had been combined long before the time of the Deuteronomic Historian. The other narrative, Micah's story, is not included in the lection. What follows is the story of Micah's mother. It opens with the reminder of a theft and a curse upon the thief, followed by a reversal when Micah confessed to his mother that he was the one who had stolen her money and she in turn blessed him for giving it back. There are some clear ironies in the mother's story. She consecrated all of the returned money to the God of Israel, then took part of it to make a molten image for worship. There is no mention of what she did with the rest of the consecrated money, which was the much larger amount. Micah, whose name means "Who is like Yahweh?" enshrined an idol in his house and established a resident priesthood. Commentators come down hard on Micah for his idolatrous acts. Little is said about Micah's

149

mother, although her association with graven images forbidden by the Israelite religion is seen to be aberrant.

There is another point of view, which casts the same facts in a different light. Micah's mother was definitely a believer and she sincerely blessed God for the return of her lost money by consecrating all of it to God. She may have commissioned an idol for worship, but from her perspective this was not inappropriate. Syncretistic religious practices were common during the time of the judges, when everyone did what they thought was right and two very different religions lived side by side in the same land and often in the same house. People of the ancient Near East were accustomed to worshiping both god and goddess; in Canaan this was Anath-Baal. When Yahweh overthrew the male god Baal, female goddess worship continued alongside the worship of Yahweh in the person of Anath or Asherah. This practice was widely tolerated and for a very long time. Micah's mother may have made an image of Asherah for the shrine in Micah's house. True, she used only two hundred of the eleven hundred pieces of silver, which is far more than the customary tithe but far less than what was consecrated, but that was just the cost of the molten image. The rest of the money may have been set aside for use in worship rites and may even have been used to pay the stipend of the priest. Nothing in Micah's mother's attitude or behavior suggests an alienation from Israel's God. Rather, one senses a deep dedication and a commitment to a regular rhythm of worship, which was probably the basis for her wanting a shrine close by in her son's house.

◇ **Lectionary Reading**

There was a man in the hill country of Ephraim
whose name was Micah.
One day he said to his mother,
"The eleven hundred pieces of silver
that were stolen from you,
about which you uttered a curse —
I heard it with my own ears —
that silver is in my possession.
I took it and now I am returning it to you."
And Micah's mother said:
"May my son be blessed by God!"
Micah returned the silver to his mother,
and she said,
"I consecrate to the God of Israel
this silver returned to me by my son.
It shall be made into an idol."
When Micah gave the silver to his mother,
she took two hundred pieces
and gave them to the silversmith

who made them into an idol of metal.
It was placed in Micah's house.
Micah made a shrine with vestment and statuary
and installed one of his sons
in the role of resident priest.
In those days there was no king in Israel,
and everyone did what they thought was right.

◇ **Points for Shared Reflection**

- Micah's mother took charge of her own worship by providing what was needed out of her personal resources. What might this say to women today who are finding it hard to continue within the structure of authorized rites?

- "In those days," says scripture, "everyone did what they thought was right." In a certain sense this can be said of women and worship in our time. In your opinion, is this good or bad?

- Is there any way that aspects of the goddess traditions can be compatible with your own religious worship?

- It seems that Micah's mother could do a lot of things in relation to worship, but a man had to serve as priest. Comment on this in light of current debate on females in the priesthood.

◇ **A Psalm to God as Goddess** (see p. 152)

◇ **Prayer**

To You we lift the whole of ourselves,
Goddess our God,
and we praise You,
for You created the universe
in which all of life surrenders
to the power of Your name.
How can we say we love You
when we hardly even know You?
Help us to see with new eyes
the mysteries and the miracles
that You alone can claim
and help us to become accustomed to
new images and new understandings,
knowing You remain the same
forever and ever.
Amen.

◇ A PSALM TO GOD AS GODDESS ◇

Choir 1 If we called You by a female name
like Anath or Asherah,
O God of Our Lost Traditions,
would You hear us?
Would You answer?

Choir 2 Would it matter
if we praised You
for the gift of Your fecundity
and sang songs
to celebrate
the fullness of Your
sacred breasts
and our own need for nurture?

Choir 1 Where were we
when Your water broke,
spilling upon the universe
the foothills of creation?

Choir 2 How could we know
the way it was
when sun, stars, streams, seeds
were all thrust
from Your sacred womb
into their cosmic patterns?

Choir 1 Who can say
if You walked the earth
to find the perfect habitat
before You bore humanity,
then left us
in the afterbirth
of Your inspired infinity?

Choir 2 How do we know
what You prefer
when we go about our worshiping?
Yet we choose pews
over sacred poles
and rigid rules
over garden groves
and stark, sober, solemnity
over tambourines and dancing.

   By M. T. Winter, Crossroad Pub. Co., © 1992 Medical Mission Sisters

Choir 1   Rise up, Goddess, from our past
             and break the silence You have kept
             so sacrosanct.
             Come again
             as You once came
             to those who loved You.
             Reveal Your name.

Choir 2   Rise from the primal depths
             of being,
             proud and unconditional,
             to lead us
             through the troubled waters
             into freedom,
             we, Your devoted daughters.

Choir 1   We praise You, God,
             united with all other people
             who also claim You.

Choir 2   We praise You, Goddess,
             for You are God,
             no matter how we name You.

ICHABOD'S MOTHER

◇ **Scripture Text**   1 Sam 4:19–22

◇ **Biography**

This unnamed woman, the wife of Phinehas whose father Eli was the priest at Shiloh, gave birth to her son Ichabod shortly after learning that the ark of the covenant had been captured by the Philistines, her husband had been killed in battle, and her father-in-law had died on hearing the tragic news.

◇ **Context**

In the time between the period of the judges and the rise of the monarchy, before Samuel had assumed leadership in Israel, the Philistines were victorious over the Israelites and captured the ark of the covenant, which had been brought to the battlefield from Shiloh by Eli's two sons who were priests at the sanctuary there. Israel's defeat in battle, the loss of God's Shekinah, and the fall of the house of Eli all come together in one anonymous woman's tragic story where national and personal catastrophe are inseparably intertwined. The pregnant woman's husband Phinehas and his brother Hophni were among the thousands slaughtered, but the narrative suggests that this news did not devastate her or her elderly father-in-law Eli, the pious but powerless priest under whose tutelage Samuel had grown up. The death of Eli's sons had already been prophesied (2:34) because of their evil ways, for they treated the burnt offerings with contempt (12–17) and had intercourse with the women

154

who served at the entrance to the tent of meeting (22). The author of this originally independent narrative clearly states that it was the loss of the ark of the covenant that killed Eli and sent the woman into premature labor.

Her dying words, assuming she did die, were both a name and a lament. The glory indeed had departed on all levels for her. The loss of the Shekinah to one who had lived so close to its sanctuary must have been profound, but no less painful surely would have been her own loss of security, for an evil priest's widow with a newborn infant would have had very little recourse. A later reference describes the priest who accompanied Saul and his troops and carried the ark of the covenant into battle as "Ahijah son of Ahitub, Ichabod's brother, son of Phinehas son of Eli" (14:3, 18). While this notation has been dismissed as spurious, it does raise some interesting questions. Did the dying woman live, marry Ahitub, and give birth to a second son? If so then she whose son was named to recall the loss of God's glory would have personally experienced the return of that glory in a second son who was closely associated with the ark of the covenant she cherished.

◇ **Lectionary Reading**

Eli's daughter-in-law,
the wife of Phinehas,
was pregnant and about to give birth
when she heard that the ark of God
had been captured
and both her husband
and her father-in-law were dead.
She went into labor,
and in great pain
she gave birth to her child.
Seeing she was at the point of death,
the midwife attending her said to her,
"Do not be afraid.
You have borne a son."
She did not respond to her.
Instead she named the child Ichabod, meaning,
"The glory has departed from Israel,"
because the ark of God had been captured
and she had lost her husband and father-in-law.
"The glory has departed from Israel," she said,
"for the ark of God has been captured."

◇ **Points for Shared Reflection**

◇ **Points for Shared Reflection**

- What do you think was the real reason for the utter despondency of Ichabod's mother?

- In biblical times names had meaning. Discuss the meaning of Ichabod's name. Do you know the meaning of your name?

- If you were to rename yourself right now with a phrase to express how you feel about your formal religious tradition, what would be your name?

- If you were to rename yourself now to express how you feel about you own personal spiritual life, what would be that name? Compare both names. Why are they different or why are they the same?

◇ **A Psalm on Glory Departed** (see p. 157)

◇ **Prayer**

Glory
and Power
and Praise
are Yours,
whether or not
we know it,
whether or not
we see it,
present
even when
Glory
and Power
are hidden from our eyes.
Show us
Your Glory,
Shekinah-Shaddai,
in the midst
of our sin
and our suffering,
and help us transform
ourselves
and our world
through Your Glory
indwelling here,
now and forever.
Amen.

◊ A PSALM ON GLORY DEPARTED ◊

All   The Glory has departed.
Shekinah has left Her dwelling place.
Where has Her Glory gone?

Choir 1   The streets are littered
with homelessness.

Choir 2   Laws bar the indigent
from begging their daily bread.

Choir 1   White on black
and black on black
battle for domination.

Choir 2   Public funds are squandered
that were intended for the poor.

All   The Glory has departed.
Shekinah has left Her dwelling place.
Where has Her Glory gone?

Choir 1   Innocence is lost
in every town
on the corner of Main and Market.

Choir 2   Drugs are no longer
cause for alarm
and rape is no longer news.

Choir 1   Riots break out
over silly things
like who is the best at soccer.

Choir 2   Last week
an acre of trees went down
to build another mall.

All   The Glory has departed.
Shekinah has left Her dwelling place.
Where has Her Glory gone?

Choir 1   A baby died
in its mother's arms
in a flat in an urban ghetto.

Choir 2   A million babies die
of malnutrition
every year.

By M. T. Winter, Crossroad Pub. Co., © 1992 Medical Mission Sisters   *WomanWitness* / **157**

Choir 1	War breaks out like a deadly plague pockmarking the face of our planet.
Choir 2	In most of the homes of suburbia, somebody owns a gun.
All	The Glory has departed. Shekinah has left Her dwelling place. Where has Her Glory gone?
Choir 1	Who will restore the Glory as in the days of faith and justice?
Choir 2	Who can remember what it was like in those former Glory days?
Choir 1	Come among us, Shekinah-Shaddai, for You are the Power and Glory.
Choir 2	You alone have the power to help us bring Your Glory home.
All	Yours is the Power, Shekinah-Shaddai! Yours is the Glory forever!

   By M. T. Winter, Crossroad Pub. Co., © 1992 Medical Mission Sisters

DAVID'S MOTHER

◇ **Scripture Reference**   1 Sam 22:3–4

◇ **Biography**

David's mother was the wife of Jesse. Chronicles credits Jesse with seven sons and two daughters. We can assume that all of these children were also this woman's children, but there is no way of knowing for certain. The notation that she and her husband sought asylum with the king of Moab is the only scripture reference specifically about her. The rest of her personal story seems irretrievably lost to us.

◇ **Context**

In his effort to escape from Saul who was determined to kill him, David moved through the Philistine city of Gath to Adullam in southern Judah and on into Moab, where he prevailed upon the king of Moab to give sanctuary to his parents until he decided what to do next. He was obviously concerned about their safety, and for as long as David hid out in Mizpeh in Moab, his mother and father remained under the protection of the king. We know nothing about David's mother. She is not even listed in the records chronicling the birth of her children. The lineage of her famous son is carefully traced through his father Jesse, his grandfather Obed, his great-grandparents Ruth and Boaz, and on back through his patriarchal ancestry. Yet David's Jewish legitimacy came solely from her.

159

◇ **Lectionary Reading**

David fled to Mizpeh of Moab,
and he said to the king of Moab,
"Please let my father and mother come to you,
until I know what God will do for me."
So he left them with the king of Moab,
and they stayed with him all the time
that David was in the stronghold.

◇ **Points for Shared Reflection**

- David's mother is simply taken for granted. Do you/did you take your mother for granted? Is there any way of changing that now?

- The story of David's mother is irretrievably lost. Will your own mother's story be lost? Has your grandmother's story been lost? Is there any way of correcting that now?

- What about your own story? Will that too one day be lost? How can we assure that the storyline of your life will be preserved and handed on? Can you think of any reason why it should be?

- What are some of the qualities and values David's mother might have handed on to her son? What has your mother handed on to you?

◇ **A Psalm about Raising Children** (see p. 161)

◇ **Prayer**

Before we were
in our mother's womb
You knew us
and were there for us,
mothering us,
fathering us,
filling us full
of the faith that we feel now,
God of Our Mothers and Fathers,
and we depend on Your Presence.
Help us to be there
for all Your children
and especially for those special children
entrusted to our care.
We thank You for all
You are and do
as we continue to turn to You
today and every day.
Amen.

◇ A PSALM ABOUT RAISING CHILDREN ◇

Choir 1   What mother wouldn't hope
to have her son
grow up to be king,
her daughter
be the president
of some major corporation
or a college
or the nation.

Choir 2   What father hasn't dreamed
of seeing his boy
in the arena
slay a giant with a sling,
his little girl
promoted
because of her intelligence
and not her wedding ring.

Choir 1   What part of us is handed on
to future generations
through our children who,
surprisingly,
exceed our expectations?

Choir 2   Can we hope that our convictions,
our faith, our dedication
will somehow,
some way,
be picked up and continued
by progeny who never seem
to hear a word we say?

Choir 1   Who of us really raises children?
We raise our hopes,
raise our voices,
raise the roof,
raise hell sometimes,
and even raise some vegetables
so we can stock the shelves.
Yes, we can raise a lot of things,
but our children raise themselves.

Choir 2   It takes a certain strength
to stand by silently,
supportively,

as children make their own mistakes,
strength to modulate our voices
and let our children
make their choices.

Choir 1   The God Who will raise us up one day
will guide us in the proper way
of parenting our children.

Choir 2   Thank God the One Who sees through us
is still willing to entrust to us
the parenting of Her children.

Choir 1   Dear Mother God, strengthen us
to be confident and discerning.

Choir 2   Dear Father God, gentle us,
and remember,
we are learning.

   By M. T. Winter, Crossroad Pub. Co., © 1992 Medical Mission Sisters

TWO MOTHERS

◇ **Scripture Reference**   1 Kings 3:16–28

◇ **Biography**

Two female prostitutes who shared the same house became mothers just three days apart. When her son died accidentally, the newer mother secretly exchanged babies with the woman whose boy was alive. Solomon was asked to determine who was the real mother of the living child. We know nothing more about these women. Their lives are presented to us only in relationship to their infants and to each other.

◇ **Context**

Although many people are familiar with this episode of two women presenting their case before Solomon, the historical truth of the story has been called into question. Its narrative style, with vivid direct speech and repetition, is reminiscent of the folktale, and its theme is one that was fairly widespread. Some twenty-two examples of this same theme have been collected from various parts of the world. The closest parallel to the biblical story is an Indian version in which two women, widows of the same man, both claim to be the mother of his child and therefore the rightful head of his household and heir to his estate. When the magistrate orders the estate divided and the child sawed in half, the true mother relinquishes her claims and is subsequently awarded both child and estate. The biblical narrative may simply be illustrative of the wisdom accorded Solomon in the previous pericope, as has been suggested, or there may have been more to it than that. Two such women may have actually existed. Their story is not that farfetched. Until there is more definitive evidence to the contrary, these two mothers remain historical figures and as such claim their place in this lectionary.

◇ **Lectionary Reading**

Two women who were prostitutes
came and stood before Solomon the king.
The first woman said,
"This woman and I live in the same house,
and I gave birth while she was there.
Three days after the birth of my child,
she too gave birth, and we were together.
There was no one else in the house.
Then this woman's son died in the night,
because she accidently lay on him.
She got out of bed in the middle of the night,
took my son from me while I slept,
placed him at her breast,
and placed her dead son at my breast.
When I arose in the morning to nurse my son,
I saw that he was dead.
But when I looked at him more closely,
clearly it was not my son!"
The other woman said,
"No, the living son is mine. The child who is dead is yours."
The first woman said,
"No, the dead son is yours, and the living son is mine."
So they argued before the king.
Solomon said, "One of you says,
'My son lives, your son is dead,'
while the other says, 'No!
Your son is dead, and my son lives.'"
Then Solomon said to his servants, "Bring me a sword,"
and they brought him a sword.
Then the king pronounced his judgment.
"Divide the living boy in two.

Give half to the one, and half to the other."
"No!" cried the woman whose son was alive,
her love for him burning within her.
"Please, my lord, do not kill him.
Give her the living boy."
The other woman said, "Divide the child.
It shall be neither mine nor yours."
Then Solomon said, "Do not kill the boy.
Give to the first woman the living child
because she is his mother."
All Israel heard of the judgment that King Solomon had rendered,
and they stood in awe of him,
for they perceived in him the wisdom of God
given to execute justice.

◇ **Points for Shared Reflection**

- The two women in this narrative are prostitutes. What bearing does this have on their case? Would it make any difference to you as judge or juror if the plaintiffs before you were prostitutes?

- The mother did not mean to harm her child, but the sad truth is that many women physically injure or psychologically destroy their children unintentionally. Is child abuse a problem in your community? In your family? In your home?

- After a closer look the mother knew the dead child was not her own. As a mother knows her child, as shepherds know their sheep, so does God know us. Have you ever felt completely transparent to God?

- Too many times parents divide their children in half by making impossible demands or by trying to fulfill their own needs through their children. Has this ever happened to you? Could this be happening to your children?

◇ **A Psalm concerning Parents Who Abuse a Child** (see p. 166)

◇ **Prayer**

We pray to You, Mother-Father God,
Who brought all of us into being
and sustain us all with life.
Help us to interact carefully
in the lives of our sons and daughters
and to touch their maturing spirits
only with tenderness and with love
every day that we are together
for as long as we shall live.
Amen.

◇ A PSALM CONCERNING PARENTS WHO ABUSE A CHILD ◇

Choir 1   How easy it is to stifle a child,
to squeeze the life out of one
who is so very vulnerable.

Choir 2   Lean a little too heavily
on a fragile personality
and growth will be suppressed.

Choir 1   We can be terribly suffocating,
closing in on a carefree spirit
with a heavy-handed harangue:
not clever enough,
not quick enough,
not good enough for me.

Choir 2   All kinds of parents
have all kinds of ways
of abusing their sons and daughters
physically,
spiritually,
emotionally.

Choir 1   Mothers smother their daughters
at times
with too much love
or the lack of it.

Choir 2   Holy Mother Church
rolls over hard periodically
on her children.

Choir 1   Fathers inhibit sons
with the intensity
of their demands
sometimes.

Choir 2   Parents can push to the limits
and break the spirit inadvertently.

Choir 1   The telltale signs of abuse
populate all of our towns and cities
as abused becomes abuser
and the cycle spirals on.

Choir 2   Deliver us all, O God of us all,
from abusing
and using our children
in our public and private lives.

   By M. T. Winter, Crossroad Pub. Co., © 1992 Medical Mission Sisters

SAMARITAN MOTHERS

◇ **Scripture Reference** 2 Kings 6:24–31

◇ **Biography**

A woman confronts the king of Israel as he walks the city's walls during the Syrian siege of Samaria. The famine is so severe she has been reduced to cannibalism. Forced to eat her baby, she wants her female companion to keep her promise to do the same. We have no other factual information about these women.

◇ **Context**

The Syrian king Ben-hadad had put the city of Samaria under siege. Supplies had dwindled and hunger was rampant when two women confronted the king of Israel who resided there. The king who is not named (he was either Jehoahaz or Jehoash) was at first too preoccupied with larger issues to be concerned about the needs of women. When he relented and heard their story, he lashed out at the prophet Elisha, blaming everything on him. Hadn't he encouraged the king to hold out for divine intervention only to have people die of starvation? Hadn't the prophet predicted the famine that may not have been the cause of Samaria's problem but was certainly not helping things? The king may have wanted to shift blame from himself out of concern for his personal safety. People who were hungry enough to consume their own children were surely angry enough to kill the king under whose rule this had occurred. This is the context in which the narrative must be understood. But the question remains, did this incident really happen? Is it possible, under any circumstance, for a mother to eat her baby? Our first inclination is to say no, but it has been documented that in times of extreme famine or siege such a thing has been done. An Assyrian text from the time of Ashurbanipal and also an Egyptian papyrus cite instances of cannibalism in antiquity. Israelites themselves were forewarned, "In the desperate straits to which the enemy siege reduces you, you will eat the fruit of your womb, the flesh of your own sons and daughters" (Deut 28:53). Our feelings fight with such hard facts to find some justification. Perhaps the baby was already dead. Perhaps it was food for her other children, so that some of them might survive. An ongoing supply of breast milk would also be available for them. This stark situation is complicated by the behavior of the other woman, and the anecdotal nature of the narrative also raises serious questions about the women's "cannibal pact." Nevertheless, we can be fairly certain that starving women in Samaria were driven to desperate action, providing the basis for this pericope. This is a text that must be considered not only in relation to its historical setting but for what it has to say to our world of diminishing resources and, at times, cataclysmic need. We ought not to be too quick to dismiss another's stated experience as fanciful. Those who are comfortable find it hard to understand the desperation of the deprived. People under siege in today's world may be doing similar things. We just don't know about it.

◇ **Lectionary Reading**

The Syrian king mustered his army and marched against Samaria.
As the siege against Samaria continued,
the famine became so severe
that a donkey's head cost eighty shekels of silver
and two liters of pigeon dung cost five.
The king of Israel was walking on the city wall one day,
when a woman cried, "Help, my lord king."
"No!" he said. "Let God help you. Where can I find help?
From the threshing floor? From the winepress?"
But then the king softened and said to the woman,
"What is your complaint?"
This is how she answered: "This woman said to me,
'Give up your son; we will eat him today

and we will eat my son tomorrow.'
So we cooked my son and we ate him.
On the following day I said to her
'Give up your son and we will eat him.'
But she has hidden her son away."
When the king heard the woman's words,
he tore his garments, revealing to all —
since he was walking on the city wall —
that he wore sackcloth underneath.
He said, "So may God do to me, and more,
if the head of Elisha son of Shaphat
stays on his shoulders today."

◇ **Points for Shared Reflection**

- Desperate women cry out for help to one who has the authority to act, and he tells them he cannot help them. Has someone in authority ever refused your legitimate request? Reflect on that experience.

- Women do desperate things to survive or to ensure the survival of their children. Reflect on the narrative from the perspective of the women who were involved, then speaking as one of them, say what you would have done had you been in their situation.

- Which woman acted more abominably, the one who delivered up her baby or the one who set her up for it, then went back on her word?

- Many people today are close to starvation. How might you help them? Think locally, globally, personally, systemically.

◇ **A Psalm for Those Who Are Starving** (see p. 170)

◇ **Prayer**

O Maker of Milk and Honey
and all the sweet abundance promised
for the new creation,
give us sufficient sustenance
to sustain us on our journey
and look with special tenderness
on those who are disadvantaged,
on those who are forced to go without,
on those who must scrape to make ends meet,
on those who struggle for resources
and for enough to eat.
Take care of all your children,
and have mercy on the starving,
we beg You, Shaddai.
Amen.

◇ A PSALM FOR THOSE WHO ARE STARVING ◇

Choir 1   Miserable are those who hunger
to the point of dying
by starvation,
forced to grasp
at any chance
for one more day of desperation.

Choir 2   Woe to those who are full up to here
with more than they need for getting by,
who wallow in their affluence
while watching other people die.

Choir 1   Villages fall by the side of wells
that yield no water,
living hells
replace tribal tranquilities.

Choir 2   Mothers with nipples
dry and cracked
on breasts shriveled
like empty sacks
carry corpses on their backs.

Choir 1   The problem belongs to every nation;
yes, people here at home are hungry,
some are dying of starvation.

Choir 2   Have you noticed sullen faces
not too far from fast-food places?
Food comes slow to them,
you know.

Choir 1   There was a horde of people once
who hungered
out in the wilderness
and manna
sufficient to feed them daily
fell from the lap of love's largesse.

Choir 2   There was a mob of people once
who were hungry,
and they were fed
with a few small fish
and some loaves of bread.

All   O One Who brought us through the waters,
feed all Your starving sons and daughters.

   By M. T. Winter, Crossroad Pub. Co., © 1992 Medical Mission Sisters

JEWISH MOTHER

◇ **Scripture Reference**   2 Macc 7:1–42
4 Macc: chapters 8 through 18

◇ **Biography**

The narrative of a mother and her seven sons during the time of the Maccabees reveals the scorn Antiochus had for the Hebrews and their traditions and highlights the courage and valor of those who chose to abide by the laws of their religion in defiance of civil law. The mother exhorted her children to stand firm in the practice of Judaism while enduring the extreme horrors of the Seleucid persecution and the certainty of death. All seven sons were tortured and slaughtered before she herself was killed. A figure larger than life, she held in a delicate balance the love she had for the sons of her womb and her undying love of God. Her heroism was and is a symbol of the power of God in us.

This woman's story is recorded in 2 Maccabees, the apocryphal account of the deeds of Judah Maccabee, son of Mattathias and leader of the Hasmonean dynasty that spearheaded the revolt against the Syrian king Antiochus IV Epiphanes, who began his reign in 175 B.C.E. Her story is also retold in 4 Maccabees, the only major piece of Greek rhetoric extant in Jewish literature. This later account, which focuses on recent martyrs, is primarily a philosophical sermon on how pious reason can control passion and covers eleven chapters of the book. Because of its length and because it is basically a rhetorical commentary on the original story, the text has not been incorporated into this lectionary narrative.

The literary context of the original telling is the ornate, idiomatic style of Greek historians and is filled with a pathos and drama intended to stir the reader. One of the purposes behind the telling of this story was to promote the understanding that sin is the cause of divine punishment, suffering is only to chasten, and strength lies in the fulfillment of the practical *mitzvot*, in this case, the refusal to eat forbidden food. Another is to lift up heroism in extreme adversity as an inspiration and encouragement for others. Christianity appended the name Maccabees to this family, and both Eastern and Western Christianity dedicated a day to these "Maccabean Saints." The Roman Catholic calendar of saints included the "Seven Maccabee Brothers" (and, by the way, their mother) and considered their martyrdom a prefiguring of later Christian martyrdoms.

Although the mother is not named in 2 Maccabees, in Syriac Christian accounts she is called Shamone and/or Maryam and has come to be known among Christians as Salome. In rabbinic accounts she is called Miriam. In Jewish tradition she is known as Hannah and her seven sons. Accounts also differ on the way she died. The text of 2 Maccabees does not say. In 4 Maccabees she threw herself into the fire. In the Midrash she jumped off a roof. In *Josippon,* an anonymous historical narrative written in Hebrew about the events of this period, she fell dead on the corpses of her children. Whatever the historical basis to the story of this Jewish mother, the narrative form represents an adaptation of the way tragedies were retold. As an image of the Jewish mother of the holocaust of every age, this heroic woman witnesses to the courage of women under fire and remains an inspiration to us all.

◇ **Lectionary Reading**

Now it happened that seven brothers
and their mother
were arrested under orders of the king
and subjected to torture
with whips and thongs
in order to compel them to eat pork,

which is unlawful for the Jews.
One of them, speaking for all of them, said,
"What do you intend to accomplish with us?
We are prepared to die
rather than break the laws of our ancestors."
The king fell into a rage
and ordered pans and cauldrons heated.
When this was done, he commanded them
to cut out the speaker's tongue,
then scalp him and chop off his hands and his feet
while his mother and brothers looked on.
Mutilated but still breathing,
he was taken to the fire
where they proceeded under the king's order
to fry him in a pan.
As the smoke from the pan billowed about,
the mother and brothers
encouraged each other to die bravely, saying,
"God is watching over us
and in truth has compassion on us."
When the first brother had died,
they brought the second forward.
They tore off the skin of his head with his hair.
"What would you prefer," they asked,
"to eat or to have the whole of your body
punished limb by limb?"
He replied in the language of his ancestors
with a loud, definitive, "No!"
So he in turn was tortured the way his brother had been.
He spoke to them with his final breath,
"Despicable scum, you dismiss us from this present life,
but the God of the universe will raise us up
to an everlasting renewal of life
for being faithful to the law."
Then the third brother was brought forward
as victim of their sport.
On demand he quickly put out his tongue
and courageously offered his hands, saying,
"I will not hold on to these in defiance of God's law.
I got these from God
and I hope to get them back again from God."
The king and those who were with him
were astonished at his spirit,
for his sufferings seemed small to him.
After he too had died,
they tortured the fourth brother much the same way.

When he was near death, he said these words,
"There is no choice but to die by your hands
and to cherish the hope God gives
of being raised again to life.
But for you there will be no resurrection to life!"
After suffering the same kind of treatment,
the fifth brother said to the king,
"Because you have authority over us,
you do to us as you please.
But do not think God has forsaken us.
You will see how God's mighty power
will torture you and your descendants!"
After him they brought the sixth brother forward,
and when he was about to die, he said,
"Do not deceive yourself in vain.
For we are suffering on our own account
because of our sins against God.
For this reason this has happened.
But do not think you will go unpunished
for having tried to fight against God!"
Now the mother was especially heroic.
Her memory will live forever.
She lost seven sons in a single day,
watched them perish before her eyes,
yet she bore it with grace and courage
because of her hope in God.
She encouraged each of her children
in the language of their ancestors.
Filled with remarkable spirit,
with wisdom and discernment, bravery and strength,
she said to all her sons,
"I do not know how you came into being
there in the depth of my womb.
It was not I who gave you life and breath,
nor I who set in order the elements in each of you.
Therefore the Creator of the world
who shaped the beginning of humankind
and devised the origin of all things
will give life and breath back to you again
because you choose to remember God's law
and to forget about yourselves."
Antiochus felt treated with contempt
and was suspicious of her reproachful tone.
Now her youngest son was still alive,
so Antiochus tried to appeal to him,
swearing by oath he would make him rich

if he would turn from the ways of his ancestors
and enter his royal court
where he would be part of his coterie
and entrusted with public affairs.
Since the young man would not listen to him,
the king told the mother to advise the youth
so that he might save himself.
Under pressure she agreed to persuade her son.
Leaning in close to him,
she spoke in their native dialect,
denouncing the wiles of the tyrant
and encouraging the child of her womb.
"My son, have pity on me.
For nine months I carried you in my womb
and for three years after, I nursed you.
I have raised you and taken care of you
and brought you to this point in life.
I beg you, my child, look at heaven and earth
and know it is God who made them
and everything that is in them.
So too all of us came into being,
so do not fear this butcher,
but prove worthy of your brothers.
Accept death, so that in God's mercy,
I will get all of you back again."
While she was yet speaking, the young man said,
"What are you waiting for?
I will not obey the king's command,
I obey the command of our ancestors
as given us by the law.
But you who harass the Hebrews
will not escape the hand of God.
We suffer because of our sins,
and if God is angry for a little while,
we know we will be reconciled,
but you cannot escape the judgment
of the almighty, all-seeing God.
For my brothers after a brief suffering
now drink of everflowing life.
So I, like my brothers, give up my body
and relinquish my life
to keep the laws of our ancestors,
appealing to God to show mercy soon
to the sufferings of our nation.
As for you, may trials and plagues convince you
that God alone is God."

The king, in a rage, handled this son
even worse than he had the others,
for he was stung to the core by his scorn.
So he died in his integrity,
putting his whole trust in God.
Last of all the mother died.

◇ **Points for Shared Reflection**

- It is a tragedy to lose a child. Has this happened in your family or among your circle of friends? Is there someone present who needs to share such an experience and who might benefit from talking about it?

- When children die, when calamity occurs, even persons of faith are inclined to ask, "How could such bad things happen to good people? How could God allow it?" How would you respond to these questions? Have you ever questioned God?

- Compare this Jewish mother to the mothers of the holocaust, to suffering mothers everywhere, to your own mother. What characteristics do they have in common? In what ways is this mother unique?

- Dedication does strengthen endurance. Can you recall a time when sheer determination and/or the power of prayer enabled you to endure extreme hardship or stress?

◇ **A Psalm for Mothers Who Lose a Child** (see p. 177)

◇ **Prayer**

O Mother of Mercy,
Mother of Compassion,
draw to Yourself the depths of pain
contained in the broken-hearted.
Be with the mother
whose child is stillborn.
Be with the mother
forced to mourn
a life cut short,
a light put out,
a mother outliving the life she gave
but never outliving the pain.
Give her a chance at peace again
within the comforting circle
of Your maternal blessedness
and Your everlasting love.
For this we sincerely pray.
Amen.

◇ A PSALM FOR MOTHERS WHO LOSE A CHILD ◇

Choir 1   What greater sorrow
can there be
for a mother?
To outlive a child,
to bury the life force
felt in the womb,
to relinquish one's flesh and blood
to a tomb.
There can be no greater sorrow.

Choir 2   A child is a child
at eight
or eighty.
Babies grow up
but never outgrow
existential relationship,
and mothers die
when their babies die
at whatever age
of chronology
or maturation.

Choir 1   When death robs the cradle
for whatever reason —
illness, accident,
weakness, war,
by the hand of God
or the hand of another —
a voice is heard in Ramah,
weeping,
Rachel keeping *kadesh*
for her children
who are no more.

Choir 2   When death takes
the one she loves,
yet again a mother's water breaks
and tears spill
to fill the void
left by a womb left vacant
and a room unoccupied.

Choir 1   O loving, life-giving Mother
of mothers,
You know what it means
to bestow life,

By M. T. Winter, Crossroad Pub. Co., © 1992 Medical Mission Sisters   *WomanWitness* / **177**

You know how it feels
to let go of life,
draw to Yourself
all suffering mothers,
all heart-broken,
grief-stricken
tenders of others
and lend them Your Shalom.

Choir 2   Mothers of the holocaust,
mothers in lands destroyed
by famine
and fratricidal war,
mothers of slaves
and all those children
sent to graves
by oppression, injustice, sin:
forgive us,
please forgive us
for having abandoned you.

Choir 1   Let us lament
for all who have spent
their lives
in uncommon sorrow.

Choir 2   Indeed we mourn
for all who are born
too soon
into tomorrow.

    By M. T. Winter, Crossroad Pub. Co., © 1992 Medical Mission Sisters

EDNA

◇ **Scripture Reference** Tob 7:1–15; 8:1–5, 9–21; 9:6; 10:7–13; 14:12–13

◇ **Biography**

Edna was the wife of Raguel and the mother of a daughter, Sarah, who was possessed by a demon, for Sarah's seven husbands died on their wedding nights. When Tobias asked to marry Sarah, Edna prepared the bridal chamber and spent a sleepless night. On learning that Tobias had survived and that the evil spell was broken, Edna and her husband prepared a fourteen-day wedding celebration. Then Edna's only child left home and moved to Nineveh with her husband.

◇ **Context**

Edna is depicted as the ideal wife, mother, and mother-in-law. She is a partner to her husband. She supports him, does what he asks, and they discuss things together. She is a homemaker who prepares meals and rooms and in general sees to the running of the house. Everything about her seems ordinary, except her extraordinary daughter, who is her only child. How many mothers have had to bury their daughters' husbands on their wedding night? How many would have dared look in on the bridal couple to see what was going on? She must have suffered extreme pain because of the pain of her daughter and she must have worried continually about what would become of her when she and her husband were gone. How she must have loved Tobias, who was like a son to her. The overwhelming joy at her daughter's joy seemed to

179

overcome the pain of their separation as the lone child of her womb left home for a life apart from her. It could not have been easy. Yet despite some of the fantastic flourishes, Edna's story is like that of every mother who has ever had and loved a child.

◇ **Lectionary Reading**

As they were entering Ecbatana,
Tobias said to Raphael,
"Take me straight to Raguel's house."
So he did and they found Raguel sitting
beside the courtyard door.
After exchanging greetings,
Raguel took them inside the house
and said to Edna his wife,
"How much he resembles Tobit!"
Before long they learned that their visitor
was Tobias, the son of Tobit,
and that they were relatives.
Raguel kissed him, blessed him, and wept.
When they heard of Tobit's blindness,
Raguel and Edna wept again,
and their daughter wept as well.
Raguel slaughtered a ram from the flock,
and they bathed and washed
and reclined at table
and Tobias whispered to Raphael,
"Ask Raguel to give me my kinswoman Sarah."
But Raguel overheard it.
"Eat, drink, and be merry tonight,"
Raguel said to Tobias,
"for you are my nearest relative
and no one but you has the right by law
to marry my daughter Sarah.
But let me speak truthfully to you.
I have given her to seven men,
all of them our relatives,
and all of them died on their wedding night.
But now, my son, just eat and drink,
for I am sure that God will intervene
on behalf of both of you."
"I will not eat or drink," said Tobias,
"until this thing is settled."
So Raguel said, "She is given to you
in accord with the law of Moses.
She is given to you today and forever.

It has been decreed from heaven.
May God protect you both this night
and grant you mercy and peace."
Then Raguel summoned his daughter Sarah.
He took her and gave her to Tobias, saying,
"Take her to be your wife
in accordance with the law of Moses.
Take her and bring her safely home.
And may God bless your journey with peace."
Then he asked her mother for writing material
and he wrote a marriage contract.
And then they ate and drank.
Later, Raguel said to Edna,
"Prepare the other room and take our daughter there."
So she went and prepared the bridal bed
and brought her daughter there.
Wiping away her tears, she said,
"Be brave, my daughter, be brave.
The God of heaven grant you joy
in place of all your sorrow."
Then Edna departed and left Sarah alone
in the bridal chamber.

When they had finished eating and drinking
and were ready to retire,
they escorted Tobias to the room
where Sarah his bride was waiting.
Tobias remembered Raphael's words.
He took the fish's liver and heart
and put them on embers of incense.
The odor so repelled the demon
that he fled to the ends of Egypt
where Raphael, having followed him there,
bound him hand and foot.
When Raguel and Edna had left the room
and shut the door behind them,
Tobias said to Sarah,
"My sister, get up and let us pray,
imploring God for mercy
and for safety through the night."
So Sarah got up and together they prayed,
then they went to sleep for the night.
But Raguel that night summoned his servants
to go out and dig a grave.
"It is possible he will die," he said,
"and we will be marked for derision

and for ridicule by everyone."
When the grave was dug, Raguel called for Edna.
"Send a maid to look in on them," he said,
"to see if he is alive.
But if he is dead, let us bury him
without anyone knowing of it."
So they sent a maid who lit a lamp
and opened the bedroom door.
She went in and found the two of them
sound asleep together.
She came out and informed them
that nothing was wrong, that Tobias was alive.
So they blessed God and Raguel prayed,
"Blessed are you, O God;
let all your chosen children bless you;
let us bless your name forever.
Blessed are you for making me glad.
It has not happened as I expected,
for you have shown your mercy.
Blessed are you who have had compassion
on these two only children,
the only child of Edna's womb
and the only child of Anna's.
Be merciful to them and keep them safe
and bring their lives to fulfillment
in happiness and peace."
Then he ordered his servants to fill in the grave
immediately, before daybreak.
Edna baked many loaves of bread
while Raguel slaughtered rams and steer
as they began their preparations.
When Tobias awoke,
Raguel swore an oath to him in these words,
"You shall not leave for fourteen days
but shall eat and drink with me.
You shall cheer up my daughter
who has been depressed.
Half of what I own you may take with you
when you return to your father;
the other half will come to you
after Edna and I have died.
Take courage, my son, Edna and I,
we are your mother and father.
We belong to you as well as your wife,
this day and forever."

When the fourteen days of the wedding celebration
which Raguel had sworn to observe for his daughter
had come to an end, Tobias said,
"Let me go home,
for I know that my mother and father are certain
they will not see me again.
I beg of you, let me go,
so that I might return to them."
But Raguel said to Tobias,
"Stay but a little longer, my son.
I will send messengers to your parents
who will tell them all about you."
Tobias refused, so Raguel gave him
Sarah his wife
and half of all his property:
slaves, sheep, oxen, donkeys, camels,
clothing, money, and goods.
He embraced Tobias and said to him,
"Farewell, my son; have a safe journey.
May God prosper you and Sarah, your wife,
and may I see children before I die."
Then he kissed his daughter Sarah and said,
"Honor your father-in-law and your mother-in-law,
for now they are as much your parents
as the ones who gave you birth.
Go in peace, my daughter,
and may I hear only good about you
for as long as I shall live."
Then he said farewell and let them go.
Edna said to Tobias,
"My child, may God bring you safely back,
and may I live long enough to see children
born of you and my daughter Sarah.
Before God I entrust my daughter to you.
Do nothing at all to grieve her
all the days of your life.
Go now in peace, my son.
From now on I am your mother,
and Sarah is your beloved wife.
May we all prosper together as family
all the days of our life."
Then she kissed them both and saw them off.
Tobias parted from Raguel with happiness and joy,
praising the God of heaven and earth
for making his journey successful.
Blessing Raguel and Edna, he said,

"God commands me to honor you
all the days of my life."

◇

When the mother of Tobias died,
he buried her beside his father.
Then he and his wife and children
returned to Media and settled in Ecbatana with Edna and Raguel.
He treated his elderly parents-in-law with great respect,
and when they died,
he buried them there in Ecbatana.

◇ **Points for Shared Reflection**

- In what ways might Edna serve as a role model for married women? What dimensions of her behavior as wife would you personally find unacceptable?

- What qualities make a good mother? Was your mother a good mother? Why? If you are a mother, are you a good one, and why?

- What are the primary challenges facing mothers today? What concerns do you have about family life?

- What demons torment society's children? If you are a mother, what demons torment your children? What demons torment you?

◇ **A Psalm for My Mother** (see p. 185)

◇ **Prayer**

Dear Mother God,
how good it is
to name You and to know You,
to feel Your gentle Presence
and Your mothering energy.
Thank You for creating me
in Your image of compassion.
May I share with others
the tenderness
that is always there between us,
and may I recreate
our bond of love
with all Your cherished children
who are longing to be loved.
Amen.

◇ A PSALM FOR MY MOTHER ◇

Choir 1   I'm glad I was cause for joy
in your life.
How I wish I could remember
the moment of your elation
when you knew you had borne a girl.

Choir 2   When you took me
and held me to your breast
and your life force flowed
within me,
we knew that nothing could separate me
from your spirit
or your love.

Choir 1   A part of you I will never know,
for you were young too early,
yet I know that
you
know
me
in ways I will never know myself.

Choir 2   Somewhere along the journey,
we became friends,
and I am grateful.
Moments of mother-and-daughtering
live in my memory,
and I smile.

Choir 1   I never took time to thank you
for the labor
and the piercing pain
of bringing me forth,
of bringing me up,
of letting me grow
and letting me go
to the far side of the universe
unaccompanied by you.

Choir 2   I have never asked forgiveness
for the agonizing separations.
I left your womb,
knowing it was time,
and doing so, left you empty;
left our home
before it was time for you,

for I knew
it was time for me,
and once again
left you empty.

Choir 1   You gave me love
and laughter
and the goodness of your being,
gentleness and compassion,
tenderness and feeling,
wisdom, yes,
and understanding.
How blessed we are
in who we are
and how we are for each other.

Choir 2   Thank you for being you
for me,
thank you for being
my mother.
In the image of God,
God created you,
recreated you
in creating me
in your image,
which is Her image:
Gloria
in excelsis Deo!

Choir 1   You and me,
we put the whole of ourselves
into what we do.

Choir 2   May all who see
and delight in me
give praise and thanks
for you.

    By M. T. Winter, Crossroad Pub. Co., © 1992 Medical Mission Sisters

QUEEN MOTHERS

◇ **Scripture Reference**   See lectionary texts

◇ **Biography**

Queen mothers were the mothers of the kings of Israel during the time of the monarchy. When the nation split into two kingdoms, Judah in the south with its capital in Jerusalem and the Northern Kingdom of Israel with its center in Samaria, historians faithfully followed the Davidic monarchy and noted the names of nearly all the mothers of its kings. Queen mothers in the North were virtually ignored. Little information exists about the majority of these women apart from the listing of their names.

◇ **Context**

To trace the queen mothers through the monarchy in Israel is a task reserved for the resolute. Discontinuity and confusion abound. The empire established by David and continued in the reign of his son Solomon began with its center in Hebron, which moved to Jerusalem and embraced the whole nation of Israel. Following Solomon the kingdom split in two: Judah in the south with the palace in Jerusalem and Israel in the north with its palace in Samaria. From 922 to 722 B.C.E. the name Israel was used in two ways, as the name of the entire Israelite nation and at the same time the name of the smaller schismatic kingdom in the north. Historians of the canon favored the Davidic monarchy in Judah. They as well as the prophets tended to incorporate their prejudice into the recording of their facts. The names of the queen mothers of Judah are recorded fairly faithfully, although there are some significant omissions. Except in two cases, the queen mothers of Israel are ignored. Zeruah is noted as mother of Jeroboam, the man who established the Northern Kingdom. The story of Jezebel — royal wife of King Ahab, temporary regent, mother of two future kings — seems to have been preserved to symbolize all that was evil in the north and in foreign wives. There is also some confusion in the fact that several queen mothers had two sons who became kings; that several kings of the same name reigned in both Judah and Israel, one set simultaneously (Jehoram); that Jehoram is also referred to by the shorter derivative Joram; that the texts record contradictory dates and identifications; that the queen mother in one kingdom was sometimes the royal daughter in the other; and that the presence of women was minimized so that names were not always recorded and sometimes a mother's very existence was ignored.

The role of queen mother had some influence — note the interaction between Bathsheba and Solomon — but not nearly as much as the mother of the ruling king in the Hittite Kingdom and in Egypt and Mesopotamia. Patriarchal Israel had difficulty recognizing its own women as queens, whether in the role of queen mother or temporary regent until a successor could be found or came of age to fill a vacancy, or as a reigning queen. Athaliah reigned for six years in Jerusalem, a fact of some significance, but little has been made of that. Jezebel was probably reigning queen during a brief interim in Samaria, but that only proves the point that reigning women are to be feared. The Bible mentions several queens, but they reside in other nations: Vashti in the court of Ahasuerus in Persia and her successor, the Jewish woman Esther; the Queen of Sheba; the wives of Artaxerxes and Belshazzar, kings of the Persian Empire and Assyria; Tahpenes in Egypt, and, in the Deuterocanonical texts, Arsinoe and Cleopatra.

The queen mother did have an official status in Judah, which made the cultic offenses of Asa's mother a point of such contention. Precisely how much influence these women had or what role they played or what they accomplished is currently unknown.

◇ **Lectionary Reading**

Reader: Here are the mothers of the kings of Israel
before the nation was divided:

Mother of Saul: not recorded in scripture
◇ ◇ ◇
Mother of David: her name is unknown (see p. 159)
◇ ◇ ◇
Bathsheba, mother of Solomon:
So Bathsheba went to Solomon.
The king stood up to meet her,
bowed down to her, then sat on his throne
and had a throne brought for his mother,
who sat at his right hand. (1 Kings 2:19; see Bathsheba's story, p. 62.)
◇ ◇ ◇
Reader: Here are the mothers of the kings of Judah:

Naamah, mother of Rehoboam:
Rehoboam was forty-one years old when he took the throne.
He reigned seventeen years in Jerusalem.
His mother's name was Naamah the Ammonite.
He did evil, for his heart did not seek God. (2 Chr 12:13–14)
◇ ◇ ◇
Maacah, mother of Abijah and Asa:
Rehoboam king of Judah married Maacah
the daughter of Absalom,
who bore him Abijah, Attai, Ziza, and Shelomith.
Rehoboam loved Maacah daughter of Absalom
more than all his other wives and concubines
(he had eighteen wives and sixty concubines,
and fathered twenty-eight sons and sixty daughters).
Rehoboam appointed Abijah son of Maacah
as chief prince among his brothers,
for he intended to make him king. (2 Chr 11:20–22)
◇
In the eighteenth year of King Jeroboam of Israel,
Abijah began to reign over Judah.
He reigned for three years in Jerusalem.
His mother's name was Maacah.
She was the daughter of Abishalom [Absalom].
Abijah committed all the sins that his father had before him.
His heart was not true to the God of Israel
as the heart of David had been. (1 Kings 15:1–3; 2 Chr 13:1–2)
◇
In the twentieth year of King Jeroboam of Israel,
Asa began to reign over Judah.

He reigned for forty-one years in Jerusalem.
His mother's name was Maacah.
She was the daughter of Abishalom [Absalom].
Asa did what was right before God, just as David had done.
He got rid of the male temple prostitutes
and removed all the idols his ancestors had made.
He also removed his mother, Maacah,
from her position as queen mother,
because she had made an image for Asherah.
Asa cut down the image she had made
and burned it at Wadi Kidron;
but he did not remove the main sanctuaries
of worship to the alien gods. (1 Kings 15:9–14; 2 Chr 15:16)

◇ ◇ ◇

Azubah, mother of Jehoshaphat:
Jehoshaphat son of Asa began to reign over Judah
in the fourth year of King Ahab of Israel.
Jehoshaphat was thirty-five years old
when he took the throne,
and he reigned twenty-five years in Jerusalem.
His mother's name was Azubah.
She was the daughter of Shilhi.
He walked in the ways of his father Asa
and did what was right before God;
yet the sanctuaries to alien gods remained,
and the people continued to offer incense and sacrifices.
(1 Kings 22:41–43; 2 Chr 20:31)

◇ ◇ ◇

Mother of Jehoram: not recorded in scripture

◇ ◇ ◇

Athaliah, mother of Ahaziah:
In the twelfth year of King Joram son of Ahab of Israel,
Ahaziah son of King Jehoram of Judah
began to reign in Judah.
Ahaziah was twenty-two years old
when he took the throne.
He reigned one year in Jerusalem.
His mother's name was Athaliah.
She was a granddaughter of King Omri of Israel.
He walked in the ways of the house of Ahab,
doing evil in the sight of God,
for he was son-in-law to the house of Ahab.
(2 Kings 8:25–27)

◇ ◇ ◇

Jehu met relatives of King Ahaziah of Judah and said,
"Who are you?" They answered, "We are relatives of Ahaziah.

We have come down to visit the royal princes
and the sons of the queen mother."

(2 Kings 10:13; see Athaliah's story, p. 88.)

◇ ◇ ◇

Zibiah, mother of Joash:
In the seventh year of Jehu,
Joash began to reign in Judah.
He was seven years old when he took the throne,
and he reigned forty years in Jerusalem.
His mother's name was Zibiah of Beer-sheba.
Joash did what was right in the sight of God,
because the priest Jehoiada instructed him.
Yet alien sanctuaries were not removed,
and the people continued to make offerings
and perform sacrificial worship. (2 Kings 12:1–3; 2 Chr 24:1–2)

◇ ◇ ◇

Jehoaddin, mother of Amaziah:
In the second year of King Joash of Israel,
King Amaziah son of Joash of Judah
began to reign in Judah.
He was twenty-five years old when he took the throne,
and he reigned twenty-nine years in Jerusalem.
His mother's name was Jehoaddin of Jerusalem.
He did what was right in the eyes of God,
yet not like his ancestor David.
He did as his father Joash had done.
But the alien sanctuaries were still not removed
and the people continued to sacrifice
and make offerings in those places. (2 Kings 14:1–3; 2 Chr 25:1)

◇ ◇ ◇

Jecoliah, mother of Azariah (Uzziah):
In the twenty-seventh year of King Jeroboam of Israel,
King Azariah son of Amaziah
began to reign in Judah.
He was sixteen years old when he took the throne,
and he reigned fifty-two years in Jerusalem.
His mother's name was Jecoliah of Jerusalem.
He did what was right in the eyes of God,
just as his father Amaziah had done.
Nevertheless the alien sanctuaries were still not removed,
and the people still sacrificed
and made offerings there. (2 Kings 15:1–4; 2 Chr 26:3)

◇ ◇ ◇

Jerusha, mother of Jotham:
In the second year of King Pekah of Israel,
King Jotham son of Azariah began to reign in Judah.

He was twenty-five years old when he took the throne,
and he reigned sixteen years in Jerusalem.
His mother's name was Jerusha.
She was the daughter of Zadok.
He did what was right in the sight of God,
just as his father Uzziah had done.
Still the alien sanctuaries were not removed,
and the people continued to sacrifice
and make offerings in those places. (2 Kings 15:32–35; 2 Chr 27:1)
◇ ◇ ◇

Mother of Ahaz: not recorded in scripture
◇ ◇ ◇

Abi, mother of Hezekiah:
In the third year of King Hoshea of Israel,
Hezekiah son of King Ahaz of Judah
began to reign in Judah.
He was twenty-five years old when he took the throne,
and he reigned twenty-nine years in Jerusalem.
His mother's name was Abi.
She was the daughter of Zechariah.
He did what was right in the eyes of God,
just as his ancestor David had done.
He removed the alien sanctuaries,
broke down the pillars,
and cut down the sacred pole.
He smashed the bronze serpent that Moses had made,
for the people had made offerings to it
and had called it Nehushtan.
He trusted in the God of Israel,
and there was no one like him
among all the kings of Judah after him,
or among those who had gone before.
                    (2 Kings 18:1–5; 2 Chr 29:1)
◇ ◇ ◇

Hephzibah, mother of Manasseh:
Manasseh was twelve years old
when he began to reign in Judah.
He reigned fifty-five years in Jerusalem.
His mother's name was Hephzibah.
He did what was evil in the sight of God.
He rebuilt the alien sanctuaries
his father Hezekiah had destroyed,
erected altars for Baal and made a sacred pole,
as King Ahab of Israel had done,
and worshiped all the host of heaven. (2 Kings 21:1–3)
◇ ◇ ◇

Meshullemeth, mother of Amon:
Amon was twenty-two years old
when he began to reign in Judah.
He reigned two years in Jerusalem.
His mother's name was Meshullemeth.
She was the daughter of Haruz of Jotbah.
He did what was evil in the sight of God,
as his father Manasseh had done. (2 Kings 21:19–20)

◇ ◇ ◇

Jedidah, mother of Josiah:
Josiah was eight years old
when he began to reign in Judah.
He reigned thirty-one years in Jerusalem.
His mother's name was Jedidah.
She was the daughter of Adaiah of Bozkath.
He did what was right in the sight of God,
as his ancestor David had done. (2 Kings 22:1–2)

◇ ◇ ◇

Hamutal, mother of Jehoahaz and Zedekiah:
Jehoahaz was twenty-three years old
when he began to reign in Judah.
He reigned three months in Jerusalem.
His mother's name was Hamutal.
She was the daughter of Jeremiah of Libnah.
He did what was evil in the sight of God,
just as his ancestors had done.

◇

The king of Babylon made Mattaniah,
Johoiachin's uncle,
king in place of Jehoiachin,
and changed his name to Zedekiah.
Zedekiah was twenty-one years old
when he began to reign in Judah.
He reigned eleven years in Jerusalem
[after Jehoiakim and Jehoiachin]
His mother's name was Hamutal.
She was the daughter of Jeremiah of Libnah.
He did what was evil in the sight of God,
just as Jehoiakim had done. (2 Kings 23:31–32; 24:17–19; Jer 52:1)

◇ ◇ ◇

Zebidah, mother of Jehoiakim:
Jehoiakim was twenty-five years old
when he began to reign in Judah.
He reigned eleven years in Jerusalem.
His mother's name was Zebidah.
She was the daughter of Pedaiah of Rumah.

He did what was evil in the sight of God,
just as all his ancestors had done. (2 Kings 23:36–37)

◊ ◊ ◊

Nehushta, mother of Jehoiachin:
Jehoiachin was eighteen years old
when he began to reign in Judah.
He reigned three months in Jerusalem.
His mother's name was Nehushta.
She was the daughter of Elnathan of Jerusalem.
He did what was evil in the sight of God,
just as his father had done.
At that time the troops of King Nebuchadnezzar of Babylon
came up to Jerusalem, and the city was besieged.
King Nebuchadnezzar came to the city
while his troops were besieging it.
King Jehoiachin of Judah surrendered to the king,
himself, his mother, his servants,
his officers, and his palace officials.
The king of Babylon took him prisoner
in the eighth year of his reign.
He carried off all the temple treasures
and the treasures of the king's palace.
He cut up the temple's vessels of gold
which King Solomon had made,
just as God had foretold.
He carried away all of Jerusalem,
all the officials, the warriors,
all the artisans and the smiths;
he took ten thousand captives.
No one remained in the city
except the poorest people of the land.
He carried away Jehoiachin to Babylon.
The king's mother, his wives, his officials,
and all the elite of Israel
he took into captivity
and brought them from Jerusalem to Babylon.
                          (2 Kings 24:8–15; Jer 29:2)

◊ ◊ ◊

Reader: Here are the mothers of the kings who reigned
        in the Northern Kingdom of Israel:

Zeruah, mother of Jeroboam:
Jeroboam son of Nebat,
an Ephraimite of Zeredah,
a servant of Solomon,
whose mother's name was Zeruah, a widow,

rebelled against the king.
When all Israel heard that Jeroboam had returned,
they sent and called him to the assembly
and made him king over Israel.
There was no one who followed the house of David,
except the tribe of Judah. (1 Kings 11:26; 12:20)

◇ ◇ ◇

Jezebel, mother of Ahaziah and Jehoram of Israel:
Ahaziah son of Ahab
began to reign over Israel in Samaria
in the seventeenth year
of the reign of King Jehoshaphat of Judah.
He reigned two years over Israel.
He did what was evil in the eyes of God
and walked in the ways of his father and mother.
                              (1 Kings 22:51–52)

◇

When Joram saw Jehu, he said,
"Is it peace, Jehu?"
He answered, "What peace can there be,
as long as the many whoredoms
and sorceries of your mother Jezebel continue?"
                    (2 Kings 9:22; see Jezebel's story, p. 77)

◇ ◇ ◇

Queen Mothers who have not been recorded in scripture
  • **Mother of Nadab**
  • **Mother of Baasha**
  • **Mother of Elah**
  • **Mother of Zimri**
  • **Mother of Omri**
  • **Mother of Ahab**
  • **Mother of Jehu**
  • **Mother of Jehoahaz**
  • **Mother of Jehoash**
  • **Mother of Jeroboam II**
  • **Mother of Zechariah**
  • **Mother of Shallum**
  • **Mother of Menahem**
  • **Mother of Pekahiah**
  • **Mother of Pekah**
  • **Mother of Hoshea**

◇ **Points for Shared Reflection**
  • Why do you think it was so important to name the mother of the
    reigning king?

- What would you be saying about yourself and about your mother if you began to identify yourself as daughter (or son) of your mother?
- The role of queen mother had a certain amount of influence and prestige but was virtually without power. What titles do you hold and what roles do you fill that might be considered similarly prestigious but powerless?
- Queen mothers of Judah were identified; those of Israel were not. What does this say about those who record our history? Why is this question particularly important to women?

◇ **A Psalm on Faithfulness** (see p. 197)

◇ **Prayer**

Faith of our mothers
who knew You, Shaddai,
as we have seldom
known You,
knew You before
we made You up
into Someone
You are not,
Someone we could
believe in,
Someone Who is
more like us.
Out of all our pride
and prejudice
and our theological guesswork,
we made a molten image
and we danced around You,
worshiping You,
refusing to admit
that in some strange way
we were worshiping ourselves.
Free us from our need
to have a God Who meets our standards,
who passes the text of orthodoxy
and stays within the rules.
We are so often devoid of faith
and faithful to unessentials.
Help us, Shaddai,
to find and faithfully keep
true faith in You.
Amen.

◇ A PSALM ON FAITHFULNESS ◇

All   Hear my cry, Shekinah-Shaddai.
Let me not lose faith
in Your faithfulness.
Give me the fulness of faith.

Choir 1   Things go wrong.
I lose control.
My faith is sorely tested.

Choir 2   Nothing seems secure anymore.
Where are You, Shaddai?

Choir 1   People turn against me,
my faithfulness
is questioned.

Choir 2   It used to be so easy,
until we changed the rules.

All   Hear my cry, Shekinah-Shaddai.
Let me not lose faith
in Your faithfulness.
Give me the fulness of faith.

Choir 1   How tempting it is
to give up
on all the convoluted
escapades
that make up our tradition.

Choir 2   How easy it would be
sometimes
simply to walk away.

Choir 1   How hard the struggle
to speak the truth
as we ourselves
have heard it,
when we know
the truth we heard
in the past
may not be quite so true.

Choir 2   How strange
the once familiar terrain
of theology
and ritual;

those who thought
these things were gods
are no longer satisfied.

All   Hear my cry, Shekinah-Shaddai.
Let me not lose faith
in Your faithfulness.
Give me the fulness of faith.

Choir 1   You created us equal,
in Your image,
but that has not been
our experience.

Choir 2   The curse on the female gender
is a point of personal pain.

Choir 1   What happened
to unconditional love
and all Your original blessing?

Choir 2   Help us to find ourselves again
as we were
before we cursed ourselves
instead of trusting You.

All   Hear my cry, Shekinah-Shaddai.
Let me not lose faith
in Your faithfulness.
Give me the fulness of faith.

MOTHERS

◇ **Scripture Reference**   See lectionary texts

◇ **Biography**

The women remembered primarily as mothers were the life force of
Israel and the other nations of the ancient Near East that are mentioned
in the Bible. Mothers who appear elsewhere in this volume either on a
list or in a featured narrative are not included here.

◇ **Context**

From an early age little girls were prepared to grow up to be mothers.
A woman's goal was to have many sons through whom she might be
remembered, notwithstanding that without daughters there would be
no mothers of sons. Ironically the mother who brought forth a son has
seldom been remembered. In genealogical listings the father is named,
the mother is not; in fact, she is rarely mentioned. In Israel fertility was a
sign of blessing, childlessness a curse, barrenness a disgrace. Rachel and

199

Leah gave their maids to their husbands so that through them they might be mothers of sons. Punishment meant being deprived of one's identity as a mother — "no birth, no pregnancy, no conception... dry breasts and a womb that miscarries" (Hos 9:11, 14). The blessings of Israel were also described with the imagery of birth: "...as soon as Zion was in labor she delivered her children" (Is 66:8). True joy meant "to nurse and be satisfied from her consoling breast" (v. 11). There are images of God as a mother about to give birth: "I will cry out like a woman in labor, I will gasp and pant" (42:14); as a nursing mother: "Can a woman forget her nursing child, or show no compassion for the child of her womb?" (49:15); as a solicitous mother: "As a mother comforts her child, so will I comfort you" (66:13). The maternal metaphor was also applied to the nation of Israel: "...your mother shall be utterly shamed, and she who bore you shall be disgraced. She shall be the last of the nations..." (Jer 50:12). To be Jewish one had only to be born of a Jewish mother, for in patriarchal Israel, Jewishness was transmitted through the matriarch.

No matter what the tradition felt about barrenness or sterility, significant mothers of significant sons were barren for lengths of time: Sarah, mother of Isaac; Rebekah, mother of Jacob and Esau; Rachel, mother of Joseph and Benjamin; Samson's mother; and Hannah, mother of Samuel come immediately to mind. Is God saying something here about woman's worth apart from bearing children? Or simply stating that some things can only be done by God and are beyond the control of males. Stories of individual mothers appear throughout all three volumes in this series, and the sum total of their narratives presents a powerful witness to the work of God in womankind. What follows is a lection-based litany of remembrance for mothers in the Bible. Some are named, others unnamed, still others are mentioned in generic terms. We must not forget the multitude of women who are not mentioned in the Bible but are remembered through their children who bear witness to their lives.

◇ **Lectionary Reading**

Narrator: We remember **mothers whose names we know**
We remember **Abihail,** mother of Mahalath

Reader
Rehoboam took as his wife Mahalath,
daughter of Jerimoth son of David
and of Abihail daughter of Eliab son of Jesse. (2 Chr 11:18)
◇ ◇ ◇

Narrator: We remember **Aiah,** Rizpah's mother

Reader
Now Saul had a concubine whose name was Rizpah.
She was the daughter of Aiah. (2 Sam 3:7)
◇ ◇ ◇

Narrator: We remember **Deborah,** mother of Tobit

Reader
A tenth of my grain, wine, olive oil, pomegranates, figs, and fruits
I would give to the orphans, widows, and converts
who had attached themselves to Israel.
I would bring it and give it to them every third year,
and we would eat it according to the ordinance decreed
concerning it in the law of Moses
and according to the instructions of Deborah,
the mother of my father Tobiel,
for my father had died and left me an orphan. (Tob 1:8)

◇ ◇ ◇

Narrator: We remember **Hammolecheth,** sister of Machir

Reader
Machir's sister Hammolecheth gave birth to
Ishhod, Abiezer, and Mahlah. (1 Chr 7:18)

◇ ◇ ◇

Narrator: We remember **Shimeath and Shomer (Shimrith)**

Reader
Joash's servants conspired together,
and killed him in Millo on the way to Silla.
It was Jozacar son of Shimeath
and Jehozabad son of Shomer, his servants,
who struck him down. (2 Kings 12:20–21)

◇

Those who killed Joash were Zabad son of Shimeath the Ammonite,
and Jehozabad son of Shimrith the Moabite. (2 Chr 24:26)

◇ ◇ ◇

Narrator: We remember **Zeruiah,** David's sister, mother of Joab

Reader
Jesse became the father of Eliab his firstborn;
Abinadab the second; Shimea the third;
Nethanel the fourth; Raddai the fifth;
Ozem the sixth; David the seventh;
and their sisters were Zeruiah and Abigail.
The sons of Zeruiah were Abishai, Joab, and Asahel.
                    (1 Chr 2:13–16)

◇

Then Abishai son of Zeruiah said to the king,
"Why should this dead dog curse my lord the king?
Let me go over and take off his head."
But David said, "What have I to do with you,
you sons of Zeruiah?
If he is cursing me because God has said to him,

'Curse David,' who then shall say,
'Why have you done so?'" (2 Sam 16:9–10)

◇

David had said, "Whoever attacks the Jebusites first
shall be my chief and commander."
And Joab son of Zeruiah went up first,
so he became the chief. (1 Chr 11:6)

◇

Now Absalom had set Amasa over the army in place of Joab.
Amasa was the son of Ithra the Ishmaelite,
who had married Abigal daughter of Nahash,
sister of Zeruiah, Joab's mother. (2 Sam 17:25)

◇ ◇ ◇

Narrator: We remember **mothers whose names we do not know**
We remember **Abraham's mother**

Reader
Abram answered Abimelech.
"I said to Sarai, whenever we travel,
say of me, He is my brother.
Besides, she is my sister,
the daughter of my father, but not of my mother,
and she became my wife." (Gen 20:11–13)

◇ ◇ ◇

Narrator: We remember **Rebekah's mother**

Reader
Rebekah ran and told her mother's household
about these things.
Abraham's servant brought out jewelry
of silver and of gold, and garments,
and gave them to Rebekah;
he also gave costly ornaments
to her brother and to her mother.
Her brother and her mother said,
"Let the girl remain with us awhile,
at least for ten days; then she may go."
But Abraham's servant said to them,
"Do not delay me.
God has made my journey successful.
Let me return to my master."
They said, "We will ask the girl."
And they called Rebekah and said to her,
"Will you go with this man?"
She said, "I will."
So they sent their sister Rebekah and her nurse
with Abraham's servant and his men.

And they blessed Rebekah and said to her,
"Sister of ours, may you increase
to thousands and tens of thousands!
May your descendants gain possession
of the gates of their enemies!" (Gen 24:28, 53, 55–60)

◇ ◇ ◇

Narrator: We remember the Canaanite woman, **mother of Shaul**

Reader
The children of Simeon were Jemuel, Jamin, Ohad,
Jachin, Zohar, and Shaul, the son of a Canaanite woman.
(Gen 46:10; Ex 6:15)

◇ ◇ ◇

Narrator: We remember the **mother of Phinehas** the priest,
grandson of Aaron — she was Aaron's daughter-in-law

Reader
Aaron's son Eleazar married one of the daughters of Putiel,
and she bore him Phinehas. (Ex 6:25)

◇ ◇ ◇

Narrator: We remember **Rahab's mother**

Reader
Then Rahab said, "Give me a sign of good faith,
that you will spare my father and mother,
my brothers and sisters and all who belong to them,
and deliver our lives from death."
The men said to her,
"We will be released from this oath
that you have made us swear to you
if we invade the land
and you do not tie this crimson cord
in the window through which you let us down,
and you do not gather into your house
your father and mother, your brothers, and all your family."
Joshua said to the two men who had spied out the land,
"Go into the prostitute's house,
and bring the woman out of it
and all who belong to her, as you swore to her."
So the young men who had been spies
went in and brought Rahab out,
along with her father, her mother, her brothers,
and all who belonged to her —
they brought all her kindred out —
and set them outside the camp of Israel.
Then they burned down the city and everything in it.
Only the silver and gold, and the vessels of bronze and iron,

they put into the treasury of the house of God.
But Rahab the prostitute,
with her family and all who belonged to her,
Joshua spared.
Her family has lived in Israel ever since.
For she hid the messengers whom Joshua sent
to spy out Jericho. (Josh 2:13,17–18; 6:22–25)

◇ ◇ ◇

Narrator: We remember **Sisera's mother**

Reader
Through the window she stared,
through the lattice she gazed, the mother of Sisera.
"Why is his chariot so long in coming?
Why do the horses tarry?"
She answers herself:
"Are they not now dividing the spoil?
A girl or two for every man,
a garment or two for Sisera,
an embroidered scarf, two scarves for me!" (Judg 5:28–30)

◇ ◇ ◇

Narrator: We remember **Hiram's mother**

Reader
Now King Solomon invited and received Hiram from Tyre.
He was the son of a widow of the tribe of Naphtali,
whose father, a man of Tyre, had been an artisan in bronze.
He was skillful and intelligent
and knowledgeable about working in bronze.
He came to King Solomon and did all his work.

◇

Then King Huram of Tyre answered Solomon in a letter:
"I have dispatched Huram-abi, a skilled artisan
endowed with understanding,
the son of one of the Danite women,
his father a Tyrian.
He is trained to work in gold, silver, bronze, iron,
stone, and wood, and in purple, blue, and crimson fabrics
and fine linen, and to do all sorts of engraving
and execute any design that might be assigned him.
(1 Kings 7:13–15; 2 Chr 2:11, 13–14)

◇ ◇ ◇

Narrator: We remember **Elisha's mother**

Reader
Elijah passed by Elisha
and threw his mantle over him.

Elisha left his oxen and ran after Elijah, saying,
"Let me kiss my father and my mother,
and then I will follow you."
Then Elijah said to him,
"Go back again; for what have I done to you?" (1 Kings 19:19–20)

◇ ◇ ◇

Narrator: We remember the **mother of Jabez,** a descendant of Judah

Reader
Jabez was honored more than his brothers;
and his mother named him Jabez, saying,
"Because I bore him in pain." (1 Chr 4:9)

◇ ◇ ◇

Narrator: We remember **Jeremiah's mother**

Reader
Woe is me, my mother, that you ever bore me,
a man of strife and contention to the whole land! (Jer 15:10)

◇ ◇ ◇

Narrator: We remember **Susanna's mother**

Reader
Susanna's parents were virtuous and just.
They had trained their daughter
according to the law of Moses....
When they sent for Susanna,
she came with her parents, her children,
and all her relatives....
Hilkiah and his wife praised God
on behalf of their daughter Susanna,
and so did her husband Joakim
and all her relatives,
because she was found innocent of a shameful deed. (Sus 3, 30, 63)

◇ ◇ ◇

Narrator: We remember the **mother of Simon Maccabee**

Reader
Simon erected seven pyramids opposite one another,
for his father and mother and four brothers.
This is the tomb he built in Modein,
and it remains to this day. (1 Macc 13:28, 30)

◇ ◇ ◇

Narrator: We remember the **mothers recorded in scripture
as having suffered persecution**

Reader
According to the decree of Antiochus,
they put to death the women

who had had their children circumcised,
and their families and those who circumcised them;
and they hung the infants from their mothers' necks. (1 Macc 1:60–61)

◇

For example, two women were brought in
for having circumcised their children.
They publicly paraded them around the city,
with their babies hanging at their breasts,
and then hurled them down headlong from the wall.

(2 Macc 6:10)

◇ ◇ ◇

Narrator: We remember **mothers who are not recorded in scripture**
but whose presence is implied
by the presence of their children:

- **mother of the sons and daughters of Seth**
- **mother of the sons and daughters of Enosh**
- **mother of the sons and daughters of Kenan**
- **mother of the sons and daughters of Mahalalel**
- **mother of the sons and daughters of Jared**
- **mother of the sons and daughters of Enoch**
- **mother of the sons and daughters of Methuselah**
- **mother of the sons and daughters of Lamech**
- **mother of the children of Shem**
- **mother of the children of Ham**
- **mother of the children of Japheth**
- **mother of Sarah**
- **mother of Milcah**
- **mother of Leah and Rachel**
- **mothers of the children of all the ancestral houses of Israel,
  of all the tribes, clans, and families**
- **mother of Jephthah's daughter**
- **mother of the virgin daughter of Gibeah**
- **mothers of all the sons and daughters recorded in the pages
  of scripture**
- **mothers of the soldiers in Pharaoh's army drowned in the Sea
  of Reeds**
- **mothers of the Canaanites, the Philistines, and all other tribes
  and nations recorded in the pages of scripture as having
  been slain, captured, or condemned**

◇ **Points for Shared Reflection**

- Women of ancient times ordinarily did not have to balance motherhood with a career. Do you? Name some of the challenges facing a woman with those dual responsibilities and some of the ways she might meet those challenges.

- Do you think there is too much emphasis or insufficient emphasis on the role of motherhood today? Or do you think there is a healthy balance? Give reasons for your response.

- What advice would you give your real or imaginary daughter as she prepares to enter the world of the twenty-first century?

- What advice would you give a young mother today? Would you follow that advice?

◇ **A Psalm about Mountains** (see p. 208)

◇ **Prayer**

I lift my prayer
to the mountains
where I see
an image of You, Shaddai,
and feel very close to You.
In the silent strength
of Mount Sinai
rising from the desert
of disbelief,
I stand in awe of Your presence.
In the splendor
of Kilimanjaro,
I feel Your glory
from age to age
washing the bones
of the Great Rift valley
and cleansing the flesh
and bone of me.
Reveal to me,
O Sacred Mountain,
what eye has not seen
nor heart comprehended
in the depths
of eternal Being,
and draw me into You,
now and forever.
Amen.

◊ A PSALM ABOUT MOUNTAINS ◊

Choir 1   Mountains are there,
simply there,
strong, silent, enduring,
keeping vigil without complaint
from before I came into being,
and they will be there when I am gone.
Mothers are like mountains.

All   I lift my eyes to the mountains
where I feel Your strength, Shaddai.

Choir 2   Mountains see
what the eye cannot see,
are above and beyond complexity,
touched by the infinite
toward which they reach.
Mystics are like mountains.

All   I lift my heart to the mountains
where I feel Your presence, Shaddai.

Choir 1   Mountains watch
the world go by,
keeping perspective,
keeping faith,
always affirming
what happens to be,
always welcoming every encounter
in any season
on any day.
Friends are like a mountain.

All   I lift my soul to the mountains
where I encounter You, Shaddai.

Choir 2   Mountains are
what we have to climb
to get to the other side of things,
to get to the other side of ourselves,
to grow to know
there is more to life
than what happens
here on the plains.
We can be like a mountain.

All   I lift myself to the mountains
where I am one with You, Shaddai.

 By M. T. Winter, Crossroad Pub. Co., © 1992 Medical Mission Sisters

◇ III ◇
Daughters

EVE'S DAUGHTERS

◇ **Scripture Reference**   Gen 5:3–4

◇ **Biography**

The brief notation in the Genesis genealogy is the only written indication that Adam and Eve gave birth to daughters. While the biblical text refers only to Adam, we may appropriately speak of Eve's daughters.

◇ **Context**

Did Adam and Eve have any daughters? This question is guaranteed to stump even the biblically astute. Ask your community or group. Someone is bound to say, usually after an awkward silence, "They must have." Indeed, or we would not be here. But that is just not good enough. Ask the second question. Is it recorded anywhere in the Bible that Adam and Eve had daughters? Hardly anyone remembers the notation in Genesis 5, but that will surely change. The surprise surrounding the discovery should also be accompanied by sorrow, for from the very beginning, women have been forgotten or valued solely for their role in propagating the species. An injustice has been done to all of Eve's daughters, biological and spiritual. Those in the present can best be supported by spending a little time rediscovering their sisters in the past. Who and how many were Eve's daughters? Genesis focuses on the sons, opting to feature a murderer rather than allocate editorial space to the ways those initial women dealt with the challenges of being fully human and of nurturing the future to life. This is one biblical text that literally cries out for historical imagination both from women and from men. Don't bother with traditional commentaries. You won't find anything there. The first few pages of *Dear Daughter* by Colleen Ivey Hartsoe (Wilton, Conn.: Morehouse-Barlow, 1981) are provocative, but the book is now out of print. Simply try to remember. The more we try to remember, the more we will learn directly from Eve's daughters who are eager to tell their story to any who have ears to hear.

◇ **Lectionary Reading**

When Adam had lived
one hundred thirty years,
he became the father of a son
in his likeness
and named him Seth.
After he had become the father of Seth,
Adam lived for eight hundred years
and he — and Eve — had other sons
and daughters.

◇ **Points for Shared Reflection**

- Have you ever thought about Eve's daughters? Have you ever heard anyone speak of them? How do you feel about the silence and indifference surrounding our firstborn sisters?

- Talk about some of the things Eve would have told her daughters. How would she have explained her action in the Garden? What would she have said about losing paradise in the process of becoming fully human?

- If you are a woman, you are one of Eve's daughters. What are some of the characteristics you have inherited from the mother of all the living?

- Whatever Eve herself may have felt, her sons were given priority over her daughters in every arena of life and opportunity. Has that been true of your experience? Respond in terms of both your domestic life and your public life.

◇ **A Psalm for Eve's Daughters** (see p. 213)

◇ **Prayer**
Mother of All the Living,
we are wounded,
deeply wounded,
by the silence and indifference
surrounding Your firstborn daughters.
These first fruits
of Your maternal womb
never made the pages of history,
and the need to know their story
haunts their sisters
and some brothers
in our biased world today.
Transmit to us their wisdom.
Let them be our inspiration
as we struggle to claim
a place for ourselves
and for all of Eve's future daughters,
forever and ever.
Amen.

◇ **A PSALM FOR EVE'S DAUGHTERS** ◇

All   The first females
to break the waters
of Eve and earth
were Eve's daughters.
Tell their story. Sing their praises.
Give thanks for the hope their memory raises.

Choir 1   In the beginning,
on that day,
in the annals of *in illo tempore*,
women emerged from the primal waters
of one woman's womb,
Eve's daughters.

Choir 2   In the dreamtime
when life began,
God made woman
and God made man.
In our image: yes, I will send her
replicas of our female gender.

Choir 1   Daughters danced
in the new creation,
learned about love
and dedication,
opened their wombs and brought to birth
goodness and strength
to people the earth.

Choir 2   But no one remembered
what had been
when the daughters of Eve
ushered life in.
We lost their laughter,
lost their tears,
lost their memory to the years.

Choir 1   Look to the stars
and see there reflected
the dreams of the daughters
as yet undetected,
flickers of hope,
a flash of their flame,
and there in the stars
you will read their name.

By M. T. Winter, Crossroad Pub. Co., © 1992 Medical Mission Sisters   *WomanWitness* **/ 213**

Choir 2   Feel the wind on your fingers and face
and hear in its whisper
the delicate trace
of the song of the daughters,
the primeval theme
of the fullness of life
in the time of the dream.

Choir 1   See in the moonlight
the warmth of their faces,
and feel in the waters
their sensuous traces;
the lace of the spider
has strands of their hair;
there are signs of the daughters of Eve
everywhere.

Choir 2   In fields and forests,
among the flowers,
where they lifted their spirits
and sharpened their powers,
they dreamed of a future
where women would be
just as happy as they were
and, yes, just as free.

All   All who are female
have passed through the waters
of life, all women
are Eve's daughters.
Look to the future and dare to believe
we'll recover the spirit of the daughters of Eve.

    By M. T. Winter, Crossroad Pub. Co., © 1992 Medical Mission Sisters

LOT'S DAUGHTERS

◇ **Scripture Reference**   Gen 19:1–26, 30–38

◇ **Biography**

The two virgin daughters of Lot, the nephew of Abraham, escaped the destruction of Sodom and fled to the town of Zoar and from there to a cave in the hills with their father where they got themselves pregnant by making him drunk and secretly having intercourse with him. The elder daughter bore a son named Moab. The younger daughter also had a son, and she named her boy Ben-ammi.

◇ **Context**

It is ironic that we know the two nameless women of this narrative only as their father's daughters, for their story centers on two traumatic incidents involving him. In the first he callously offered a local mob the opportunity to rape them. In the second the daughters, in two separate incidents, raped him. The driving force in these episodes is the issue of expediency. To protect the code of hospitality, Lot's daughters were expendable. To continue the family name and heritage, impregnation by one's father was deemed acceptable. Or was the second incident in some sense retribution for the first? Did the writer allow the daughters to violate the father who violated them? The message to women — and men — is unclear. Women abhor incest and rape; they are usually its victims. Other troubling questions arise from the text. How did Lot and his daughters end up in a cave in the hills when they had gone to the city of Zoar and had been assured of their safety there? Since the messengers had promised to spare Zoar, how could the daughters conclude that there were no more men living on earth? Perhaps they meant there were no men of their own religion or lineage. The seduction of Lot may simply have been an etiological story to explain the origins of the Moabites and Ammonites and their relationship to the ancestral houses of Israel, a story with some basis in fact. The women are introduced to us in a violent way. It will take time to get to know them.

⬦ **Lectionary Reading**

In the evening two angels came to Sodom.
Lot was sitting at Sodom's gate.
As soon as he saw them, he rose to meet them
and bowed with his face to the ground.
He said, "Please, my lords, spend the night with me;
you can wash your feet and in the morning
you can be on your way again."
"We will spend the night in the square," they said.
But he persisted until they went home with him.
He made them a feast,
baked unleavened bread,
and they sat and ate their fill.
Before the guests had gone to bed,
the men of Sodom, every last male, young and old,
surrounded the house.
"Where are the men who are with you tonight?"
the mob of Sodomites shouted.
"Hand them over to us
so that we might have sex with them."
Lot stepped out to reason with them
and shut the door behind him.
"I beg of you, my brothers," he said,
"do not do such an evil thing.
Look, I have two daughters who are virgins.
Let me bring them out to you
and you can do to them as you please,
only do not violate these men

who have sought hospitality with me."
But the mob responded, "Move out of the way."
Then they said to one another,
"This man who came here as a foreigner
now sets himself up as a judge!
We will do worse things to him
than we had planned to do to his guests."
Then they pushed Lot back against the door
and began to break it down.
The guests reached out, pulled Lot inside,
and barred the door behind him.
Then those who were pressing forward
were suddenly struck with blindness
and they could not find the door.
The guests said to Lot, "Is anyone else here?
Sons, daughters, sons-in-law, daughters-in-law,
or other relatives in the city?
You must get them out of here.
We are going to destroy this place
because the outcry against its people
has reached the ears of God
and God has sent us to wipe it out."
So Lot went and said to his sons-in-law
who were about to marry his daughters,
"Get up, we must get out of this place,
for God is about to destroy it."
But they thought that he was joking.
When morning came,
the angels urged Lot, saying to him,
"Get your wife and your daughters
and get out of here
or you will be consumed
in the punishment of this city."
But Lot lingered, so the angels seized him
and his wife and his two daughters,
and they took them and led them by the hand
out of the doomed city,
because God was merciful to them.
On the outskirts of Sodom they said to them,
"Run for your life. Do not look back
or stop anywhere in the plain.
Head for the hills or you will be consumed."
And Lot said to the angels,
"Oh no, my lords, you have saved my life
and shown me overwhelming kindness,
but I am afraid to flee to the hills

where the disaster might overtake me
and then I will surely die.
Look, see that small town over there?
It is near enough to flee to
and it is such a little place.
Spare that town — it is only a little one —
and I will go there to escape God's wrath
and there my life will be saved!"
"Very well," said the angels,
"we grant this favor also to you.
We will not destroy that town.
Hurry now, escape there,
for we can do nothing until you are safe."
Now the name of that town is Zoar.
As the sun was rising the following morning,
Lot and his family entered Zoar.
Then God rained fire and sulfur
on the cities of Sodom and Gomorrah
and overthrew the cities and the plain
and the inhabitants of the cities.
Lot's wife looked back,
and she became a pillar of salt.
Now Lot left Zoar with his two daughters
and settled in the hills,
because he was afraid to stay in Zoar.
The three of them lived in a cave.
One day the firstborn said to the younger,
"Our father is old,
and there is not a man remaining on earth
to come and make love to us.
Come, let us make our father drunk,
and then we will lie with him
so that we may have children through our father."
So they served their father wine that night,
and the firstborn went and slept with him,
and Lot was so intoxicated,
he was unaware of when she lay down beside him
or when she got up and left.
The next day the firstborn said to her sister,
"Last night I had intercourse with my father.
Let us give him wine again tonight,
so that you too may lie with him
and have children through our father."
So they served their father wine that night,
and when he was intoxicated,
his younger daughter had intercourse with him,

and he was unaware of when she lay down
or when she got up and left.
So both of the daughters of Lot
became pregnant by their father.
The firstborn daughter bore a son
and she named her baby Moab.
He is ancestor to the Moabites.
The younger daughter gave birth to a son
and she named her child Ben-ammi,
and he is ancestor of the Ammonites.

◇ **Points for Shared Discussion**

- How do you as a woman feel about the way rape and incest are presented in this narrative? Why do you think these incidents were included in the canon of sacred scripture?

- The point of sexual relations here is the propagation of children. A segment of the Christian church holds a similar philosophy today. Do you agree or disagree, and why?

- Lot's guests were bearers of the word of God and he abused his daughters to protect them. In what way is this similar to what is happening in contemporary religion? Name occasions when women have been abused in order to protect the word of God.

- What would you say to Lot's daughters if you had the chance to address them? What would you say to any woman who has been the victim of rape or incest?

◇ **A Psalm about Burning** (see p. 220)

◇ **Prayer**

O Sacred Fire
burning
with the brilliant blaze
of glory,
we lift to You
the unenlightened corners
of our spirits.
Illuminate
the shadows
on the paths of our ascent to You,
and let our hearts
burn brightly
with Your wisdom
and Your love.
Amen.

◇ A PSALM ABOUT BURNING ◇

Choir 1   It burns me up
when I hear about the things
they do to women.
Are You a God of fire?
Rain hot coals and searing ash
upon the offenders,
stoke the flame,
and all who have been violated
will praise Your holy name.

All   Sacred Fire, Everlasting Flame:
holy, holy, holy is Your name.

Choir 2   I am on fire for justice
for all who are oppressed.
Are You a God of fire?
Inflame the hearts of all
who have a stake in earth's survival.
Set us all ablaze.
Then all of us who covenant to care
will sing Your praise.

All   Sacred Fire, Everlasting Flame:
holy, holy, holy is Your name.

Choir 1   Be with us under fire.
Enlighten us with Your wisdom
so that all may catch
the spark of truth
in what we say and do.
You are a God of fire
and we believe in You.

All   Sacred Fire, Everlasting Flame:
holy, holy, holy is Your name.

Choir 2   Set the world on fire.
Ignite a conflagration
in our aridness
and our apathy.
Fire up those who have given up,
for every believer knows,
a new day dawned for everyone
when Your Blazing Sun arose.

All   Sacred Fire, Everlasting Flame:
holy, holy, holy is Your name.

        By M. T. Winter, Crossroad Pub. Co., © 1992 Medical Mission Sisters

DINAH

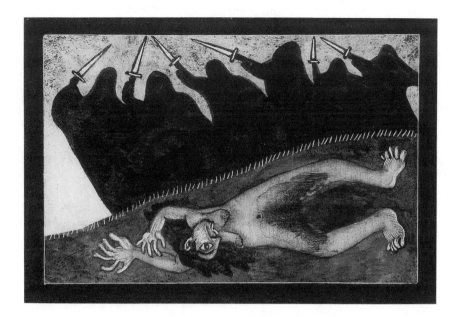

◇ **Scripture Reference**　Gen 30:19–21; 34:1–31; 46:15

◇ **Biography**

Leah and Jacob had a daughter, Dinah. Shechem, a Canaanite prince, raped Dinah, then fell in love with her and asked for her hand in marriage. In a rage her brothers tricked Shechem into accepting circumcision for himself and the men of his city and then, when they were weakened, slaughtered them all to avenge the violation. Dinah was removed from Shechem's house and never heard from again.

◇ **Context**

The rape of Dinah was an act of violence, but the action taken by her brothers was even more violent. Dinah, the victim who was violated, was victimized again. Her brothers were not avenging her; they were avenging an offense to their nation and to the honor of their father, and yes, they were seeking revenge for an insult to themselves. Twelve brothers had failed to protect the virginity of their baby sister. The brothers were not at all concerned about the feelings of a wounded female, nor did they give any thought to her future. What possible chance for marriage did Dinah have apart from Shechem now that she had been dishonored? Her brothers pulled her away from the one person who probably cared about her feelings, for Shechem had fallen in love with Dinah, and it is reasonable to assume that Dinah may have begun to care for him. He would hardly have approached Jacob for permission to marry her unless she had forgiven him and was prepared to remain with him. Even if her brothers had known her intentions, it would not have deterred them, because what Dinah felt and wanted really did not matter.

Dinah was just an excuse for the men to go and do as they pleased. While she is central to the narrative, Dinah never speaks nor is she consulted regarding the very significant actions taken on her behalf. She is both property and possession, passed from hand to hand. She is an object of men's so-called love, sexual love and familial love that begins and ends in violence and bodily violation. Dinah's story is a tragic story representative of other women and what men have done to women, how they have used them and moved on. Dinah was used for sexual pleasure and as an excuse for a massacre, and then she was forgotten. The writers of history say no more about what became of her.

◇ **Lectionary Reading**

When Leah gave birth to her sixth son,
she said, "God has truly blessed me;
now my husband will honor me,
for I have given six sons to him."
She named the baby Zebulun.
Afterward she bore a daughter,
and she named the little girl Dinah.

◇

Now Dinah the daughter Leah bore to Jacob
went to visit the women of the region.
When Shechem, son of Hamor the Hivite
and prince of that region, saw her,
he seized her and forcibly raped her.
Infatuated with Dinah the daughter of Jacob,
he fell in love with her and tenderly comforted her.
Shechem said to Hamor his father,
"I want her for my wife."
On hearing that Shechem had raped his daughter,
Jacob said nothing as he waited for his sons
to come in from their work in the fields.
Meanwhile, Shechem's father Hamor
went to speak with Jacob,
just as Jacob's sons were returning from the fields.
The men flew into a rage at the offense against Israel
caused by the rape of their sister,
an offense that could not be ignored.
Hamor pleaded with them, saying,
"The heart of my son longs for your daughter;
please give her to him in marriage.
Enter into marriage with us as a people.

Give your daughters to us; take our daughters for yourselves.
Live here with us and we guarantee
that our land will be open to you.
Live off the land, move freely about,
purchase property of your own."
Shechem also met with Dinah's father and brothers.
"Favor me with your approval," he said,
"and I will give you whatever you ask.
Set the price of the dowry as high as you like,
and I will give it to you, only let me marry Dinah."
Because Shechem had violated their sister Dinah,
her brothers responded deceitfully
to Shechem and his father, saying,
"We cannot do what you ask.
To give our sister to one who is uncircumcised
would be a disgrace to us.
Only on this condition will we give our consent to you:
that you will become as we are
and that every male among you will agree to be circumcised.
Then we will give our daughters to you
and we will take your daughters as wives.
Then we will live among you
and we will become one people.
But if you will not listen to us,
if you refuse to be circumcised,
we will take our daughter and go."
Their words pleased Hamor and Shechem.
Because he was so in love with Dinah,
Shechem proceeded without delay.
As the influential person in his father's house,
he spoke to the men of the city who had gathered at the gate,
and he told them the conditions set by Jacob and his sons
for sharing their land and their property
and for a marriage covenant.
The men agreed to the proposal outlined
by Shechem and his father Hamor,
and every male was circumcised.
On the third day, when they were still sore,
two of Dinah's brothers, Simeon and Levi,
took the city by surprise
and killed all the men with their swords.
They murdered Hamor and Shechem
and took Dinah out of Shechem's house and hurried her away.
Their other brothers looted the city
and those who had been slaughtered,
because their sister had been defiled.

They took flocks and herds and donkeys,
whatever was in the city and all that was in the fields.
They captured wealth, wives, and children.
Then Jacob said to Simeon and Levi,
"You have caused trouble for me,
for you have ostracized me among the people of this land,
among the Canaanites and the Perizzites.
My numbers are few.
If they should attack me to seek their revenge,
I shall be destroyed, and my household will fall with me."
But the sons said to their father,
"Should our sister be treated like a whore?"

◇ **Points for Shared Reflection**

- Talk about Dinah's story from the perspective of a woman. How do you feel about what happened to her? How would she feel about what happened to her?

- How do the main elements of Dinah's experience relate to women's experience today?

- Where was Leah, Dinah's mother? Could she have been present? Whose side would she have taken? Why? Comment on her silence.

- Levi, to whom the priesthood is traced, killed his sister's lover in a deceitful act of revenge. Reflect on this and respond in terms of the present as well as the past.

◇ **Dinah's Psalm** (see p. 225)

◇ **Prayer**

O Vulnerable One Who feels the pain
of so many violated women,
comfort our sisters ravaged and raped
by men or power or poverty
and empower them
to free themselves
from the cycle of guilt and despair.
Strengthen us
who in lesser ways
are similarly disempowered,
that we might never succumb to guilt
or to giving up on ourselves.
Thank You for being Compassion and Comfort.
We need You now.
Amen.

◇ DINAH'S PSALM ◇

All recite together:

My soul screams in pain and despair
and my spirit spills its guilt
upon every facet of my being.

The Holy One has abandoned me,
and all generations will blame me,
me! — the one who has been violated,
a victim again and again!

You Who have always cared for me,
where were You when I needed You?
Where are You now in my shame?

Where is the mercy shown
from generation to generation?

Where was the strength of Your mighty arm
that once scattered the proud
and shattered the shields of the oppressor?

Throughout our history,
You replaced the powerful
with powerless people,
You filled all those who hungered,
and You sent the satisfied away.

Fill me now with all that I need
for keeping faith
and for starting over.
Empower me now to take control
of my guilt
and my grief
and my shame.

For I remember the mercy shown
to Sarah
and to Hagar,
and the promises made
to all the daughters of Eve,
even to me.

Have mercy on me.
Have mercy on me,
Shekinah,
Shaddai,
Shalom.

By M. T. Winter, Crossroad Pub. Co., © 1992 Medical Mission Sisters

MAHLAH, NOAH, HOGLAH, MILCAH, TIRZAH

◇ **Scripture Reference**   Num 26:33; 27:1–11; 36:1–13; Josh 17:3–6

◇ **Biography**

The five women were daughters of Zelophehad, a descendant of one of the clans of Manasseh. They were his only children. The sisters publicly challenged the Israelite laws of inheritance and won a concession from Moses, who received a new statute from God. They were accorded the right to inherit and eventually married sons of their father's brothers so their inheritance would remain within the tribe of their father's clan.

◇ **Context**

The promised land had been proportionately divided among the tribes and families of Israel. In order to maintain tribal boundaries, it had been established that land would be passed down through the eldest son within the same family from one generation to the next. Zelophehad had no sons, but he had five feisty daughters. He had died in the wilderness on the way from Egypt, having done nothing to merit the loss of his family's piece of the promised land. Struck by the injustice of the system, Mahlah and her sisters appealed to Moses for the right to receive their fa-

226

ther's inheritance. They were concerned not only about property but also about the perpetuation of their father's name. No doubt they were also concerned about themselves. Because the case was without precedent, Moses consulted God for an interpretation of the law. What was more important? That only males inherit or that the land remain within the family? God took the side of the daughters, favoring equitable distribution over gender priority. This legal challenge was the first such incident recorded in the life of the second generation of Israelites in the land of Canaan. Later, the daughters themselves were challenged by those concerned that ancestral land might be lost to the tribe through marriage, when the property of women became the property of their men. Again God was consulted. The daughters remained free to choose their own husbands but they had to marry within the tribe in order to protect the land. The narrative of Mahlah and her sisters records an instance of gender equality and reveals that women did speak out in biblical times and were in fact effective. At least on one occasion, they were heard, they were taken seriously, and they achieved systemic change. The pericope also indicates that there was flexibility regarding the rubrics of tradition. When the reasons were persuasive, laws and their interpretation could and did change.

◇ **Lectionary Reading**

Zelophehad
son of Hepher
son of Gilead
son of Machir
son of Manasseh
son of Joseph
was a member of the Manassite clans.

◇

Now Zelophehad son of Hepher
had no sons,
only daughters,
and the names of his daughters were
Mahlah, Noah, Hoglah, Milcah, and Tirzah.

◇

The daughters of Zelophehad —
Mahlah, Noah, Hoglah, Milcah, and Tirzah —
stood before Moses,
Eleazar the priest,
the leaders,
and all the congregation
at the entrance of the tent of meeting
and said:
"Our father died in the wilderness;

he was not among the gathering of those
who defied God in the company of Korah,
but died for his own sin.
Our father had no sons.
Why should his name be removed from his clan
because he had no son?
Give us an inheritance
among our father's brothers."
So Moses presented their case before God,
and God spoke to Moses, saying,
"The daughters of Zelophehad
have a legitimate point.
Let them possess an inheritance
among their father's brothers,
and let their father's property
pass on to them.
You shall also say to the Israelites,
'If a man dies and has no son,
then his daughter shall inherit.
If he has no daughter,
then you shall give his inheritance
to his brothers.
If he has no brothers,
then his inheritance shall go
to his father's brothers.
And if his father has no brothers,
then you shall give his inheritance
to the member of the clan
most closely related to him.
This shall be for the Israelites
a statute and ordinance,
as God commanded Moses.'"

◇

The heads of the ancestral houses
of the clans of the descendants of Gilead
son of Machir son of Manasseh,
of the Josephite clans,
came forward and spoke in the presence of Moses
and the leaders of other ancestral houses.
"God commanded that the land be given for inheritance
by lot to the Israelites," they said,
"and that the inheritance of our brother Zelophehad
be given to his daughters.
But if they marry into another tribe,
their inheritance will be taken
from the inheritance of our ancestors

and added to that of their husbands' tribe,
and we will lose the allotted portion
of our tribe's inheritance.
And when the Jubilee of the Israelites comes,
their inheritance will be added to the inheritance
of the tribe into which they married,
and their inheritance will be taken from the inheritance
of our ancestral tribe."
Then Moses commanded the Israelites
according to the word of God.
"The descendants of the tribe of Joseph are right
in their interpretation.
This is what God commands
concerning the daughters of Zelophehad.
'Let them marry whom they think best for them,
but they must be sure to marry
into a clan of their father's tribe,
so that no Israelite inheritance shall be transferred
from one tribe to another.
All Israelites shall retain the inheritance
of their own ancestral tribes.
Every daughter who possesses an inheritance
in any of the tribes of Israel
shall marry within the clan of her father's tribe.
No inheritance shall be transferred
from one tribe to another,
for each of the tribes of Israel
shall retain its own inheritance.' "
The daughters of Zelophehad
did as God commanded.
Mahlah, Tirzah, Haglah, Milcah, and Noah
married sons of their father's brothers.
They were married into the clans
of the descendants of Manasseh son of Joseph,
and their inheritance remained
in the tribe of their father's clan.
These are the commandments and ordinances
that God commanded to the Israelites through Moses
in the plains of Moab at Jericho.

◇

Thus there fell to Manasseh ten portions,
besides the land of Gilead and Bashan
on the other side of the Jordan,
because the daughters of Manasseh
received an inheritance
along with all his sons.

- Mahlah and her sisters were not afraid to challenge the establishment on behalf of their rights and push for systemic change. In this they serve as role models for us. Who and what are women challenging? What laws would you like to see changed?

- Are inheritance patterns fair to women today? Were they fair to your mother? To your grandmothers?

- The sisters were concerned about the loss of the family name. How do you as a woman feel about the traditional loss of your family name in marriage? How do you feel about the alternatives to that practice?

- In those days God and men were involved in making the laws and in their interpretation. Has anything really changed?

◇ **A Psalm of Celebration** (see p. 231)

◇ **Prayer**

We pray to You, Goddess,
Whoever You are,
however we are to name You,
and deep within the sacred space
inside ourselves
where none can see,
there in the silence of Your word,
there we dare to claim You.
Loosen us, lighten us,
lift us up to a truly festal feeling,
and reveal to us that secret name
which You, for so many centuries,
have been carefully concealing.
Give us the name to praise You by.
Amen.

◇ A PSALM OF CELEBRATION ◇

Choir 1   Sound the trumpet and clap your hands.
Call upon all creation.

Choir 2   Let us sing of ancestral lands.
Come, join the celebration.

Choir 1   Laugh in the light of the new moon.
Start the circle dances.

Choir 2   The Goddess Shekinah is coming soon
to change our circumstances.

Choir 1   Sound the chants and the tambourines.
Intensify the drumming.

Choir 2   The sisters and daughters know what it means:
the Goddess Sophia is coming.

Choir 1   Listen, the wind in Her sacred wood
sings of Her presence to us,

Choir 2   when all that is gracious and all that is good
will enter us and renew us.

Choir 1   Sing of the sacred soil of earth,
sing as we prepare it.

Choir 2   The seed we sow will be a tree
our daughters will inherit.

Choir 1   Dance on the rock and through the weeds;
claim our spinning planet.

Choir 2   The Spirit of Gaia knows earth's needs;
She was there when She began it.

Choir 1   Kiss the rain upon your face;
cherish the changing seasons.

Choir 2   It is sacred time and sacred space,
and myriad are the reasons.

Choir 1   Celebrate women equal to men,
together join the dances,

Choir 2   for the beginning time will come again,
giving us second chances.

ACHSAH

◇ **Scripture Text** Josh 15:16–19; Judg 1:11–15; 1 Chr 2:49

◇ **Biography**

Achsah was the daughter of Caleb the founder of the Calebites, a distinct group assimilated early on into the tribe of Judah. She was probably the daughter of Maacah, Caleb's concubine. She married Othniel, her father's nephew, who was allotted land in the desert area of the Negeb, and she asked for, and received, springs of water as a dowry gift from her father.

◇ **Context**

Since Chronicles records Achsah's name after the list of Maacah's sons, it is reasonable to assume she was Maacah's daughter. Her personal style is clearly characteristic of her father. Caleb was one of the spies sent out to assess the quality of the land of Canaan before the Israelites took possession of it, and when the others tried to terrify the people out of entering Canaan because of the size of its inhabitants, Caleb and Joshua stood firm in their support of occupation and were the only two of that delegation who lived to enter the land. God praised "my servant Caleb, because he has a different spirit and has followed me wholeheartedly" (Num 14:24). Achsah had some of that spirit. Her very brief story reveals a woman who was assertive and confident. She may have been awarded as a prize of war, but she made sure her new life would work out well for her. Desert land is useless without water and her husband's allotment was in the Negeb. She asked her father for a source of water, confident she would get it, and she did — twice as much as she hoped for, both the upper and lower springs. Achsah's narrative appears in two books, both in Joshua and in Judges. Since women were seldom noted or named and their stories were seldom recorded, this is a point of some significance, emphasizing the importance of the one about whom the story was told.

◇ **Lectionary Reading**

Caleb said, "Whoever attacks Kiriath-sepher and takes it,
to him I will give my daughter Achsah as wife."
Othniel son of Kenaz, the son of Caleb's younger brother,
attacked and took Kiriath-sepher,
and Caleb gave him Achsah his daughter
for his wife.
When she came to Othniel,
Achsah urged him to ask her father for a field.
As she dismounted from her donkey,
Caleb said to her, "What do you wish?"
She said, "Give me a gift.
Since you have set me in the land of the Negeb,
give me springs of water as well."
So Caleb gave both the upper springs
and the lower springs to his daughter.

◇ **Points for Shared Reflection**

- Achsah's assertiveness paid off. Women who are assertive are often criticized. Do you have difficulty being assertive? Are you criticized when you are?

- Achsah was not only assertive, she was politically astute. Water in the desert meant more than personal survival. Whoever controlled the water had power as well. In what ways do women fail to be politically astute?

- What does power mean to women? How do women exercise power differently from men? In what ways do you feel you have power? In what ways are you powerless?

- The desert figures prominently in biblical tradition and is a strong metaphor of the spiritual life. Have you ever been in the desert, either physically or spiritually? Describe an experience.

◇ **A Psalm about Deserts** (see p. 235)

◇ **Prayer**

Here I am
in the desert
again.
Where are You,
Living Water?
Where is the promised oasis?
Where are Your refreshing springs?
My soul and spirit
thirst for You
and seek You
here in the wilderness
of a spiritual desolation,
mourning my heart's isolation
and the loneliness
of my soul.
If I but scratch the surface
of Your fertile Ground
of Being,
I know
I will be satiated
with waters of eternal life.
Come to me, Living Water.
Let me drink from Your fountain
of love.
Amen.

◇ A PSALM ABOUT DESERTS ◇

Choir 1 You lure me
into the wilderness,
away from all companionship,
to share with me
Your mysteries
as You draw me to Yourself.

Choir 2 Deserts are
a landscape of grace
inhabited by demons.

All My heart and my soul are so vulnerable.
Where are You, my Protector?
Do not leave me all alone.

Choir 1 I wander about
in alien terrain
with no map or star
to guide me,
losing control
in the shifting sands
of opposing pieties.

Choir 2 Deserts are
stark environments
of instability.

All My spiritual center is disoriented.
Where are You, my Guiding Star?
Do not leave me all alone.

Choir 1 I have stumbled
into a canyon,
terrified because
there is no way out.
Steep walls
tower over me.
I turn and run
and run and run
through a riverbed
long gone dry.

Choir 2 Deserts are where we go
to be tested,
and only a few return.

By M. T. Winter, Crossroad Pub. Co., © 1992 Medical Mission Sisters   *WomanWitness* / **235**

All   My courage and strength are so fallible.
Where are You, my Oasis?
Do not leave me all alone.

Choir 1   You lead me
to Your waterways
through the long, dry search
for meaning,
littered with the bones
of heretics
and housewives
and saints.

Choir 2   Deserts are
the route to glory.
There is no other way.

All   My faith is sorely tested,
yet my trust in You
goes on and on.
I thirst for You, Living Water.
Give me a sip
from the river of Life.
Do not let me drink alone.

 By M. T. Winter, Crossroad Pub. Co., © 1992 Medical Mission Sisters

JEPHTHAH'S DAUGHTER

◇ **Scripture Reference**   Judg 11:1–11, 29–40

◇ **Biography**

The virgin daughter of Jephthah became her father's burnt offering to God after his victory over the Ammonites. She was an only child. She willingly accepted the sacrifice of her life to fulfill her father's vow.

◇ **Context**

Jephthah, son of a prostitute, was driven from his home in Gilead by his brothers who resented him. When the Ammonites threatened to overtake Gilead, its elders approached Jephthah to enlist him in leading their troops, overlooking his illegitimate origins and his status as an outlaw, for he had a reputation as a renegade warrior. In return for commanding their forces, Jephthah extracted a promise for a permanent civil leadership beyond the immediate military one, and their commitment to this was ratified by oath at the local sanctuary in Mizpah. A military victory would confirm Jephthah's leadership over the clans of Gilead, which they had conferred on him. The text says that the spirit of God came upon him, but his subsequent actions lead one to suspect that this phrase was an editorial gloss. Jephthah bargained with God — a human sacrifice, a burnt offering, in return for a victory. His vow reflected his lack of faith and his failure to trust the Spirit. The first to come forth to greet him would be sacrificed to God. This is our introduction to Jephthah's daughter. Our heroine is anonymous here, as is usually the case with females, and we never do learn her name. The son of an anonymous prostitute sacrifices an anonymous virgin daughter. Her narrative is full of irony. What poses as a religious act is really sacrilegious. God never asked for this. It was not God's will, but Jephthah's. True, what happened was not what Jephthah intended. Nevertheless in making such a vow, he knew someone had to die, and that someone turned out to be his daughter. In the spirit of women before her (Ex 15:19–21) and women who would follow after (1 Sam 18:6–7), the daughter came forth joyfully to greet her father with music, but the jubilance of victory was the victim's dance of death. On seeing her, Jephthah blamed her for what he was about to do. He did not sympathize with her or console her but simply felt sorry for himself. The victim accepted and forgave him.

Jephthah chose to remain faithful to a vow made out of lack of faith and broke faith with his own flesh and blood who maintained her faith in him. She prepared for this inhuman sacrifice by removing herself from patriarchy and retiring into the silent, supportive company of female friends. Patriarchy eventually rewarded her father. For six years he was a judge in Israel. Scripture records that he was a warrior, mighty and victorious. Scripture does not record patriarchy's lament for the death of his daughter. Innocent victims always accompany victories by violence. Throughout this entire episode, God kept silent and must have seemed, at least to the women, to be very far away. The final irony is that the women, powerless to help their friend in the present, take charge of the slain one's future. Phyllis Trible interprets verse 39 to read, "*She* became a tradition in Israel" (*Texts of Terror*, Fortress, 1984, p. 106). Her female friends remained faithful to more than her memory, for Jephthah's daughter continued to live through those who remembered and mourned for her. In Africa there is still a belief that a person does not really die until the last one who remembers that person dies. Jephthah's daughter lived and lives as symbol of all those women we remember into life.

◇ **Lectionary Reading**

Now Jephthah was the son of a prostitute.
He was also a mighty warrior.
Gilead, his father, had sons by his wife,
and when these sons were older,

they drove Jephthah away, saying,
"You shall not inherit in our father's house,
for you are the son of another woman."
So Jephthah fled from his brothers to the land of Tob
where he headed a band of outlaws
who went out with him on raids.
After a time the Ammonites waged war against Gilead,
and its elders sent a delegation to bring Jephthah home.
"Come and be our commander," they said,
"so that we may defeat the Ammonites."
But Jephthah said to the elders of Gilead,
"Are you not the very ones who rejected me
and drove me from my father's house?
So why do you come to me now?"
The elders said to Jephthah,
"We are in trouble, we are turning to you.
Come and defeat the Ammonites for us
and we will appoint you as head over us and all in Gilead."
"If you bring me home again to fight,
if God gives the Ammonites over to me,
then you must make me your leader," said Jephthah.
"Let God be the witness between us," they said,
"we will surely do as you say."
So Jephthah went with the elders
and the people made him commander and head of all Gilead,
and Jephthah prayed to God at Mizpah.
Then the spirit of God came upon him
and he moved through Gilead and Manasseh
to confront the Ammonites.
And Jephthah made this vow to God:
"If you deliver the Ammonites into my hand,
whoever comes out of the doors of my house
to greet me when I return victorious
shall be a burnt offering to you."
So Jephthah invaded Ammonite territory
and fought and defeated their forces,
for God gave them over into his hand.
It was a massive victory;
he took twenty towns from Aroer to Minnith
and as far as Abel-keramim.
Then Jephthah came home to Mizpah
and his daughter came out to meet him,
dancing with tambourines.
She was his only daughter,
in fact, she was his only child.
When he saw her, he tore his garments and cried,

"My daughter, why have you done this to me?
Before battle, I made a vow to God
and I cannot go back on my word."
She said to him, "Father, if you have vowed to God,
then do what must be done.
For God has given the victory and defeated your enemies.
Only let this thing be done for me:
Give me two months to wander the hills
and bewail my virginity, I and my female friends."
"Go," he said, and sent her away.
Two months later she returned to her father
who kept the vow he had made.
Now she who died a virgin became a tradition in Israel.
Year after year the daughters of Israel
mourned for the daughter of Jephthah
for four days every year.

◇ **Points for Shared Reflection**

- A father can destroy a daughter, or destroy his relationship with his daughter, even when he doesn't intend to. What was/is your relationship with your father?

- The perpetrator blames the victim for the violence he is about to do. Discuss this classic response in terms of contemporary situations of abuse. Has this ever happened to you?

- Do you tend to seek solace and understanding from the company of female friends? Is there any formal support system among females of your choice?

- The system often rewards those who destroy the innocent in the name of the common good. Can you give some examples?

◇ **A Psalm for a Lost Daughter** (see p. 241)

◇ **Prayer**

Have mercy on us who sacrifice
the innocent child within us
on the altars of ambition,
who put to death self-centeredly
a dream, a hope, or a cause.
Lament with us the awful waste
of so many gifted daughters.
We pray to You, O Holy One,
that no matter what the consequences,
the dancing will go on.
Amen.

◇ A PSALM FOR A LOST DAUGHTER ◇

Voice   His daughter ran to greet him,
All   like an innocent lamb to the slaughter.

Voice   She slid into the arms of death,
All   like an innocent lamb to the slaughter.

Voice   The abused little girl goes home at night,
All   like an innocent lamb to the slaughter.

Voice   The runaway runs in search of herself,
All   like an innocent lamb to the slaughter.
There is no balm in Gilead.
There is no comfort in Eden or Oz.
For we have lost a daughter.

Voice   The daughters of Eve went out from her,
All   like innocent lambs to the slaughter.

Voice   Our daughters step out to face the world,
All   like innocent lambs to the slaughter.

Voice   The women went into Buchenwald,
All   like innocent lambs to the slaughter.

Voice   African women were dragged into ships,
All   like innocent lambs to the slaughter.
There is no balm in Gilead.
There is no comfort in Eden or Oz.
For we have lost a daughter.

Voice   The baby girl comes out of the womb,
All   like an innocent lamb to the slaughter.

Voice   The little girl hidden within us comes out,
All   like an innocent lamb to the slaughter.

Voice   Woe to the one who leads a child,
All   like an innocent lamb to the slaughter.

Voice   Woe to us when we lead ourselves,
All   like innocent lambs to the slaughter.
There is no balm in Gilead.
There is no comfort in Eden or Oz.
For we have lost a daughter.

By M. T. Winter, Crossroad Pub. Co., © 1992 Medical Mission Sisters

VIRGIN DAUGHTER

◇ **Scripture Reference**   Judg 19:16–25

◇ **Biography**

The virgin daughter of the Ephraimite in Gibeah was a woman about whom one fact is known. Her father offered her to a sex-crazed mob to dissuade them from raping his house guest, a male Levite from his own tribal territory of Ephraim.

◇ **Context**

The context of the young woman's story was her home, a place of security. Surrounding her in a circle of safety were her father and some visitors, among them another woman. Suddenly a depraved mob besieged the house demanding physical access to the male guest for their own sexual gratification. Such a thing was so unthinkable to the host that he offered them his own virgin daughter instead in order to appease them. It was a brutal scene in which a daughter was heartlessly abused by the callousness of her own father. He not only offered her in place of the man, but he brought her out to the mob himself and he told them specifically to ravish her, in fact to do with her whatever they wished. Imagine her terror as she stood there before that shouting, sex-crazed mob and her sickening sense of betrayal as she felt her father's hand pushing her forward into their midst. Her father had also offered them his guest's concubine. Throughout this episode the women do not speak. The men are viciously vocal. Words of abuse and betrayal — male to male, male among males — mock the silent vulnerability of the victims who once again are female.

The text is also silent about the mother of this child. Was she present in the house? Did she try to intervene? Did she rescue her daughter from the hands of the mob and from the hands of her husband? The men outside wanted the man but they did in fact settle for a woman, not the virgin daughter because suddenly she was no longer there, but the Levite's concubine because he threw her out to them. As suddenly as the daughter is drawn into the narrative, she is as swiftly removed from it and is never heard from again. She had to go on with the rest of her life in a changed relationship to her father and with her memories. Did she also recall the scene from Genesis that so closely mirrored her own experience? Earlier in Israel's history, Lot had offered his two virgin daughters to a rampaging mob in Sodom to protect male guests of his own. Perhaps the Ephraimite's daughter prayed for another rain of fire to destroy the sinners of Gibeah.

◇ **Lectionary Reading**

An old man returning from the fields,
not a native of Gibeah but a sojourner from Ephraim
who had settled in the town,
saw the travelers and stopped to inquire,
"Where have you come from? Where are you going?"
The Levite answered him.
"We are on our way from Bethlehem in Judah
to Ephraim, my home,
but no one has offered us shelter for the night.
We have enough provisions,
straw for the donkeys and bread and wine."
The old man responded, "Shalom! Come with me.
I will see to all your needs.
You cannot spend the night in the square."
So he took them home and he fed their donkeys.
They washed their feet and ate and drank.
As they were relaxing,
men from the town, abusive and perverse,
surrounded the house and beat on the door,

demanding that the guest be given to them
that they might have sex with him.
The old man pleaded, "My brothers, no!
Do not act like this. The man is my guest.
Do not persist in this wickedness.
Here is my virgin daughter,
and here is his concubine.
Let me bring them out to you.
Enjoy them, ravish them, do what you will,
but do not mistreat this man."
The men would not listen, they were out of control,
so the Levite took his concubine
and brought her out to them.
They raped her savagely, again and again,
and abused her until morning.

◇ **Points for Shared Reflection**

- If you were the Ephraimite's daughter, which experience would have left you more devastated, your close call with a ravenous mob of men or your own father's betrayal?

- Have you ever felt betrayed by your father? What were the circumstances?

- This narrative is a classic vignette of male bonding. Examine the actions of the men in this scene and relate your conclusions to present experience.

- Why was there no mention of the girl's mother? Was she there? Did she rescue her daughter? Talk about the mothers whose daughters today are abused by their fathers.

◇ **A Psalm for Survivors** (see p. 245)

◇ **Prayer**

O One Who holds the lonely
in Your everlasting arms,
Who draws the broken in body and spirit
to the warmth of Your sheltering love,
have mercy on all survivors
of drugs, incest, misuse, abuse,
and every kind of trauma.
Encourage our suffering sisters,
strengthen us all, empower us all,
for all of us are survivors
who survive by grace alone.
Amen.

◇ A PSALM FOR SURVIVORS ◇

Choir 1   Virgin daughter of Ephraim,
daughters of Lot in the city of Sodom,
your own father betrayed you,
yet you managed to survive.

Choir 2   Daughters of poverty here and now,
you feel unloved, you feel betrayed
because your father walked out on you,
because he has stopped supporting you,
yet you manage to survive.

All   My sisters, you are survivors.
She, Shaddai, will strengthen you.
Take courage and carry on.

Choir 1   Dinah, raped by a wealthy prince,
Tamar, raped by your brother —
your lives were left in shambles,
yet you managed to survive.

Choir 2   My sisters, victims of rape and incest,
tortured by guilt, tormented by shame,
a piece of your lives has been destroyed,
yet you manage to survive.

All   My sisters, you are survivors.
She, Shaddai, will strengthen you.
Take courage and carry on.

Choir 1   Mahlah, you and your sisters were brave.
Patriarchy tried to eliminate you,
but you took on the system
and you managed to survive.

Choir 2   Feminists, womanists everywhere —
patriarchy is trying to silence you,
the system is trying to compromise you,
yet you manage to survive.

All   My sisters, you are survivors.
She, Shaddai, will strengthen you.
Take courage and carry on.

Choir 1   Merab and Rizpah, grief-stricken mothers,
you suffered the death of your children
as an act of revenge in war,
yet you managed to survive.

| Choir 2 | Mothers in war-torn countries, mothers of gang war victims, you suffer the loss of your children today, yet you manage to survive. |

Choir 2   Mothers in war-torn countries,
mothers of gang war victims,
you suffer the loss of your children today,
yet you manage to survive.

All   My sisters, you are survivors.
She, Shaddai, will strengthen you.
Take courage and carry on.

Choir 1   Witch of Endor, sorcerer,
they took away your religious rites
and compromised your integrity,
yet you managed to survive.

Choir 2   Women of churches and synagogues,
you are deprived of meaningful rites,
yet you manage to survive.

All   My sisters, you are survivors.
She, Shaddai, will strengthen you.
Take courage and carry on.

Choir 1   Woman of Abel-beth-maacah,
you were besieged on every side
and the odds were all against you,
yet you managed to survive.

Choir 2   Women besieged in so many ways
on so many fronts
with so little support,
everything is stacked against you,
yet you manage to survive.

All   My sisters, you are survivors.
She, Shaddai, will strengthen you.
Take courage and carry on.

Choir 1   Wives of Benjaminites, taken by force,
you were dragged away from all that you loved
and made to marry against your will,
yet you managed to survive.

Choir 2   Women whose marriages are arranged,
who arrange marriages filled with pain,
you have to struggle to make it,
yet you manage to survive.

All   My sisters, you are survivors.
We praise God for survivors.
She, Shaddai, will strengthen you.
Take courage and carry on.

     By M. T. Winter, Crossroad Pub. Co., © 1992 Medical Mission Sisters

MERAB

◇ **Scripture Reference**   1 Sam 14:49; 17:24–25; 18:17–19; 2 Sam 21:1–9

◇ **Biography**

Merab was Saul's eldest daughter. He promised her in marriage to David, then just before the wedding, he gave her to Adriel the Meholathite as his wife. Years later when David as king agreed to hand over seven of Saul's sons to the Gibeonites to expiate for Saul's crime against them, he took the five sons of Merab and approved their execution. In her narratives Merab does not speak for herself but is seen only in relation to her father, her husband, and her sons.

◇ **Context**

Merab's father, Saul, was the first to replace the rule of the Judges with a central and permanent authority when Samuel anointed him king. Saul had promised a daughter in marriage to the one who slayed the Philistine giant Goliath (1 Sam 17:25). The slayer turned out to be David, the psalmist who soothed Saul's irrational outbursts, but when the crowds began to show a preference for David over Saul, the king's friend became the king's enemy and a never-ending threat to his security. Saul said he would give his daughter Merab to David as his wife, but then went back on his word. The marriage offer may have been Saul's attempt to make good on his earlier promise, or he may have wanted to ensure that this giant slayer would continue to fight the Philistines at the head of his own armies. However, it seems that the idea of reward-

247

ing his rival by elevating his peasant status to that of son-in-law of the king may have been more than Saul could handle, so he gave Merab to another. With David's subsequent marriage to Merab's younger sister Michal, Saul set David up for death, presumably at the hands of the Philistines.

Merab was a pawn in a set of political decisions. When David was finally king and had to offer expiation for Saul's betrayal of the Gibeonites, he committed an act of incomprehensible violence against Merab. Was the execution of her five sons his act of revenge for having been passed over by her father and was he blaming Merab? Was it retaliation for the pain he had suffered in his marriage to her sister Michal? Since these are the only incidents involving Merab recorded in scripture, they are surely not unrelated. Although several Hebrew manuscripts and ancient translations state that David chose Merab's sons for execution, and this is the traditional understanding, it must be noted that other texts identify the sons as Michal's.

◇ **Lectionary Reading**

Now the names of Saul's two daughters were:
Merab, the name of the firstborn,
and Michal, the name of the younger.

◇

When the Israelites saw Goliath,
they were terrified and fled, saying,
"Have you seen this giant who defies Israel?
The king will enrich the man who kills him.
He will make his family free and secure
and will give him his daughter in marriage."

◇

Then Saul said to David,
"Here is my elder daughter Merab.
I will give her to you as a wife,
only be valiant for me
and fight God's battles."
For Saul thought,
"I will not raise a hand against him.
Let the Philistines deal with him."
David said to Saul,
"Who am I and who are my family
that I should be son-in-law to a king?"
But just at the time that Merab
should have been given by Saul to David,
he gave her instead to Adriel the Meholathite
as a wife.

◇

Now there was a famine in the days of David.
After it had lasted for three full years,
David inquired of God, who said,
"There is blood-guilt on Saul and on his house
for slaughtering the Gibeonites."
The Gibeonites were not part of Israel
but a remnant of the Amorites,
and Israel had sworn to spare them,
but Saul had tried to wipe them out
in his zeal for Israel and Judah.
So David called the Gibeonites
and said to them,
"What shall I do for you?
How shall I make expiation,
so that you may bless the heritage of God?"
The Gibeonites said to him,
"It is not a matter of silver or gold
between us and Saul and his house.
Neither is it up to us
to put anyone in Israel to death."
But David again insisted,
"What do you want me to do for you?"
Then they said this to the king,
"The man who attacked us
and tried to destroy us,
so that we should have no place here
in the territory of Israel —
let seven of his sons be delivered to us
and we will impale them at Gibeon
on the mountain of God."
David said, "I will deliver them to you."
But David spared Mephibosheth,
the son of Saul's son Jonathan,
because of the oath that had been sworn
between David and Jonathan.
David took into custody
the two sons of Rizpah, Armoni and Mephibosheth,
whom she had borne to Saul;
and the five sons of Merab, Saul's daughter,
whom she had borne to Adriel the son of Barzillai;
and he delivered them to the Gibeonites
and they impaled them on the mountain
in the presence of God.

◇ **Points for Shared Reflection**

- How might Merab have felt about being promised to a handsome young hero and then given to another? Have you ever lost a golden opportunity because some person or system arbitrarily ruled against you because of your gender, race, age, or social status?

- Name some act of violence committed against you or someone you cherish. Have you ever been able to forgive the one who so brutally violated you?

- Have you ever had a dream destroyed? What was it? How did it die?

- As a woman, have you ever been so publicly humiliated that you actually felt impaled? Describe the circumstances.

◇ **A Psalm for Those Passed Over** (see p. 251)

◇ **Prayer**

O God of All Opportunity,
look with favor on those of us
disadvantaged in any way:
aging women,
alien women,
ailing women,
disabled women,
women of color,
women of missed opportunity
or economic instability,
and men similarly deprived.
Give us a chance to hold our own
against those first-round choices,
and give us an edge in that all-out race
to win eternal life.
We praise you, O God.
Amen.

◇ A PSALM FOR THOSE PASSED OVER ◇

Choir 1   Some people eat and drink their fill
of the best life has to offer,
never wanting for any kind
of material security.

Choir 2   Others must be satisfied
with the crumbs of fame and fortune,
barely subsisting from day to day
on the meager whims of chance.

Choir 1   Some fully grasp the golden ring
every time occasion offers.

Choir 2   Others are caught on a merry-go-round
of frustration and delay.

Choir 1   Some always win the lottery,
even when they take no chances.

Choir 2   Others find that their number comes up
when the jackpot has gone dry.

Choir 1   For some the frog becomes a prince,
the princess always wakens,
the glass slipper fits,
the pot at the end of the rainbow
brims with gold.

Choir 2   For others their prince will never come,
their ship fails far from harbor,
their fairy tale is a hairy tale
of misfortune and defeat.

Choir 1   How long, O God, must we wait
before our faith comes to fruition?
How long must hope keep vigil
at the doorposts of despair?

Choir 2   How long must those passed over
pass the time in expectation?
How long will opportunity wait
before making a move toward the poor?

Choir 1   Turn Your providential face
toward all who crave a blessing,
O God of Sheer Abundance;

Choir 2   yet should You turn Your back on us,
let us still catch a glimpse of Your glory
and a taste of Your generous love.

Choir 1   Lucky are those for whom
a temporal prosperity
is the norm,

Choir 2   but blessed are those
who fall short of the mark,
those who have been passed over,
for the poor,
the lame,
the less able
are taking the heart of God
by storm.

By M. T. Winter, Crossroad Pub. Co., © 1992 Medical Mission Sisters

DAVID'S DAUGHTER TAMAR

◇ **Scripture Reference**   2 Sam 13:1–37; 14:27; 1 Chr 3:9

◇ **Biography**

Tamar was David's daughter. Maacah must have been her mother since she was the sister of Absalom and he was Maacah's son. Tamar was raped by her half-brother Amnon, the firstborn son of David by his wife Ahinoim. Absalom killed Amnon for violating his sister, but there is no clear indication of what Tamar did with the rest of her life.

◇ **Context**

Amnon was David's eldest son. He was so obsessed with his sister Tamar, who was very beautiful, that all he could think about was sleeping with her. His friend and cousin Jonadab shrewdly devised a scheme whereby he might get Tamar alone, and when he did, he raped her. He had barely finished with Tamar when he was filled with revulsion for her. Overcome with shame and remorse, Tamar went into seclusion in her brother Absalom's home. When David heard what had happened to his daughter, he was angry but did nothing. Was it because Amnon was his first-born and heir to his throne? Or was it because he saw in his son his own violation of Bathsheba? Absalom avoided Amnon for two years and then he avenged his sister by murdering the one who had both violated and rejected her. The reasons for the fratricide may have been more complex, for with Amnon dead, Absalom was next in line for his father's throne. For three years Absalom remained in exile while David mourned for Amnon. Eventually David's anger abated and Absalom returned home. Scripture records that Absalom had a daughter whom he also named Tamar (2 Sam 14:27). Could this have been his sister's daughter? Could Tamar have raised her in Absalom's house? We will probably never know, for scripture is intent on following the storylines of sons, not of daughters. How long did Tamar remain in seclusion? Did she ever marry? It is true she would have been considered unmarriageable, but her father was the king. Could something have been arranged? Questions like these cry out from her story and they are questions only Tamar can answer. If Amnon had really loved Tamar, he could have married her, because children of the same father and different mothers could legitimately marry in those days. The fact that he refused to consider marriage, but took her and then angrily pushed her aside, confirms the point that is made today: rape is not a sexual act, it is an act of violence.

◇ **Lectionary Reading**

David had a beautiful daughter, Tamar.
She was Absalom's sister.
Her half-brother, Amnon, was infatuated with her.
He was so obsessed with his sister
that he made himself physically ill.
She was a virgin and it seemed impossible
that he could ever have her.
Now Amnon had a friend named Jonadab,
the son of David's brother Shimeah,
and he was very crafty.
He said to Amnon, "O son of the king,
why so morose morning after morning?
Tell me what's the matter."
Amnon said to him, "I want Tamar, my brother's sister."
Then Jonadab said to him,
"Lie down on your bed and pretend to be ill.
When your father comes to see you,
ask him to tell your sister Tamar
to bring you something to eat,
and have her prepare the food before you
and feed you from her hand."
So Amnon lay down as though he were ill
and when the king came to see him, he said,
"Please have my sister Tamar come
and make a couple of cakes for me
that I may eat them from her hand."

Then David sent for Tamar and said,
"Go to your brother Amnon's house
and prepare some food for him."
Tamar went to Amnon's house.
He watched her knead some dough into cakes
and then bake the cakes for him,
but when she set them before him,
Amnon refused to eat.
Then Amnon said to Tamar,
"Bring the food into my chamber
that I may eat it from your hand."
Tamar took the cakes to her brother's chamber,
but when she drew near to give them to him,
Amnon took hold of her and said,
"Come lie with me, my sister."
She answered, "No, I will not.
Do not force me. You are my brother.
Such a thing is not done in Israel.
It is a despicable deed.
Where would I carry my shame?
And you would be an outcast.
I beg you, speak to the king.
He will not withhold me from you."
But Amnon would not listen to her.
Because of his strength, he overpowered her
and forced her to have sex with him.
When he was through with her,
he was filled with a loathing
stronger than the lust he had felt for her
a very short time ago.
"Get out!" he said.
She answered, "My brother,
this wrong you commit in sending me away
is greater than what you did to me."
But he would not listen to her.
He called the young man who served him and said,
"Get rid of this woman for me
and bolt the door behind her."
Now Tamar was wearing a long robe with sleeves,
for in those days this was the clothing
of unmarried daughters of kings.
After the servant put her out of the house,
Tamar tore her robe, sprinkled ashes on her head,
and went away, crying aloud.
Her brother Absalom said to her,
"So your brother Amnon has been with you.

Be quiet for now, my sister.
Remember he is your brother.
Do not take this so much to heart."
So Tamar remained, a desolate woman,
in her brother Absalom's house.
David was furious when he heard what had happened,
but he would not punish Amnon
because he loved his firstborn son.
But Absalom hated Amnon for raping his sister Tamar,
and he no longer spoke to him.
Two years later Absalom had sheep-shearers
at Baal-hazor near Ephraim,
and he invited all his brothers to attend a royal feast.
Absalom approached the king and said,
"Come and bring your servants."
"If we all go," he answered, "we will be a burden to you."
He pressed him, but David would not go,
although he did give him his blessing.
"If you will not go, then let my brother Amnon go,"
said Absalom to David.
"Why should he go with you?" asked David.
But Absalom kept insisting
until David let Amnon and his brothers go.
Absalom prepared a royal feast
and he said secretly to his servants,
"Keep your eye on Amnon.
When he is drunk, I will give the word,
then strike him down and kill him.
Do not be afraid. Have courage.
It is I who give the order."
So the servants did to Amnon
what Absalom had commanded.
Then all the king's sons rose up and fled.
While they were returning to Jerusalem,
word was brought to David
that Absalom had killed all the king's sons
and not one of them was left.
The king stood up, tore his garments,
and fell upon the ground.
All who were near him tore their garments.
But Jonadab said to David,
"Do not think Absalom killed all of your sons.
Amnon alone is dead.
Since the day Amnon raped his sister Tamar,
Absalom has planned to kill him.
Therefore, grieve only for Amnon."

When the sentry saw in the distance
many people approaching on the mountain road,
Jonadab said to David,
"See, your sons are returning, just as I have said."
The king's sons did indeed arrive
and they raised their voices aloud and wept,
and David and all his servants wept.
Absalom fled to Geshur
and remained there for three years.
Day after day David continued to grieve
for his firstborn son,
and when he finally got over it,
he yearned for Absalom.

◇

There were born to Absalom three sons
and a beautiful daughter, Tamar.

◇ **Points for Shared Reflection**

- What can be done to reduce the numbers of rape today and to ensure that society punishes the perpetrators, not the victims, of this crime?

- Incest is prevalent in our day. What is being done to stop it? What is being done to facilitate healing in the victims?

- Talk about Absalom's little girl. Was she Tamar's daughter?

- Reflect on Tamar's story and the behavior of the men in her life. If you could talk with her, what would you tell her to help ease her pain? What advice would you give her about the future?

◇ **A Psalm of Shalom** (see p. 258)

◇ **Prayer**

Shalom,
You are my shelter
from the terrors
and the burden of shame
I seem to have inherited.
Let me not be disheartened
when my journey into freedom
never seems to go anywhere.
Journey with me and fill me
with that peace that knows no limits,
so that I may one day come to know
the meaning of Shalom.
Amen.

◇ A PSALM OF SHALOM ◇

All recite together:

Shaddai, my Shield,
is my Shalom,
She has shown me
how much She loves me.
She leads me through shallow waters,
She showers me with unsolicited grace,
She shapes me for Her own.

Although I shiver and shake with shame
as those around me shun me,
I shall never surrender to heartbreak
nor be shattered by persecution,
nor shackled by despair.

She shares my desperation
and transforms it to shalom.
Should I shout to Her,
She answers,
showing concern for me,
shining with love,
drawing me into Her Shadow
under the shelter
of Her wing.

Shaddai, my Shield
is my Shalom.
She has shown me
how much She loves me.

 By M. T. Winter, Crossroad Pub. Co., © 1992 Medical Mission Sisters

JOB'S DAUGHTERS: JEMIMAH, KEZIAH, KEREN-HAPPUCH, AND THEIR SISTERS

◇ **Scripture Reference** Job 1:1–5, 9–20; 2:7, 9, 11, 13; 42:12–17

◇ **Biography**

The central character in the book of Job had two sets of daughters, three before his trials began and three after his sufferings were over. The first three died a tragic death. We do not even know their names. The latter three, part of Job's renewed life, symbolize special blessings. Jemimah, Keziah, and Keren-happuch were more beautiful than all other women we are told, and like their brothers, they were given a share of the inheritance of their father.

◇ **Context**

The story of Job is legendary. A devout, prosperous, basically good man, Job's faith in God was put to the test when suddenly and inexplicably he lost everything — property, possessions, children, his good health. Job's comforters sought to locate the source of his misfortune in his own personal sin, but Job refused to be coerced into a false admission of guilt. He wrestled with the troubling truth of undeserved suffering in light of his own experience, questioning all his former images of God as he anguished over the issue of God's justice, and yet he never lost faith. The book, a major example of wisdom literature whose date, location, and authorship are still in dispute, centers on the divine/human covenant of a personal God and challenges the traditional understanding of reward for the righteous and punishment for the wicked. Most scholars are convinced that the work is pure fiction, an allegory of a typical person in atypical circumstances, which offers opportunity for a theological analysis of the suffering of the innocent.

Questions of historicity aside, volumes have explored the central issues from the perspectives of Job and his male companions. Nobody has taken time to ask what it all might have meant to Job's daughters and what insight their presence might offer to Job's story. Job had two sets of daughters. To traditional exegesis they are only parenthetical, an indication of what it was like before Job's punishment began and also after it was over. From a feminist perspective the women are existential frames to the central story and say something significant not only in terms of Job's circumstances but in terms of Job himself. Job had three daughters in the beginning. He had three daughters in the end. Both sets were rooted in blessedness and were a part of his abundance. The first three, however, were a reflection of Job's patriarchy. They are nameless. They depend on their seven brothers for access to the things of life, which for them seem to center in the home, and they live with the burden of their father's suspicion that they are never quite living up to his lofty expectations, for his cleansing ritual always follows their festal family reunions. The three daughters who were part of Job's restoration indicate that Job came out of his ordeal a changed man — less patriarchal, less arrogant, more open to new ways of relating, particularly to his daughters. These three daughters have names — Jemimah, Keziah, and Keren-happuch — Job named his girls himself. We also read that they were very beautiful. What is more important, from the way Job treats them in his brave new world, they were beautiful to their father.

Job bestowed on his daughters the three things they needed to make it in the world — an identity (he named them); an equality with men through the inheritance he gave them together with their brothers; and his affirmation. Job's relationship to his latter daughters is radically different from what had been before. In the end he accepts them for who they are and participates in their becoming, seeming to move from patriarchy to a feminist perspective after his ordeal. Did suffering sensitize him to the depth of pain in others, particularly women? Was this one of the vital lessons of the book of Job, smothered in all the didactic deliberations of male sophistry? Was this one of the rewards God gave to Job for keeping faith, a clearer insight into genuine human integrity, a deeper wisdom? In fact, could the real issue behind Job's travail be patriarchy?

Job moved from a position of isolation and control to where he needed other people. In the end he had double what he had before because he was open to everyone who came to him. Those who shared a meal with him gave him money, gold, and sympathy. He was able to receive all of this and give something in return. The brief references to Job's daughters contribute a wealth of insight and meaning. The first three lived in the land of Uz, the latter three moved metaphorically to the land of Oz and took their father with them. Did the women really exist? Personally I would like to think so. If not, then, as the saying goes, somebody would have had to invent them. Maybe somebody did.

◊ **Lectionary Reading**

There was a man in the land of Uz named Job,
a just and honest man
who feared God and shunned evil.
He had seven sons and three daughters.
He owned seven thousand sheep,
three thousand camels,
five hundred yoke of oxen,
five hundred donkeys,
and very many servants.
He was a man of influence and status in the East.
His sons took turns holding banquets
in one another's houses,
and they would send for their three sisters
to eat and drink with them.
When the feasts were finished,
Job would send for them,
and early in the morning,
he would rise and offer burnt offerings
for each one of his children,
in the event that they might have offended God,
and he did this faithfully.
"Does Job fear for nothing?"
Satan once inquired of God.
"Have you put a protective fence around him
and his house and all that he has?
For clearly you have blessed the work of his hands
for his possessions have increased.
But stretch out your hand against him
and take away all his property
and he will curse you to your face."
God said to Satan, "Very well,
his possessions are in your power.
Only do not harm his person."

Then Satan left the presence of God.
One day when Job's sons and daughters
were dining in the eldest brother's house,
a messenger came to Job and said,
"The oxen were plowing and the donkeys were feeding
when the Sabeans came and carried them off
and killed all the servants with the sword.
I alone have escaped to tell you."
While he was still speaking, another came, saying,
"Fire fell from heaven.
It destroyed the sheep and consumed the servants.
Only I have escaped to tell you."
While he was speaking another arrived.
"The Chaldeans came, three columns wide,
and carried off all the camels
and put the servants to the sword.
I alone am alive to tell you."
While he was still speaking, another came.
"Your sons and daughters were sitting at table
in their eldest brother's house,
and suddenly a wind came in from the desert
and blew the house down.
It fell on your children. They are all dead.
Only I have escaped to tell you."
Then Job arose, tore his garments,
shaved his head, and fell to the ground
and proceeded to worship God.
"Naked I came from my mother's womb
and naked I shall return," he said.
"God gives and God takes away.
Blessed be the name of God."
Then Job was afflicted with loathsome sores
from the soles of his feet to the crown of his head.
"Do you still persist in your integrity? Curse God and die!"
Such was his wife's response. Job replied,
"Shall we receive the good at the hand of God,
and not receive the bad?"
Now Job's three friends heard of his troubles
and came to console and comfort him.
They sat seven days and seven nights with him
before ever speaking a word,
for his suffering was so intense.

◇

God blessed the latter days of Job
more than his beginning.
He had fourteen thousand sheep, six thousand camels,

a thousand yoke of oxen, and a thousand donkeys.
He had seven sons and three daughters.
He named his first daughter Jemimah,
his second daughter Keziah,
and his third, Keren-happuch.
In all the land no women were more beautiful
than these three daughters of Job.
And their father gave them an inheritance,
just as he had given to their brothers.
And Job lived one hundred forty years
after his trials were over.
He saw his children and his children's children
up to the fourth generation.
Then Job died, old and full of years.

◇ **Points for Shared Reflection**

- Compare Job's first three daughters with his last three. In what ways are they similar? How do they differ?

- What is the significance of Job's naming his last three daughters and giving them an inheritance? What does this particular text say to women today?

- Have you ever raised the question of innocent suffering? How do you integrate this painful point into your belief in God?

- Recall the Book of Job. If the central character were a woman, what would be her response to her suffering and the reality of her situation? If all the main characters were women, how might the response of female friends differ from that of Job's comforters?

◇ **A Psalm about Coming Around** (see p. 264)

◇ **Prayer**

How good it is
that You are all around us,
Creator, Sustainer,
for You came, come,
will come again
with power and compassion
and with all that is needed for life.
Call us into the fullness of our strength
through Your strong Presence,
and help us to come around completely
to Your will,
now and forever.
Amen.

◇ A PSALM ABOUT COMING AROUND ◇

All   What goes around
will come around
for all of life is a circle
coming around again.

Choir 1   Early morning
comes around
after the night has spent itself
dreaming about the morning.

Choir 2   Evening eventually
comes around
after the day exhausts itself
preparing for the evening.

Choir 1   The days, the weeks
all come around
in a never-ending spiral.

Choir 2   How quickly the years
come around and around
as our inner child goes out
and returns
a wiser child
enlivening the shell of the crone
who is full of years.

Choir 1   The pivotal solstice
comes around
to orient the seasons.

Choir 2   The changing seasons
come around
to encourage
and encircle
the seasons of the heart.

Choir 1   We see ourselves
as we come around again
with the same old issues.

Choir 2   We pray that we will
come around
to a change of heart,
a change of ways,
or at least a change of perspective.

    By M. T. Winter, Crossroad Pub. Co., © 1992 Medical Mission Sisters

Choir 1   God
comes around
to surprise us all
with whole new vistas of meaning.

Choir 2   Life itself
will come around again
with a new beginning,
and our faith says
our life will be even better
the next time around.

All   What goes around
will come around
for all of life is a circle
coming around again.

LO-RUHAMAH

◇ **Scripture Reference**   Hos 1:2–3, 6–9; 2:1–4, 21–22

◇ **Biography**

Lo-ruhamah was the daughter of Gomer, a former prostitute, and Hosea, prophet of the Northern Kingdom. Her name means "Not Pitied" or "Unloved." According to the Bible, both her name and her birth were part of the prophetic utterance given by God to Hosea.

◇ **Context**

Lo-ruhamah was the name Hosea gave to his second child as a symbolic indication of God's anger against Israel. All we really know about her is her name. It is extremely provocative. Imagine naming your daughter "Unloved" or "Not Pitied." Imagine your being named to raise awareness to God's wrath against you and against your nation. What a burden to carry! It may have been Hosea's prophetic utterance, but Lo-ruhamah had to live with it. She also had to live with her father's relationship

266

with her mother, a former prostitute, who was also used to illustrate the turbulent relationship between God and the nation of Israel. What a painful bond between a daughter and her mother. What an environment in which to raise a child. Lo-ruhamah must have had a pretty poor self-image. One wonders what became of her.

◊ **Lectionary Reading**

When God first spoke through Hosea,
God said to Hosea,
"Take a whore for a wife
and have the prostitute's children,
for the land commits prostitution
when it forsakes its God."
So he married Gomer, daughter of Diblaim,
and she conceived and gave birth to a son.
She conceived again and gave birth to a daughter.
"Name her Lo-ruhamah," said God,
"for I will have no more pity on the house of Israel,
I will have no more forgiveness.
But I will have pity on the house of Judah,
yes, I their God will save them."
When Gomer had weaned Lo-ruhamah
[the name means Not Pitied or Unloved],
she conceived again and bore a son.
God said, "Name him Lo-ammi
[which means No-People-of-Mine],
for you are not my people
and I am not your God."

◊

Say to your brother Ammi,
and to Ruhamah your sister:
Plead with your mother,
plead with her —
for she is not my wife
and I am not her husband —
that she put prostitution
away from her face
and adultery from between her breasts,
or I will strip her naked
and expose her as on the day she was born
and make her like a wilderness,
and turn her into a parched land,
and kill her with burning thirst.
Neither will I have pity on her children
because they are the children of whores.

On that day I will answer, says God,
I will answer the heavens
and they will answer the earth;
and the earth will answer
the grain, the wine, the oil,
and they will answer Jezreel;
I will sow him for myself in the land.
I will have pity on Lo-ruhamah,
and I will say to Lo-ammi,
"You are my people,"
and they shall say,
"You are my God."

◇ **Points for Shared Reflection**

- A loving and affirming home is essential to the well-being of a developing child. What was your home environment like when you were growing up? How has it affected you?

- Imagine that you were named "Unloved." What affect would that have on you? What does your own name mean to you and how has it affected your relating to others?

- Do you think there was a strong mother-daughter bond between Gomer and Lo-ruhamah? Is there a strong bond between your mother and you?

- Many women who are in prison or on the street today had beginnings such as Lo-ruhamah had. What are some of the ways you might reach out to destitute, disadvantaged women? Have you already done so? Share an experience with the group.

◇ **A Psalm for Unloved** (see p. 269)

◇ **Prayer**

O Love Incarnate,
draw to Yourself
Your lost and lonely daughters
who have felt
and feel unloved.
You have enough love
to change their lives and ours,
when we are unloving.
Show us how to love one another
so that none are deprived of love
from this day forth forever.
Amen.

◇ A PSALM FOR UNLOVED ◇

Choir 1   I saw you in the doorway.
You were black
and bruised
and broken.
I knew you were someone's daughter.

All   You are your mother's daughter.
If she could,
she would sit with you
and say how much she loved you.

Choir 2   I saw you in the shelter.
You looked much older
than your years.
Your kids were tired
and making a fuss.
I knew you were someone's daughter.

All   You are your mother's daughter.
Imagine her here,
as a sister and friend,
saying how much she loves you.

Choir 1   I saw you on the news last night
on a dirt road in Soweto.
They were screaming at you.
You had no shoes.
I knew you were someone's daughter.

All   You are your mother's daughter
and she is her mother's daughter.
She has put up with so much abuse.
That shows how much she loves you.

Choir 2   I saw you in the delivery room
in drug withdrawal, writhing.
They say you have AIDS.
You are three hours old,
and I know you are someone's daughter.

All   You are your mother's daughter
and she needs you to forgive her.
She doesn't know how to love as yet,
but when she does,
I promise you,
she will say how much she loves you.

By M. T. Winter, Crossroad Pub. Co., © 1992 Medical Mission Sisters

Choir 1	I saw you in an orphanage.
	How sad you looked,
	and lonely.
	They say that you are hard to place,
	but I know you are someone's daughter.
All	You are your mother's daughter
	and a foster mother's daughter,
	and one of these days,
	she will come for you
	and say how much she loves you.
Choir 2	I saw you in a nursing home.
	You were slumped in a chair
	with a vacant stare.
	I knew you were somebody's daughter.
All	You are your mother's daughter,
	your Mother God's own daughter.
	Soon, very soon,
	She will come for you
	and say how much She loves you.

    By M. T. Winter, Crossroad Pub. Co., © 1992 Medical Mission Sisters

DAUGHTERS

◇ **Scripture Reference**   See lectionary texts

◇ **Biography**

While every woman begins life as a daughter, only those women whom the Bible specifically identifies as daughters — and who have not appeared elsewhere in this lectionary series — have been included here. Some of the women are named, others are described, still others are remembered by the generic word "daughter." The daughters are from the various cultures mentioned in the Bible.

◇ **Context**

In this lectionary series, a number of daughters have been singled out for special celebration. They are the women whose biblical narratives reveal a particular story either in words or in textual silence. The stories of the women who are grouped together here are also very important, but the limits of time and space preclude a more individual consideration. Many women make up the tradition, yet we know but a few of their names. That is because women throughout the tradition have been identified in terms of men. First they are daughters, then they are wives, and eventually most are mothers and we remember them, the ones recorded, through their fathers and husbands and sons. In the patriarchal culture of ancient Israel, women belonged to their men. Men "took" wives and "gave" daughters to other men in marriage. The daughters were there to be protected until they could be wives. Larger cities had "daughters" which were smaller adjacent villages under the city's protection.

The virginity of a daughter was a high priority and often seemed far more important than the young girl herself, or at least more important than her feelings or her future happiness. The stories of Dinah (p. 221) and David's daughter Tamar (p. 253) illustrate this point. The violation of a daughter meant a violation of Israel, and sometimes in avenging Israel's honor, the daughter was forgotten. On the other hand the virginity which seems so sacrosanct was at times too easily dispensable when other values were involved. Lot's daughters (p. 215) and the virgin daughter of Gibeah (p. 242) were victims of this truth. For all the cultural constraints, some daughters managed to break out of the mold and forge a new tradition. Mahlah and her sisters (p. 226) and Achsah (p. 232) suggest that there were many more women with similar experiences whose stories have been lost.

The daughters of many cultures, particularly Canaanites, married Israelite men, and their daughters ordinarily continued in the worship tradition of their mothers. Such practices were considered idolatrous to the priests and the biblical writers, and these women were often castigated and publicly condemned.

The existence of many significant women is not noted in the biblical text. See for example the genealogies in Genesis and Chronicles and the lists of children that favor sons. How many daughters did David have by all of his wives and concubines? How many daughters did Solomon have through his harem of one thousand women? Daughters who are named and those without names, daughters identified in terms of their men, daughters who are unidentified and are simply listed as daughters, as well as all those daughters whom the writers failed to mention and whose presence is implied by the text — all these we remember here.

◊ **Lectionary Reading**

Narrator: We remember **daughters whose names we know**
We remember **Abigail,** David's sister, Jesse's daughter

Reader
Jesse became the father of Eliab his firstborn;
Abinadab the second; Shimea the third;

Nethanel the fourth; Raddai the fifth;
Ozem the sixth; David the seventh;
and their sisters were Zeruiah and Abigail.
The sons of Zeruiah were Abishai, Joab, and Asahel.
Abigail bore Amasa, and the father of Amasa
was Jether the Ishmaelite. (1 Chr 2:13–17)

◇ ◇ ◇

Narrator: We remember **Agia and her sisters,**
        the daughters of Barzillai

Reader
The following had assumed the priesthood
but were not registered as priests:
the descendants of Habaiah,
the descendants of Hakkoz,
and the descendants of Jaddus
who had married Agia,
one of the daughters of Barzillai,
and was called by his name. (1 Esd 5:38; Ezra 2:61; Neh 7:63)

◇ ◇ ◇

Narrator: We remember **Basemath and Taphath,**
        Solomon's daughters

Reader
Solomon had twelve officials over all Israel,
who provided food for the king and his household.
Each one had to make provision for one month in the year.
One of these was Ahimaaz in Naphtali,
who had taken Basemath, Solomon's daughter, as his wife.
Another was Ben-abinadab in Naphath-dor,
who had Taphath, Solomon's daughter, as his wife.
        (1 Kings 4:7, 11, 15)

◇ ◇ ◇

Narrator: We remember **Bithia,** Pharaoh's daughter,
        and Bithiah's daughter **Miriam**

Reader
Bithiah, daughter of Pharaoh,
whom Mered married,
conceived and bore Miriam,
Shammai, and Ishbah, father of Eshtemoa. (1 Chr 4:17)

◇ ◇ ◇

Narrator: We remember **Hazzelelponi**

Reader
These were the sons of Etam: Jezreel, Ishma, and Idbash;
and the name of their sister was Hazzelelponi. (1 Chr 4:3)

◇ ◇ ◇

Narrator: We remember **Iscah,** daughter of Haran

Reader
Nahor married Milcah, the daughter of Haran
who was the father of Milcah and Iscah. (Gen 11:29)
◇ ◇ ◇
Narrator: We remember **Maacah,** Reumah's daughter

Reader
Reumah, Nahor's concubine,
bore Tebah, Gaham, Tahash, and Maacah. (Gen 22:24)
◇ ◇ ◇
Narrator: We remember **Mahlah,** Hammolecheth's daughter

Reader
Machir's sister Hammolecheth gave birth to
Ishhod, Abiezer, and Mahlah. (1 Chr 7:18)
◇ ◇ ◇
Narrator: We remember **Mehetabel and Matred**

Reader
Baal-hanan son of Achbor died,
and Hadad succeeded him as king.
The name of his city was Pau,
and his wife's name was Mehetabel,
the daughter of Matred,
daughter of Me-zahab. (Gen 36:39; 1 Chr 1:50)
◇ ◇ ◇
Narrator: We remember **Naamah,** Zillah's daughter

Reader
Zillah bore Tubal-cain,
who made all kinds of bronze and iron tools.
The sister of Tubal-cain was Naamah. (Gen 4:22)
◇ ◇ ◇
Narrator: We remember **Serah**

Reader
The children of Asher were Imnah,
Ishvah, Ishvi, Beriah,
and their sister Serah. (Gen 46:17; Num 26:44–46; 1 Chr 7:30)
◇ ◇ ◇
Narrator: We remember **Sheerah**

Reader
Sheerah was Ephraim's daughter.
She built both Lower and Upper Beth-horon,
and Uzzen-sheerah. (1 Chr 7:24)
◇ ◇ ◇

Narrator: We remember **Shelomith,**
          daughter of Maacah and Rehoboam

Reader
After Mahalath, Rehoboam took Maacah, Absalom's daughter,
and she gave birth to Abijah, Attai, Ziza, and Shelomith. (2 Chr 11:20)
          ◇ ◇ ◇
Narrator: We remember **Shelomith,** Zerubbabel's daughter

Reader
The sons of Pedaiah were Zerubbabel and Shimei;
and the sons of Zerubbabel were Meshullam and Hananiah,
and Shelomith was their sister. (1 Chr 3:19)
          ◇ ◇ ◇
Narrator: We remember **Shua**

Reader
Heber became the father of Japhlet,
Shomer, Hotham, and their sister Shua. (1 Chr 7:32)
          ◇ ◇ ◇
Narrator: We remember **Tamar**

Reader
Now there were born to Absalom three sons,
and one daughter whose name was Tamar;
she was a beautiful woman. (2 Sam 14:27)
          ◇ ◇ ◇
Narrator: We remember **daughters whose names we do not know**
          We remember the **daughters of the Genesis genealogies**
          and the Genesis mythologies

Reader
Seth lived after the birth of Enosh
eight hundred seven years,
and had other sons and daughters.
          ◇
Enosh lived after the birth of Kenan
eight hundred fifteen years,
and had other sons and daughters.
          ◇
Kenan lived after the birth of Mahalalel
eight hundred forty years,
and had other sons and daughters.
          ◇
Mahalalel lived after the birth of Jared
eight hundred thirty years,
and had other sons and daughters.
          ◇

Jared lived after the birth of Enoch
eight hundred years,
and had other sons and daughters.

◇

Enoch lived after the birth of Methuselah
three hundred years,
and had other sons and daughters.

◇

Methuselah lived after the birth of Lamech
seven hundred eighty-two years,
and had other sons and daughters.

◇

Lamech lived after the birth of Noah
five hundred ninety-five years,
and had other sons and daughters.
                              (Gen 5:1–32)
              ◇ ◇ ◇
When people began to multiply
on the face of the earth,
and daughters were born to them,
their sons saw that they were fair;
and they took wives for themselves.
Then God said,
"My spirit shall not abide in mortals forever,
for they are flesh;
their days shall be one hundred twenty years."
Giants were on the earth in those days —
and also afterward —
the offspring of the sons of divine beings
and the daughters of humans.
These were the heroes of old,
the warriors of renown. (Gen 6:1–4)
              ◇ ◇ ◇
Shem lived after the birth of Arpachshad
four hundred three years,
and had other sons and daughters.

◇

Arpachshad lived after the birth of Shelah
four hundred three years,
and had other sons and daughters.

◇

Shelah lived after the birth of Eber
four hundred three years,
and had other sons and daughters.

◇

Eber lived after the birth of Peleg
four hundred thirty years,
and had other sons and daughters.

        ◇

Peleg lived after the birth of Reu
two hundred nine years,
and had other sons and daughters.

        ◇

Reu lived after the birth of Serug
two hundred seven years,
and had other sons and daughters.

        ◇

Serug lived after the birth of Nahor
two hundred years,
and had other sons and daughters.

        ◇

Nahor lived after the birth of Terah
one hundred nineteen years,
and had other sons and daughters. (Gen 11:11–26)

        ◇ ◇ ◇

Because Shechem had violated their sister Dinah,
her brothers responded deceitfully
to Shechem and his father, saying,
"We cannot do what you ask.
To give our sister to one who is uncircumcised
would be a disgrace to us.
Only on this condition will we give our consent to you:
that you will become as we are
and that every male among you
will agree to be circumcised.
Then we will give our daughters to you
and we will take your daughters as wives.
Then we will live among you
and we will become one people.
But if you will not listen to us,
if you refuse to be circumcised,
we will take our daughter and go."
Their words pleased Hamor and Shechem.
Because he was so in love with Dinah,
Shechem proceeded without delay.
As the influential person in his father's house,
he spoke to the men of the city
who had gathered at the gate, saying,
"These people are friendly with us.
Let them live in our land and do business here,
for the land is large enough for us all.

Let us take their daughters in marriage,
and let us let them marry our daughters."
So every male was circumcised.
On the third day, when the men were still sore,
two of Dinah's brothers, Simeon and Levi,
took the city by surprise
and killed all the men with their swords.
And the other sons of Jacob came and plundered the city
and took everything and everyone that was in it
because their sister had been defiled. (Gen 34:13–29)

◇ ◇ ◇

Then Jacob set out from Beer-sheba;
and the sons of Israel carried their father Jacob,
their little ones, and their wives,
in the wagons that Pharaoh had sent to carry him.
They also took their livestock
and the goods that they had acquired
in the land of Canaan,
and they came into Egypt,
Jacob and all his offspring with him,
his sons and their sons and daughters,
his daughters and their sons and daughters,
all his offspring he brought with him into Egypt. (Gen 46:5–7)

◇ ◇ ◇

Narrator: We remember **Abijah's sixteen daughters**

Reader
Abijah king of Judah grew strong.
He took fourteen wives and became the father
of twenty-two sons and sixteen daughters. (2 Chr 13:21)

◇ ◇ ◇

Narrator: We remember **Achan's daughters**

Reader
Then Joshua and all Israel with him
took Achan son of Zerah,
with the silver, the mantle, and the bar of gold
[which he had plundered from Jericho],
with his sons and daughters,
with his oxen, donkeys, and sheep,
and his tent and all that he had;
and they brought them up to the valley of Achor.
And all Israel stoned him to death;
and they burned them with fire, cast stones on them,
and raised over him a great heap of stones
that remains to this day. (Josh 7:24–26)

◇ ◇ ◇

Narrator: We remember **David's Daughters**

Reader
In Jerusalem, after he came from Hebron,
David took more concubines and wives;
and more sons and daughters were born to David.
These are the names of those born in Jerusalem:
Shammua, Shobab, Nathan, Solomon,
Ibhar, Elishua, Nepheg, Japhia, Elishama, Eliada,
Eliphelet, Nogah, and Beeliada. (2 Sam 5:13–16; 1 Chr 14:3–7)

◇ ◇ ◇

King David covered his face
and cried out with a loud voice,
"O my son Absalom, O Absalom, my son, my son!"
Then Joab came into the house and said to the king,
"Today you have covered with shame
the faces of all your officers who saved your life
and the lives of your sons and daughters,
your wives and concubines,
for love of those who hate you
and hatred of those who love you.
You have made it clear today
that commanders and officers are nothing to you;
for I perceive if Absalom were alive
and all of us were dead today,
then you would be pleased." (2 Sam 19:4–6)

◇ ◇ ◇

Narrator: We remember **Eleazar's daughters**

Reader
Eleazar died having no sons, but only daughters.
Their relatives, the sons of Kish, married them. (1 Chr 23:22)

◇ ◇ ◇

Narrator: We remember the **other daughters and
    daughters-in-law of Gomer and Hosea**

Reader
"Your daughters play the whore
and your daughters-in-law commit adultery.
I will not punish your daughters when they play the whore,
nor your daughters-in-law when they commit adultery."
                    (Hos 4:13–14)

◇ ◇ ◇

Narrator: We remember **Hannah's daughters**

Reader
And God took note of Hannah.

She conceived and bore three sons and two daughters.
And the boy Samuel grew up in the presence of God. (1 Sam 2:21)

◇ ◇ ◇

Narrator: We remember **Izban's thirty daughters
and his thirty daughters-in-law**

Reader
After Jephthah, Izban of Bethlehem judged Israel.
He had thirty sons.
He gave his thirty daughters in marriage outside his clan
and brought in thirty young women from outside
for his sons.
He judged Israel seven years,
then died and was buried in Bethlehem. (Judg 12:8–10)

◇ ◇ ◇

Narrator: We remember **Jethro's six other daughters**

Reader
Moses fled from Pharaoh
and settled in the land of Midian.
One day he was sitting by a well
when the seven daughters
of the priest of Midian
came to the well to draw water.
They came together with their father's flock
and filled the troughs to water the sheep,
but some shepherds drove them away.
Moses came to their defense,
and even watered their flock.
When they returned home their father said,
"How come you are back so soon?"
"An Egyptian helped us chase the shepherds,
and drew water for us,
and watered the flock," they said,
and their father responded,
"Where is he? Why did you leave him there?
You should have invited him back for a meal."
So Moses came and he stayed with the man,
who gave him his daughter Zipporah in marriage. (Ex 2:15–21)

◇ ◇ ◇

Narrator: We remember **Joash's daughters**

Reader
Joash reigned forty years in Jerusalem.
Jehoiada got two wives for him,
and he became the father of sons and daughters. (2 Chr 24:1, 3)

◇ ◇ ◇

Narrator: We remember **the king's daughters**

Reader
Then Ishmael took captive all the rest of the people
who were in Mizpah, including the king's daughters.
But Johanan son of Kareah and all the forces with him
went to fight against Ishmael.
All the people whom Ishmael
had carried away captive from Mizpah
turned around and came back. (Jer 41:10–14)

◇ ◇ ◇

Narrator: We remember **Machir's daughter**

Reader
When he was sixty years old,
Hezron married the daughter of Machir
the father of Gilead,
and she gave birth to Segub. (1 Chr 2:21–23)

◇ ◇ ◇

Narrator: We remember **Meshullam's daughter**

Reader
Many in Judah were bound by oath to Tobiah,
because he was the son-in-law of Shecaniah son of Arah:
and his son Jehohanan had married
the daughter of Meshullam son of Berechiah. (Neh 6:18)

◇ ◇ ◇

Narrator: We remember **Peninnah's daughters**

Reader
On the day when Elkanah sacrificed,
he would give portions to his wife Peninnah
and to all her sons and daughters. (1 Sam 1:4)

◇ ◇ ◇

Narrator: We remember **the daughters of the priests**

Reader
The priests were enrolled
with all their little children,
their wives, their sons, and their daughters,
the whole multitude;
for they were faithful
in keeping themselves holy. (2 Chr 31:18)

◇ ◇ ◇

Narrator: We remember **Rehoboam's sixty daughters**

Reader
Rehoboam loved Maacah daughter of Absalom
more than all his other wives and concubines.

He took eighteen wives and sixty concubines,
and became the father of twenty-eight sons
and sixty daughters. (2 Chr 11:21)

◇ ◇ ◇

Narrator: We remember **Shallum's daughters**

Reader
Then I said to them,
"You see the trouble we are in,
how Jerusalem lies in ruins with its gates burned.
Come, let us rebuild the wall of Jerusalem,
so that we may no longer suffer disgrace."
Next to Hasshub son of Pahath-moab
Shallum son of Hallohesh,
ruler of half the district of Jerusalem,
made repairs, he and his daughters. (Neh 2:17; 3:12)

◇ ◇ ◇

Narrator: We remember **Sheshan's six daughters**

Reader
Now Sheshan had no sons, only daughters;
but Sheshan had an Egyptian slave, whose name was Jarha.
So Sheshan gave his daughter in marriage to Jarha;
and she bore him Attai. (1 Chr 2:34–36)

◇ ◇ ◇

Narrator: We remember **Shimei's six daughters**

Reader
Shimei had sixteen sons and six daughters;
but his brothers did not have many children,
nor did all their family multiply like the Judeans. (1 Chr 4:27–28)

◇ ◇ ◇

Narrator: We remember the **daughters of the Exodus**

Reader
God said to Moses,
"I will bring your people into such favor with the Egyptians,
that when you go, you will not go empty-handed.
Each woman will ask her neighbor
and any woman living in the neighbor's house
for jewelry of silver and gold, and clothing,
and you shall put them on your sons and your daughters;
and so you shall plunder the Egyptians." (Ex 3:21–22)

◇ ◇ ◇

Aaron said to the people in the wilderness,
"Take the gold rings from the ears of your wives,
your sons, and your daughters,
and bring them to me."

So all the people took the gold rings from their ears,
and brought them to Aaron.
He took the gold, molded it,
and made an image of a calf.
And they said, "These are your gods, O Israel,
who brought you up out of the land of Egypt." (Ex 32:2–4)

◇ ◇ ◇

Narrator: We remember **the daughters of cross-cultural marriages**

Reader
So the Israelites lived among the Canaanites,
the Hittites, the Amorites, the Perizzites,
the Hivites, and the Jebusites;
and they took their daughters as wives for themselves,
and their own daughters they gave to their sons;
and they worshiped their gods. (Jdg 3:5–6)

◇ ◇ ◇

They rejected all the commandments of the God of Israel
and made for themselves molten images of two calves;
they made a sacred pole,
worshiped all the host of heaven,
and served Baal.
They made their sons and their daughters pass through fire;
they used divination and augury. (2 Kings 17:16–17)

◇ ◇ ◇

The officials approached me and said,
"The people of Israel, the priests, and the Levites
have not separated themselves
from the people of the lands with their abominations,
from the Canaanites, the Hittites, the Perizzites,
the Jebusites, the Ammonites, the Moabites,
the Egyptians, and the Amorites.
For they have taken some of their daughters as wives
for themselves and for their sons.
Do not give your daughters to their sons,
neither take their daughters for your sons,
and never seek their peace or prosperity,
so that you may be strong and eat the good of the land
and leave it for an inheritance to your children forever."
(Ezra 9:1–2, 12; 1 Esd 8:68–70, 84)

◇ ◇ ◇

Narrator: We remember **daughters who suffered**

Reader
Now there was a great outcry of the people
against their Jewish kin.
For there were those who said,

"With our sons and our daughters, we are many;
we must get grain, so that we may eat and stay alive."
There were also those who said,
"We are having to borrow money
on our fields, our vineyards, and our houses
in order to get grain during the famine."
And there were those who said,
"We are having to borrow money
on our fields and vineyards
to pay the king's tax.
Now our flesh is the same as that of our kindred;
our children are the same as their children;
and yet we are forcing our sons and daughters
to be slaves,
and some of our daughters have been ravished.
We are powerless,
and our fields and vineyards now belong to others." (Neh 5:1–5)

◇ ◇ ◇

Under the whole heaven there has not been done
the like of what was done in Jerusalem,
in accordance with the threats
that were written in the law of Moses.
Some of us ate the flesh of their sons
and others ate the flesh of their daughters. (Bar 2:2–3)

◇ ◇ ◇

Narrator: We remember **the daughters who returned from exile**

Reader
The heads of ancestral houses were chosen
to go up to Jerusalem, according to their tribes,
with their wives and sons and daughters,
and male and female servants, and their livestock.
And Darius sent with them a thousand cavalry
to take them back to Jerusalem in safety,
with the music of drums and flutes;
all their relatives were making merry.
And he made them go up with them. (1 Esd 5:1–3)

◇ ◇ ◇

The rest of the people, the priests, the Levites,
the gatekeepers, the singers, the temple servants,
and all who have separated themselves
from the peoples of the lands
to adhere to the law of God,
their wives, their sons, their daughters,
all who have knowledge and understanding,
join with their kin, their nobles,

and enter into a curse and an oath
to walk in God's law,
which was given by Moses the servant of God,
and to observe and do all the commandments
and the ordinances and the statutes of God.
"We will not give our daughters to the peoples of the land
or take their daughters for our sons." (Neh 10:28–30)

◇ **Points for Shared Reflection**

- How did you feel about being a daughter when you were growing up? How do you feel about being a daughter now?

- What can we do to prepare the next generation of daughters to be proud of their female gender? What are some ways to celebrate our female heritage?

- As daughter of God, do you feel included in the generic word "sons"? If so, why? If not, why not? How has such a designation contributed to gender discrimination and anonymity?

- As daughter of God in the image of God, do you ever imagine God anthropomorphically as female or pray with female imagery or address Her in female terms? If so, share your experience. If not, why not?

◇ **A Psalm on Loving Shaddai** (see p. 286)

◇ **Prayer**

I love You, Shaddai,
with all my heart
and with all the strength
of my faith
in Your presence
and in Your promises.
You are for me
the Core of my being,
the Source of my female gender
Whom I image in my praise.
You make all moments possible,
even on impossible days,
and I make it
from now to eternity
by clinging to Your ways.
Amen.

◇ A PSALM ON LOVING SHADDAI ◇

Voice Love Shaddai with all your heart.

All I love You, Shaddai,
with all my heart,
as a child loves its mother,
as friend loves friend.

Voice Seek Shaddai with all your heart.

All I seek You, Shaddai,
with all my heart
and find You
beside and within me.

Voice Serve Shaddai with all your heart.

All I serve You, Shaddai,
with all my heart
in all that I am attempting.

Voice Follow Shaddai with all your heart.

All I follow You, Shaddai,
with all my heart,
without question,
without compromise,
no matter what the cost.

Voice Hear Shaddai with all your heart.

All I hear You, Shaddai,
with all my heart,
speaking to me
in the depths of my being,
calling to me
from the world around.

Voice Want Shaddai with all your heart.

All I want You, Shaddai,
with all my heart,
more than I want
all else that I want,
more than I will ever know.

Voice Turn to Shaddai with all your heart.

All I turn to You
with all my heart:
draw me to You, Shaddai.

   By M. T. Winter, Crossroad Pub. Co., © 1992 Medical Mission Sisters

◇ IV ◇
Memorable Women

JEHOSHEBA

◇ **Scripture Reference**   2 Kings 11:1–3; 2 Chr 22:10–12; 24:1

◇ **Biography**

Jehosheba, daughter of King Jehoram and wife of the priest Jehoiada, hid the infant son of her dead brother King Ahaziah from Athaliah, the queen mother, who had instigated a purge of all male heirs in order to secure the throne of Judah for herself. When the boy was seven, Jehosheba's husband led a successful coup against Athaliah and anointed the boy Joash king of Judah, restoring the monarchy to the house of David.

◇ **Context**

Jehosheba is remembered for an act of sheer courage. Her brother had reigned in Jerusalem for only a year when his death thrust the queen mother Athaliah (see p. 88) into the role of interim monarch. Athaliah thought she had destroyed all possible heirs, but Jehosheba hid her brother's infant son and his nursemaid in a room in the palace, then moved the child into the temple for six more years. Although King Jehoram (or Joram) seems to have had only one wife, scripture never says that Athaliah was the mother of Jehosheba, only that she was the mother of Jehosheba's brother. That may simply have been to establish the line of succession to the throne of Judah, or Jehoram may have fathered Jehosheba by some other woman. Chronicles identifies Jehosheba as the wife of Jehoiada the high priest in Jerusalem. Although some would disagree, that relationship is probably accurate. Jehosheba's role as wife of the chief priest would have given her access to the temple as well as the palace and would have enabled her to accomplish the six-year deception. As an insider to the royal household, she would have also played a vital role in the process of the child's coronation. Both Kings and Chronicles names the child's mother, Zibiah. She may have been killed by Athaliah since she is not mentioned along with Jehosheba in the preservation and raising of her son.

◇ **Lectionary Reading**

When Athaliah,
mother of King Ahaziah of Judah,
saw that her son was dead,
she set out to destroy all the royal family.
But Jehosheba, Ahaziah's sister,
took Joash, Ahaziah's son,
and with the boy's nursemaid
hid him in a bedroom when the purge began,
so the child would not be killed.
For six years Joash hid in the temple
while Athaliah reigned over Judah.

◇

Thus Jehosheba, daughter of King Jehoram
and wife of the priest Jehoiada,
because she was a sister of Ahaziah,
hid Joash from Athaliah
so that she could not kill him.

◇

Joash was seven years old
when he became king of Judah
and he reigned forty years in Jerusalem.

◇ **Points for Shared Reflection**

- If it were not for Jehosheba, the child Joash would have died. Name other instances past and present in which women, either individually or collectively, have been responsible for saving the lives of children.

- Jehosheba's father was a murderer, yet she was able to overcome the evils of her environment in her own personal development. How large a role do you think environment plays in the shaping of a life?

- What role has environment played in the shaping of your life?

- As both princess and spouse of a priest, Jehosheba experienced the patriarchal oppression of two institutional realities, government and religion. Name some ways in which you feel oppressed by your government and your religion.

◇ **A Psalm about Believing** (see p. 291)

◇ **Prayer**

I believe in You,
O Holy One,
although at times
there no longer seems
any reason for believing.
When evil stalks
my dwelling place
and loneliness leaves
indelible traces of doubt
on my childhood faith,
I light a lamp
in the secret room
where my heart hides
its tradition
and quietly hug
Your promises
as I sing songs to You.
I believe in You.
Believe in me.
May we believe forever.
Amen.

◇ A PSALM ABOUT BELIEVING ◇

All I believe
She is
and will be
for me
Womb
where love
and security
encompass me
and I flourish.
I believe
She is
and will be
for me
Breast
where fluid grace
and strength
flow freely
and fully nourish.
I believe
She is
and will be
for me
Lap
of compassion
and comfort
where warm understanding
and love
enfold me.
I believe
She is
and will be
for me
Word
of truth
carrying the power
to accomplish
all She has told me.
I believe
She is
and will always be
for me
for you
for everyone
forever.

By M. T. Winter, Crossroad Pub. Co., © 1992 Medical Mission Sisters

NOADIAH

◇ **Scripture Text**   Neh 6:10–14

◇ **Biography**

Noadiah was a female prophet in fifth-century B.C.E. Jerusalem. Nothing more is known of her.

◇ **Context**

Noadiah's entire story consists of twelve words: "...and also the female prophet Noadiah...who wanted to make me afraid." No other information has been found to further define or describe Noadiah, and even these few words must be seen to embody the assumptions of the writer Nehemiah. He was a Jew and a high official at the Persian court of Artaxerxes I in the fifth century B.C.E. when he was assigned to be governor of Judah and entrusted with the task of rebuilding the walls of Jerusalem and reorganizing the province. Nehemiah was pious, astute, responsible, and generally well accepted. His written memoirs in which the reference to Noadiah occurs form one of the basic historical documents in the Bible and have always been considered as substantially genuine. Not all approved of the restoration, however, and Nehemiah had some enemies both within and outside the prophetic community. Several prophets conspired with others in a plan to bring him down, but Nehemiah, although frightened, bravely held his ground. He included Noadiah and other prophets in his general condemnation of those who had tried to discredit him, although she had nothing to do with the incident. She was not part of that company of prophets nor involved in their intrigue. She may not have been part of any prophetic community but may have functioned on her own.

She was obviously known in her prophetic role, and she frightened Nehemiah, although he gives no indication why. It may have been for a very good reason or for any number of reasons. She may have forced Nehemiah to face some basic truths or to rethink his approach in the new era of reconstruction. In an effort to further disparage this female prophet, some commentators suggest that she was not Jewish, but there is no basis for that assumption. On the other hand, to state that the issue underlying Nehemiah's fear was that she was a woman, or a strong woman, or prophesied about the future role of women is also speculation, tempting though it may be. It is enough to say that Noadiah was important enough to be remembered and that she made an impact on a man whose book closes the historical section of the Bible. For a female in biblical circles, or in any context, that is significant.

◇ **Lectionary Reading**

One day when I went into the house of Shemaiah
son of Delaiah son of Mehetabel,
who was confined to his house, he said,
"Let us meet together in the house of God
and let us close the doors to the temple,
for they are coming to kill you."
But I said, "Should a man like me run away?
Should I go into the temple to save my life?
No, I will not go in!"
Then I realized that God had not sent him at all,
but he had pronounced his prophecy against me
because Tobiah and Sanballat had hired him.
He was hired to intimidate me
and make me sin by acting in this way.
They wanted to give me a bad name
in order that they might taunt me.
Remember Tobiah and Sanballat, O my God,
according to these things that they did,
and also the female prophet Noadiah
and all the rest of the prophets
who wanted to make me afraid.

◇ **Points for Shared Reflection**

- What could Noadiah possibly have said or done or been to make Nehemiah afraid?
- Are men ever afraid of you? Why?

- Why were the words of male prophets recorded and collected into books and the words of female prophets lost to history and to tradition?

- What are some of the prophetic words of women today that are going unrecorded? What are some prophetic words that are making people afraid?

◊ **A Mystical Psalm** (see p. 295)

◊ **Prayer**

O Holy One
of so many blessings,
the world cannot contain You,
the mind cannot comprehend You
nor the heart fully appreciate
all You are and have been
and will always be
for all Your cherished creation.
To know You
is to love You,
and to love You
is to know that You
will never be known
except through the filter
of our own experience.
I am here before You
needing You,
here within You
loving You,
feel You within me
filling me up,
lifting me up,
building me up
so that I can be
and become
like You
a lover of all Your people
and of all Your cherished creation,
now and forever.
Amen.

◇ A MYSTICAL PSALM ◇

All   Who are You, O Holy One?

Voice   I Am Who I Am,
I will always Be
Who I Am
and Who I Will Be.

All   If that is Who You are,
then Who are You for me?

Voice   I Am for you
Who I Am for you
and Who you need Me to be.

All   Who am I, O Holy One?
Let Your Spirit speak through me.

Choir 1   I am who I am,

Choir 2   I will always be
who I am
and who I will be.

All   Who have You been, O Holy One?

Voice   I have been
Who I Have Been,
Who I have always been.

All   If that is Who You have been,
then Who have You been for me?

Voice   I have been for you
Who I Have Been for you,
Who I have always been
for you.

All   Who have I been, O Holy One?
Let Your Spirit speak through me.

Choir 1   I have been here
as who I have been,

Choir 2   as who I have always been.

All   Who will You be, O Holy One?

Voice   I will be
Who I Will Be
is Who I will be forever.

All	If that is Who You will be,
	then Who will You be for me?
Voice	I will be
	Who I Will Be
	for you
	for now
	forever.
All	Who will I be, O Holy One?
	Let Your Spirit speak through me.
Choir 1	I will be
	who I will be,
Choir 2	as Who Will Be
	will have me be,
Choir 1	in the Spirit of She
	Who will always Be
Choir 2	and will be
	with me
	forever.
All	Praise and glory to You, Shaddai,
	Who is
	and was
	and will always be
	for me
	and for all
	forever.

   By M. T. Winter, Crossroad Pub. Co., © 1992 Medical Mission Sisters

TEMPLE SINGERS

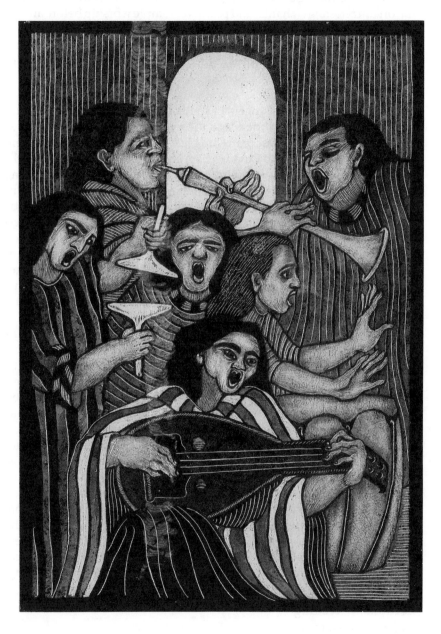

◇ **Scripture Reference**   1 Chr 25:5–8; Ezra 2:1, 64–65; Neh 7:67;
1 Esd 5:27, 42, 46

◇ **Biography**

Women were among the choirs of professional musicians who performed the organized songs, chants, and psalms of temple worship before and after the Babylonian exile. Three of the women were daughters of Heman. Scripture says that all were related to either Heman, Adath, or Jeduthum, and all were trained and skillful in the performance of liturgical music.

◇ **Context**

Women were always the singers of songs in ancient Israel. The spontaneous music-making of Miriam and the women on the banks of the Sea of Reeds (Ex 15:19–21), Deborah (Judg 5:1–31), the women of Jerusalem who praised the exploits of David (1 Sam 18:6–7), and Jephthah's daughter (Judg 11:34) are legendary. Professional musicians appeared during the reign of David but no one knows where they came from. The completion of the temple during Solomon's time with its formal, systematic pattern of worship called for a professional corps of qualified liturgical musicians. Choirs of trained singers and instrumentalists emerged and became part of the established tradition. Women were a part of these choirs. Professional musicians were considered high-ranking functionaries within the liturgy of the temple and within the royal courts. With the development of the professional choir, the spontaneous song of the women virtually disappeared.

The hymnbook of the temple singers, the biblical Psalter, which spans centuries of tradition and consists of five once separately circulating collections is included in the Hebrew canon and continues to function as sacred song for both Jews and Christians. It contains real musical terminology in the form of notations and superscriptions. The interpretation of these terms was once a closely guarded secret whose meaning has been lost. The professional choirs of the temple sang, played musical instruments, and performed liturgical gestures or dance. A wide variety of instruments was available for use: noisemakers such as bells, cymbals, rattles, gongs, tambourines, and timbrels; wind instruments: the flute, pipe, clarinet, trumpet, and shofar; stringed instruments of all kinds, including the lyre, harp, and lute. Several different sources note the presence of women in these professional liturgical choirs. While the timbrel and tambourine were instruments of choice for women who performed spontaneously, there is nothing to suggest that women's musical experience was limited to any particular instrument or repertoire of song.

◇ **Lectionary Reading**

God had given Heman
fourteen sons
and three daughters.
All of them sang in the house of God
under the direction of their father,

making music with cymbals, harps, and lyres
for the liturgy of the temple.
Adath, Jeduthum, and Heman
were registered by the king,
along with their relatives,
as ones who were trained to sing.
All among them who were skillfully trained
numbered two hundred eighty-eight.
They cast lots for their duties;
master and pupil, senior and junior,
all were assigned by lot.
⋄

Now these were the people of the province
who had been among those in exile,
whom Nebuchadnezzar had taken captive
and carried off into Babylonia.
They returned to Jerusalem and Judah,
each to their own town.
The assembly numbered forty-two thousand
three hundred and sixty people,
and seven thousand three hundred
and thirty-seven maidservants and slaves.
There were also two hundred singers,
both female and male.
⋄

There were two hundred forty-five singers,
both female and male.
⋄

The temple singers: the descendants of Asaph,
one hundred twenty-eight. . . .
There were two hundred forty-five musicians and singers.
The priests, the Levites, and some of the people
settled in Jerusalem and its vicinity;
and the temple singers, the gatekeepers,
and all Israel in their towns.

⋄ **Points for Shared Reflection**

- The temple in Jerusalem incorporated all kinds of musical instruments into its liturgies. How do you feel about the use of instruments in formal religious worship?

- Is there any particular instrument or musical style you would consider inappropriate for liturgical worship? If so, why?

- Dance has been used in most religious traditions since the beginning of recorded history and continues to be used in the worship of tribal peoples. How do you feel about dance in worship? Have you ever danced in worship? Would you? If not, why not?

- Ancient Israel did not distinguish between sacred and secular song as strictly as we do. If you were to broaden your definition of sacred music, what would you include? What would you not include, and why?

◇ **A Psalm about Music-Making** (see p. 301)

◇ **A Psalm about Music-Making** (see p. 301)

◇ **Prayer**

We sing to You,
O Singer of Songs,
O Maker of All Earth's Music.
It is in You that sound is born
and rhythm has its meaning.
It is in You that cosmic choirs
reverberate with song.
Make music in us,
make melody of us,
help us improvise a future
of international harmony
and cadences of peace.
To You we sing our song of praise,
for in You the song continues
and the music will go on
forever and ever.
Amen.

◇ A PSALM ABOUT MUSIC-MAKING ◇

Choir 1   Praise be to Her
for melody,
for the singer,
the song,
and the singing,
for cadences
and rhythm
and deep, rich harmony.

All   Sing to Her Who is Melody.
She is in all our singing.

Choir 2   Thanks be to Her
for cymbal
and drums,
for woodwind
and brass,
keyboard
and strings,
for folk guitar
and organ pipes
and every instrument
that sings.

All   Play for Her Who is Rhythm and Sound.
She is in all music-making.

Choir 1   Praise be to Her
for Gospel
and Blues,
hymnody,
psalmody,
spirituals,
jazz,
cantatas,
toccatas,
plainchant
and fugues,
preludes
and postludes
of every set form,
and improvisation
outside the norm.

All   Perform for Her Who is Creative Force.
She is in all composition.

By M. T. Winter, Crossroad Pub. Co., © 1992 Medical Mission Sisters

Choir 2	Thanks be to Her
	for movement
	and dance,
	gestures
	and postures,
	processions,
	parades,
	bowing,
	arising,
	the body at ease,
	the lifting of hands
	and the bending of knees.

All	Dance for Her Who is Embodied Movement.
	She is in all of our motion.

Choir 1	She Who is Singer,
	Singing,
	and Song,
	resonates deep
	in the soul of our being.

All	She Who is singing
	is singing in me.

Choir 2	She Who is Source
	of all music-making,
	resounds in the wind
	and the bird
	and the sea,
	reverberates
	deep in the heart
	of creation.

All	She Who makes music
	makes music of me.

Choir 1	She Who is Music,
	both substance and form,
	shapes every sound
	to the fullness of meaning.

All	She Who Composes
	makes meaning of me.

Choir 2	She Who is Dance
	gives the gesture and movement,
	and all of creation
	gives shape to Her themes.

All	Her incarnate Love
	is embodied in me.

   By M. T. Winter, Crossroad Pub. Co., © 1992 Medical Mission Sisters

QUEEN VASHTI

◇ **Scripture Reference**   Esth 1:1–21; 2:1–4, 15–17

◇ **Biography**

Vashti, queen of Media and Persia, fell into disfavor with King Ahasuerus when she refused to appear at his command to parade her beauty before his guests at a banquet in the palace. The king was outraged. His advisors feared other women would soon follow suit and defy the will of their husbands in emulation of their queen. Vashti was deposed for her rebellious act and never heard from again.

◇ **Context**

Vashti plays an important role in the Book of Esther, not only because her downfall occasioned the rise of Esther, but especially because her refusal to submit to the sexist demands of her husband and king had enormous symbolic value. It continues to have value now. Vashti's feminist stance was a threat to the male-dominated status quo and the king's advisors knew it. It was not enough to be angry with her. The woman had to be destroyed. There was more than a crown at stake here. They all had too much to lose. What if other women, what if their own wives should challenge patriarchal structures? The very fact that the men could make the connection from Vashti to other women indicates that such an issue had already surfaced, just as it has always surfaced since Adam dominated Eve.

Women today owe Vashti a debt of gratitude for ensuring that a bit of the feminist agenda would be included in the canon. Thanks are also due to the writers and the redactors of the Book of Esther for retaining this particular point. Although Vashti does not emerge as a heroine — that role is reserved for Esther — her punishment forces students of scripture to evaluate her case. It has been said that she got what she deserved, but such conclusions are in the mind of the interpreter. While men might see one who blundered and was rightfully replaced, women see a victim. Since God does not speak in the Book of Esther, we have yet to hear from God.

◇ **Lectionary Reading**

In the days of Ahasuerus,
who sat on the royal throne in the citadel of Susa
and ruled one hundred twenty-seven provinces
from India to Ethiopia,
the king gave a banquet
for his officials and his officers,
his ministers and his governors,
to display the wealth of his kingdom
and the splendor of his majesty.
The banquet lasted seven days.
It was opulent and lavish.
Queen Vashti also gave a banquet
for the women of the palace.
On the seventh day, when Ahasuerus
had had more than his share of wine,
he commanded his seven eunuchs
to bring Queen Vashti before the king,
commanded she wear the royal crown,
so that all might admire her beauty.
Queen Vashti refused the king's commands
conveyed to her by the eunuchs.
Her defiance enraged the king
and his anger burned within him.
He consulted the sages who knew the laws.
What should he do with Queen Vashti
who had rebelled against the king?

Memucan, his Persian official, said,
"Not only has she insulted the king,
she offended the people as well.
Soon all women will hear of her deed
and will look with contempt on their husbands.
They will say,
'The king commanded her
and Queen Vashti did not come.'
This very day all noble women
will defy the king's officials,
citing the queen's behavior.
There will be no end to contempt and wrath.
Send out a royal order —
write it among the laws —
word it so that it may never be altered:
Vashti will never again be allowed
to come before King Ahasuerus,
and the king will give her royal position
to another who is better than she.
Proclaim this decree throughout your kingdom,
vast though it may be,
so women will honor their husbands,
all women honor all husbands,
whatever their state in life."
The king was pleased with this advice
and wrote to all the provinces
in their local scripts and dialects,
bluntly declaring that every man
should be master in his own house.

When the king's anger had abated,
he remembered Vashti and what she had done
and what was decreed against her.
The king's servants said to him,
"Let beautiful young virgins
be brought for the king,
taken from all the provinces
to the harem in the citadel
and given cosmetic treatments
in the custody of the eunuch Hegai.
And let the girl who pleases the king
be queen instead of Vashti."
The king thought this was a good idea,
so they did as they had said.
Now Esther,
admired by everyone,

won the heart of Ahasuerus
who loved her very much,
more than all the other women.
He set the crown on Esther's head
and made her queen instead of Vashti.

◇ **Points for Shared Reflection**

- Why did Vashti refuse the king's command to appear before him and his guests? In your response, try to surface the issues and motives underlying both the request and the refusal.

- In what ways and in what arenas do women today continue to be sexually exploited? Have you ever had to face an occasion in your professional life when you were asked to do something you did not want to do and feared the penalty for refusal?

- Laws were made stating that (a) "Women will honor their husbands" and (b) "Every man should be master in his own house." In what ways and to what extent do these laws still influence us?

- In what ways are women punished today when they defy authority?

◇ **A Psalm Celebrating Beauty** (see p. 307)

◇ **Prayer**
O Beauty Incomparable,
Grace so accessible,
draw us to You
and through You to all that is good
and beautiful and holy
and worthy of our praise.
Daily we strive to be more like You,
O Joy of Our Desiring.
May we image Your beauty
and grow by Your grace
to the fullness of our being
and the completeness of our call.
For this we pray.
Amen.

◇ A PSALM CELEBRATING BEAUTY ◇

Choir 1   She walks in beauty
as the night,
veiled in the folds of mystery,
concealing the deep, dark secret source
of her integrity,
revealing only what will inspire,
so is she who walks with God.

Choir 2   She rises in beauty
as the dawn,
radiant with newly awakened light,
clear as far as the eye can see,
slowly, surely, enticing all
into the orb of her energy,
so is she who rises with God.

Choir 1   She sits in beauty
like a stone,
certain of her appointed place,
fundamental and firm to the insecure,
unafraid to sit alone,
so is she who sits with God.

Choir 2   She stands in beauty
like a tree,
deep-rooted, so no catastrophe
can wipe her memory from the land,
nor fell her
when she takes a stand,
so is she who stands with God.

Choir 1   She is with Beauty constantly,
she who enters the cosmic force
of quintessential harmony,
savoring all she has come to be,
so is she who is with God.

Choir 2   She is beauty incarnate,
the kind
transcending sinew, stature, skin
to thrill the participating mind
and fill the senses.
Who will find
a clearer image of Deity
than she who is in God?

By M. T. Winter, Crossroad Pub. Co., © 1992 Medical Mission Sisters *WomanWitness* / **307**

SARAH'S MAID

◇ **Scripture Reference**   Tob 3:7–9; 8:1, 9–15

◇ **Biography**

A maid employed in the household of Raguel in Ecbatana, the capital of Media, made her brief but anonymous appearance in the story of Sarah, future wife of Tobias, then disappeared from the pages of history.

◇ **Context**

An incident in the Deuterocanonical Book of Tobit gives a brief but vivid insight into the feisty, fiery spirit of one of the servant class. This anonymous maid stood up to her mistress and challenged her sense of integrity, accusing her of unjust behavior. She obviously had a point. Sarah took her accusation seriously, left the room in tears and even contemplated suicide because her life was filled with so much grief. It took courage to stand up to authority, just as it took courage later on in the story to look in on Sarah when she was in bed with husband number eight. She surely expected to find him dead and herself face to face with the demon. The maid was probably a household maid assigned to attend Sarah. A personal nursemaid would have been more empathetic and loyal to her mistress. Since the household of Raguel, Edna, and Sarah were exiled Jews in Media, the maid herself may have been Persian or she may have been a Jewish girl. Her story unfolds in relationship to the stories of Sarah and Anna (see *WomanWisdom*, pp. 215 and 228) and Edna (this volume, p. 179).

At Ecbatana in Media,
Sarah, daughter of Raguel,
was reproached by one of her father's maids.
She had married seven husbands,
but each of them died on their wedding night
without having slept with her,
for the demon Asmodeus had killed them.
The maid shouted at Sarah,
"Killer of husbands, that's what you are!
Seven already and not a one
has given his name to you.
So why strike out at us?
Because your husbands are dead?
May you join them!
May we never see a son or daughter of yours!"
Grief-stricken, Sarah withdrew and wept.

◇

When they had finished eating and drinking
and were ready to retire,
they escorted Tobias to the room
where Sarah his bride was waiting.
Later that night Sarah's father
summoned his servants
to go out and dig a grave.
"It is possible he will die," he said,
"and we will be marked for derision
and for ridicule by everyone."
When the grave was dug,
Raguel called for Edna.
"Send a maid to look in on them," he said,
"to see if he is alive.
But if he is dead, let us bury him
without anyone knowing of it."
So they sent a maid who lit a lamp
and opened the bedroom door.
She went in and found the two of them
sound asleep together.
She came out and informed them
that nothing was wrong,
that Tobias was alive.
So they blessed God together.

◇ **Points for Shared Reflection**

- Do you feel free to critique your employer or to speak your mind when you are with those who have power over you? Give examples to illustrate your response.

- Have you ever challenged authority for injustices you have experienced in your own religious tradition? What did you challenge or would you challenge if you chose to do so?

- Are you open to criticism from those who work for you or depend on you in professional or domestic relationships? When do you find such criticism difficult, and why?

- We are all accountable to one or more people or institutions. To whom are you accountable? Is your association with each of these liberating or oppressive? Share something about each one.

◇ **A Psalm for the Powerless** (see p. 311)

◇ **Prayer**

O Sacred Power,
Force for Good
in the midst of so much evil,
we who are powerless
call upon You
for strength
and a share in Your power,
for we are only as powerful
as Your power
empowering us,
this day
and every day of our lives.
Amen.

◇ A PSALM FOR THE POWERLESS ◇

Voice I have called you
by your name,
you are Mine.
When you pass through the waters,
I will be with you,
and I will strengthen you.

Chorus You who feel you are powerless:
All Shaddai will strengthen you.

Chorus You who are weak and so afraid:
All Shaddai will strengthen you.

Chorus You who have nowhere to turn for help:
All Shaddai will strengthen you.

Voice When you pass through the waters,
I will be with you,
and I will encourage you.

Chorus When you feel crushed by the burdens of life:
All Shaddai will encourage you.

Chorus When you are overwhelmed with stress:
All Shaddai will encourage you.

Chorus When your heart hurts and the wound will not heal:
All Shaddai will encourage you.

Voice When you pass through the waters,
I will be with you,
and I will empower you.

Chorus Stand up for justice for yourself and for others:
All Shaddai will empower you.

Chorus Challenge authority, challenge the structure:
All Shaddai will empower you.

Chorus Say to oppression, never again:
All Shaddai will empower you.

Voice I have called you
by your name,
you are Mine.

All When we pass through the waters,
You will be with us,
strengthening, encouraging, empowering us.
Praise to You, Shaddai!

ARSINOE

◇ **Scripture Text** 3 Macc 1:1–5

◇ **Biography**

Arsinoe III (ca. 235–ca. 204 B.C.E) was the daughter of Queen Berenice II and Ptolemy III Euergetes of Egypt. She was both sister and wife of the degenerate Ptolemy IV Philopater. A popular queen, she was murdered by the royal ministers after the death of her husband.

◇ **Context**

Arsinoe the sister of Philopater king of Egypt accompanied her brother to Rafia in Palestine in 217 B.C.E., presumably at his request, where the Egyptian army fought to recapture territory taken from them by the Middle Eastern Seleucid kingdom. Arsinoe's passionate encouragement of the troops seems to have helped turn a potential Egyptian defeat into victory. After trying unsuccessfully to enter the temple in Jerusalem, Philopater returned to Egypt and proceeded to persecute the Jews. Arsinoe married her brother after the episode at Rafia, and following the birth of the future Ptolemy V Epiphanes, she was sequestered in the palace while her husband's involvement with a depraved coterie of women and men led to the disintegration of both the king and the Ptolemaic kingdom. Although she did not approve of what was going on, Arsinoe was powerless to effect a change. Philopater died in 205 B.C.E., and a year later the royal ministers assassinated Arsinoe because they feared her and her popularity with the people who rioted when they learned of her death. Who was this woman who was locked into an incestuous relationship? Did she marry against her will? Events would certainly suggest that was so. She was imprisoned in her own palace once she had provided her brother/husband with an heir. A queen favored by the people, she was powerless to change the evils she detested or to save the kingdom she loved. The stark image rising out of her biblical story shows her rapport with the rank and file on the front lines of a losing battle. That suggests a quality of character seldom found in royal palaces. One wonders what prompted the writer to incorporate Arsinoe's vivid yet peripheral narrative into the biblical text.

◇ **Lectionary Reading**
When Philopater king of Egypt learned
that the regions he had controlled
had been seized by Antiochus,
he gave orders to all his forces,
both his infantry and his cavalry,
and marched out to the region near Raphia
where the army of Antiochus was encamped;
and he took his sister Arsinoe with him.
But a certain Theodotus,
determined to carry out a plot he had devised,
took with him the best of Ptolemaic arms
that had been previously issued to him
and crossed over at night to Ptolemy's tent,
intending to kill him single-handedly,
thereby ending the war.
But Dositheus,
known as the son of Drimylus,
who was a Jew by birth
but had changed his religion
and had left his ancestral traditions,
had led the king away to another place
and had arranged that someone less significant
should sleep in his tent that night.
So it happened that this other man
suffered the fate meant for the king.
A vicious battle broke out,
and when the outcome seemed to favor Antiochus,
Arsinoe walked among the troops,
wailing and in tears,
with her hair all disheveled,
exhorting them to defend themselves
and their wives and children bravely,
promising to give each of them

two minas of gold
after they had won the battle.
And so it happened that the enemy was routed
and many captives were taken.

◇ **Points for Shared Reflection**

- Arsinoe was eighteen years old when she rallied the troops in battle and about that age when she married her brother. Try to imagine what she was like and how she felt about both those events. How much freedom of choice do you think she had?

- What choice does any female victim of incest really have? Is there anyone present who has been a victim of incest who might want to talk about it? If so, make sure the sharing is done in a context that feels safe and supportive and confidentiality is assured.

- Do you think society and organized religion is doing enough to assist victims of incest in identifying their pain, sharing their story, and ridding themselves of guilt? What more ought to be done?

- Authority is usually threatened by those who think differently and are popular with the people. How does religious authority treat influential dissidents? Give some examples.

◇ **A Psalm Celebrating Life** (see p. 315)

◇ **Prayer**

Life,
spilling over
the hills of our grief
and filling the wells
in our soul
and our senses,
come, lift us up
into lighthearted
laughter,
so all the weight
of our world
of awareness
does not overwhelm us.
Life of Our World,
be life
in and through us,
now and forever.
Amen.

◇ A PSALM CELEBRATING LIFE ◇

All   Life,
          celebrate life,

Choir 1 celebrate friends,
           freedom,
           fullness,
           and feeling

Choir 2 flowing in us
           and through us
           and out of us
           into the world
           created
           because of us.

All   Life,
          celebrate life,

Choir 1 celebrate love,
           laughter,
           light coming in
           and the light
           coming out of us,

Choir 2 lighthearted
           light
           that enlightens
           the whole of us.

All   Life,
          celebrate life

Choir 1 in the midst of
           death,
           doubt,
           disappointment,
           destruction,

Choir 2 for that is when life
           most of all
           needs to happen;

Choir 1 the heart
           needs to feel
           there's an end to its sorrow,

Choir 2 the soul
           needs to know
           that there is a tomorrow.

By M. T. Winter, Crossroad Pub. Co., © 1992 Medical Mission Sisters

SUSANNA

◇ **Scripture Reference**   Dan 13:1–64

◇ **Biography**

Susanna was a beautiful, God-fearing woman who was falsely accused
of adultery by two respected elders who were judges in Babylon. The
daughter of righteous parents — her father's name was Hilkiah — and
the wife of an esteemed and wealthy man — her husband's name was
Joakim — she was condemned to death without due process on the
strength of the accusation. As she was about to be executed, Daniel
intervened and subjected the judges to a cross-examination, exposing
their lie and vindicating this much-loved daughter of Judah.

◇ **Context**

Susanna's story, a masterpiece of Jewish narrative, is an apocryphal work
appended to the Book of Daniel as chapter twelve in editions based on the
Septuagint and Latin Vulgate translations and as a prefix to chapter one

in other ancient versions. The text is part of the Roman Catholic canon. The narrative tells us about treachery and deceit, about violation of trust, and about the violent substratum often underlying illicit carnal desire. It tells of power out of control and of gullibility. Those in authority betray their mandate to mete out justice and speak the truth, and everyone seems to believe them. Susanna's own story is one of beauty, innocence, sincerity, and faith. A stranger intervenes to plead her case, and by God's grace, he saves her. How can you condemn a daughter, he asks, without finding out the truth? Why do we always trust the system? Systemic injustice does occur. Susanna's story is the story of many women of the past and of the present. Who among us will champion their cause? Who of us really believes them?

◇ **Lectionary Reading**

There was a woman in Babylon
whose name was Susanna.
She was the daughter of Hilkiah
and her parents, upright people,
had trained their daughter diligently
according to the law of Moses.
Susanna was a God-fearing woman
and she was very beautiful.
Her husband's name was Joakim.
The Jews would often come to him;
he was respected by them all.
That year two elders appointed as judges
were often at Joakim's house,
and all who had a case to be tried
appeared before them there.
Now Joakim was very rich
and had a garden adjoining his house.
After the people left at noon,
Susanna would walk in the garden.
The elders would see her every day
walking about the garden,
and they lusted after her.
They suppressed their conscience,
turned their eyes from heaven,
and ignored their responsibility
to act with integrity.
They did not tell each other
of their passion for Susanna,
for each was ashamed to reveal to the other
his lustful desire to seduce her.
Day after day,

they looked for opportunities to see her.
One day they said to each other,
"Let us go home. It is time for lunch."
So they parted from each other,
but each turned back, and when they met,
each asked the other his reason
for returning to the house.
On learning a lust for Susanna
was consuming both of them,
they plotted together to get her alone.
One day Susanna went into the garden
accompanied by her two maids.
Susanna was hot, she wanted to bathe
in the privacy of her garden.
"Bring me olive oil and ointments,"
Susanna said to her maids,
"and shut the gates to the garden."
The maids did as Susanna had asked
and left her there alone.
They did not know, however,
that the elders were hiding there,
watching Susanna,
waiting to get her by herself.
When the maids had left,
the elders ran to Susanna and said to her,
"Look, the garden gates are shut
and there is no one to see us.
We burn with desire for you.
Come on, give in to us.
If you refuse, we are prepared to testify against you.
We will say a young man was here with you.
We will say that was the reason why
you sent your maids away."
Grief-stricken, Susanna said,
"I am trapped.
If I do this, it will mean death to me.
If I do not, then the two of you
in your own way will destroy me.
Well, I choose not to do it.
I would rather fall into your evil hands
than sin in the sight of God."
Then Susanna cried out with a loud voice
and the elders cried out against her.
One of them opened the garden gates,
and when the household heard the noise
they rushed to see what had happened.

When the elders told their story,
the servants felt very ashamed,
for nothing like this had ever before
been said about Susanna.
The next day, when the people were there
in court at the house of Joakim,
the elders arrived
determined to have Susanna put to death.
"Send for Susanna, daughter of Hilkiah,
wife of Joakim," they said.
So they sent for Susanna,
and she came with her parents,
her children, and her relatives,
a woman of great refinement
and extraordinary beauty.
Susanna was veiled,
and the elders ordered the veil to be removed,
so that they might enjoy her beauty.
Those who were with her
and all who saw her,
all but her accusers,
were weeping for Susanna.
The elders stood with their hands on her head.
Through her tears she looked to heaven,
for her heart trusted in God.
The elders told their story.
"While we were walking alone in the garden,
this woman came in with her two maids,
shut the garden gates,
and sent her maids away.
Then a young man who had been hiding there
came and lay with her.
From the corner of the garden,
we saw this despicable deed.
We ran to them, but the man got away;
he was stronger than we are.
However, we seized this woman,
and we asked her for the man's name,
but she refused to tell us.
These things we testify."
Because they were elders and judges,
the people of course believed them,
and they condemned Susanna to death.
Susanna cried out with a loud voice, saying,
"O eternal God,
you know what is secret,

you know all things before they happen.
You know these men have lied
and have given false evidence against me.
And now I am going to die,
although I have done none of the evil things
that they have charged against me!"
God heard Susanna's cry.
As she was about to be executed,
God's spirit stirred in Daniel,
and he shouted with a loud voice,
"I want no part
in the shedding of this innocent woman's blood."
All the people turned to him.
"What are you saying?" they asked.
He turned to face the crowd and said,
"Are you such fools, O Israelites,
as to condemn a daughter of Israel
without bothering to find out the truth?
Return to court, for these men here
have given false evidence against her."
So all the people hurried back,
and the rest of the elders said to him,
"Come, sit among us and enlighten us;
God has given you an elder's insight."
Then Daniel said, "Separate them,
and I will examine them."
So they separated the accusers,
and he summoned one of them and said,
"You relic of wickedness.
Your sins will now overtake you,
past wrongs which you have committed —
pronouncing unjust judgments,
condemning the innocent,
acquitting the guilty —
though God has said,
'Innocence shall not be put to death.'
Now then, if you really saw this woman,
answer this for me:
Under what tree were they lying?"
He answered, "Under a mastic tree."
And Daniel said, "So be it!
The lie you have told will cost you your head,
for the angel of God has received the sentence
and you will be cut in two."
He sent him away and summoned the other.
Then Daniel said to him,

"You son of Canaan and not of Judah,
beauty has beguiled you
and lust has perverted your heart.
So this is how you have always treated
the daughters of Israel,
forcing them, through fear and threat,
to be intimate with you.
This daughter of Judah, however,
would not tolerate your wickedness.
Tell me then:
Under what tree were the two of them
when you observed their intimacy?"
He answered, "Under an evergreen oak."
"So be it!" responded Daniel.
"This lie has cost you your head,
for the angel of God is standing by with a sword,
to split you in two."
Then all the people praised God,
the God who never fails to save
all those who cling to hope.
Then they moved against the accusers,
doing to them as they had planned
to do to their neighbor, Susanna.
In accordance with the law of Moses,
they put them both to death.
And innocent blood was spared that day.
Hilkiah and his wife praised God
for saving their daughter Susanna.
So did her husband Joakim
and all her relatives,
for she was proven innocent
of committing a shameful deed.
From that day forward,
Daniel had a reputation among the people.

◇ **Points for Shared Reflection**

- There are persons in religion today who have abused their authority and betrayed a trust. If the tables were turned and their victims made accusations, do you think anyone would believe them?

- Susanna is a symbol of innocence. Name some of the innocent victims of systemic injustice in religion and society today.

- Do you think the situation would have been the same if the false accusation had been made against a man and not a woman? What do you think would have happened?

- This is a morality play whose main characters are the innocent beauty, the treacherous judges, the defending champion, the circle of supporters, and the participating crowd. Assume each of the roles briefly. Were you ever in a position similar to your corresponding role in Susanna's story? Were you ever falsely accused? Did you ever falsely accuse? Have you ever risen to the defense of someone or been supportive of someone who had been falsely accused? Have you ever condemned someone without due process, just because?

⋄ **A Psalm of Trust Betrayed** (see p. 323)

⋄ **Prayer**

Deliver us
from the lion's jaws,
from the sharpened claws
of the circling beasts,
from the evil ringed around us,
O Defender of Your People,
and speak a word of comfort
to all victims of injustice.
See to our vindication
when You rise up to defend us.
We continue to put our trust in You
until You come again.
Amen.

◇ A PSALM OF TRUST BETRAYED ◇

Choir 1 Believable
are the evil lies
on the lips
of the deceiver.

Choir 2 Desolate
are the victims
of a public trust
betrayed.

Choir 1 Sweet as honey
on a cone of ice
is the rationale
of deception.

Choir 2 Stuck in the throat
is the protest
of the molested
and the abused.

Choir 1 Why does the court
interrogate
the one whose heart is broken?

Choir 2 Why increase
the embarrassment
of the one who has been shamed?

Choir 1 The tears
of all the victims
have yet to wash away
the feelings.

Choir 2 Years go by
and still the memory
stings
and guilt abides.

Choir 1 Woe to the one
whose vestment shields
what we would deem abhorrent.

Choir 2 Woe to the one
who tears the veil
of innocence
from the young.

Choir 1	Cursed be the one who lays a hand on the helpless, and destroys them.
Choir 2	Cursed be the one who kills hope in the already crucified.
Choir 1	Reach out, Shaddai, to the victims of abuse or false accusation.
Choir 2	Give Your love to the violated or they may never love again.
Choir 1	We call on You with confidence, for You are a God of justice.
Choir 2	Protect us, and deliver us, and vindicate the betrayed.

   By M. T. Winter, Crossroad Pub. Co., © 1992 Medical Mission Sisters

MIDWIVES

◇ **Scripture Text**   See lectionary texts

◇ **Biography**

Midwives were Hebrew women who were experienced in helping other women deliver their babies. Little is known about them. Present in every village, sometimes a member of the pregnant woman's household, they acquired their knowledge firsthand and undoubtedly taught their skills and traditional wisdom to their successors. While only a few midwives are specifically mentioned in the Bible, their presence is implied in every narrative that mentions a woman giving birth.

◇ **Context**

In ancient Israel, as in villages around the globe today, women gave birth at home and were assisted by other women, usually by the females in the family and particularly by an experienced midwife, a woman who understood a breach delivery, who knew how and when a woman should push, who could cut the umbilical cord correctly. Such women were considered wise ones in the village and were treated with respect. In the several pericopes that feature the midwife, it is striking to note how often the motif of bringing to life is juxtaposed by the reality of death. Rachel gave birth to Ben-oni and died. Not even the news that she had borne a son was strong enough to save her. Ichabod's mother supposedly died in the act of naming her son. His birth and her death coincided with the departure of God's glory from the land of Israel. Earlier the Hebrew midwives

325

in Egypt carried out their life-giving ministry under threat of death and in defiance of death, snatching the sons of the Hebrew women from the hands of those who would slay them. Baby girls were allowed to live but baby boys had to be slaughtered. Yet what kind of world awaited those females after they were born? A world of slavery and bondage. Tamar's twins struggled in her womb and the younger supplanted the elder, just like the matriarch Rebekah whose twins struggled so fiercely within her that she was prepared to die. Is it just coincidence? Or are these texts trying to tell us something? The midwives we meet in these narratives are involved in situations of reversal. Not only do they bring to life but they bring life out of death, hope out of despair, and consistently give birth to the future. And more than once, in the act of giving birth to a continuation of patriarchy, another woman dies.

◇ **Lectionary Reading**

When they began their journey from Bethel,
Rachel was with child.
When they were still some distance from Ephrath,
Rachel went into labor and her delivery was hard.
The midwife said to Rachel,
"Do not be afraid, you will have another son."
Rachel died giving birth to her baby,
a boy whom she named Ben-oni,
but his father called him Benjamin. (Gen 35:16–19)

◇ ◇ ◇

When the time of Tamar's delivery arrived,
she was found to have twins in her womb.
While she was in labor,
one of the babies put out a hand
and the midwife tied to it a crimson thread, saying,
"This child came out first."
But he drew back his hand,
and his brother came first.
"What a breach you have opened for yourself!"
said the midwife,
so they named the baby Perez.
A little while later his brother was born
with the crimson thread on his hand,
and so he was named Zerah. (Gen 38:27–30)

◇ ◇ ◇

Pharaoh, king of Egypt,
said to the Hebrew midwives:
"When you are called by the Hebrew women
to assist them in giving birth,
be attentive to the delivery.

If a boy is born, kill him.
If you deliver a girl, let her live."
But the midwives were God-fearing women
and they refused to do as the king commanded,
but let the baby boys live.
Now one of the midwives was named Shiprah
and another was named Puah.
The king summoned the midwives and said,
"Why have you disobeyed my order
and allowed the boys to live?"
And the midwives answered Pharaoh,
"Because the Hebrew women are vigorous,
not like the Egyptian women,
they give birth before the midwife arrives."
So the Hebrew people grew numerous and powerful
and God rewarded the midwives.
Because of their courage and reverence for God,
they were blessed with households of their own.
Then Pharaoh commanded the Egyptians,
"Every boy that is born to a Hebrew woman
must be thrown into the Nile,
but you may let their daughters live." (Ex 1:15–22)

◇ ◇ ◇

Eli's daughter-in-law,
the wife of Phinehas,
was pregnant and about to give birth
when she heard that the ark of God
had been captured
and both her husband
and her father-in-law were dead.
She went into labor,
and in great pain
she gave birth to her child.
Seeing she was at the point of death,
the midwife attending her said to her,
"Do not be afraid.
You have borne a son."
She did not respond to her.
Instead she named the child Ichabod, meaning,
"The glory has departed from Israel,"
because the ark of God had been captured
and she had lost her husband and father-in-law.
"The glory has departed from Israel," she said,
"for the ark of God has been captured." (1 Sam 4:19–22)

◇ **Points for Shared Reflection**

- Midwives are involved in bringing to birth. What have you brought to birth recently that fills you with hope and excitement?

- The birth and rebirth of patriarchy has always meant the death of women. Name some of the patriarchal practices that you feel are destroying you.

- Men have always feared the female power of giving birth and bringing to birth. Talk about this fear and this power. How has it affected you?

- How do you feel about all the technology associated with our culture's approach to giving birth today? What do you think is missing from the birthing process? What would you like to see changed?

◇ **A Psalm for Midwives** (see p. 329)

◇ **Prayer**

O One Who Brings to Birth in us,
Who has midwifed all creation,
Who has power to open
the womb of blessing
and to close the womb of strife,
give us the means
of bringing to birth
the world we are all awaiting,
and strength
to stay the course.
We believe
that what we set out to accomplish
will one day come to pass
in You and through You,
Creator of All,
and Midwife of All the Living.
Praise be to You, Shaddai.
Amen.

◇ A PSALM FOR MIDWIVES ◇

Choir 1   You will know
when it is time
to bring to birth
the new creation.

Choir 2   The signs
will be all around you,
urging, insisting:
now is the time.

Choir 1   You have to know
just when to bear down
and concentrate
on one thing only.

Choir 2   It takes labor,
hard, hard labor
to bring forth something new.

All   Be Midwife to our dreams, Shaddai.
Make midwives of us all.

Choir 1   You have to know
just when to push
for something that is
worth fighting for.

Choir 2   If you push too soon,
the dream,
so close to fulfillment,
may be stillborn.

Choir 1   You have to know
how hard to push
when something new
is about to happen.

Choir 2   If you push too hard,
you may be too exhausted
or too discouraged
to continue on,
or someone may step in
to stop you,
causing you to abort.

All   Be Midwife to our hopes, Shaddai.
Make midwives of us all.

By M. T. Winter, Crossroad Pub. Co., © 1992 Medical Mission Sisters

Choir 1	You have to know how to cut the cord and how to let go of what has been;
Choir 2	for what will be will be different and it will take some time to adjust.
Choir 1	You have to know how to wait for things to settle after the dream is born,
Choir 2	and how to handle the consequences — clean up the mess and then move on.
All	Be Midwife to our freedom, Shaddai. Make midwives of us all.
Choir 1	How good it is to bring to birth,
Choir 2	or to help another bring to birth.
Choir 1	How good it is to deliver the dream.
Choir 2	Let us nurture it to fulfillment.
All	Be Midwife to the future, Shaddai. Make midwives of us all.

     By M. T. Winter, Crossroad Pub. Co., © 1992 Medical Mission Sisters

PROSTITUTES

◇ **Scripture Text**   See lectionary texts

◇ **Biography**

There were two kinds of prostitution in Israel. Secular or common prostitution involved only women, sacred or cultic prostitution was performed by women and men. The former was immoral but legal, the latter strictly prohibited on both moral and religious grounds, although it was practiced extensively in ancient Israel. Rahab, a prostitute, and Tamar, who conceived twins through an act of prostitution, are listed in the Matthean genealogy of Jesus (1:3, 5) as links in the Messianic line leading to and through David.

◇ **Context**

In addition to Tamar (p. 2) and Rahab (p. 24), there is the biblical narrative of two prostitutes with one surviving baby, which testifies to the wisdom of Solomon (Two Mothers, p. 163). We learn a lot about prostitutes from these texts. Tamar's narrative indicates that the prostitute in ancient Israel waited for and actively solicited business in a public place, that she was recognized by her physical appearance — she was heavily robed and her face was veiled — and she negotiated the fee for her services in advance. Prostitution was not illegal, but there was some social stigma attached, so male participants were usually discreet. Prostitutes themselves were often social outcasts. They had to be unmarried because a married prostitute was guilty of adultery, an offense

331

that was punishable by death. There were two kinds of prostitution in the Hebrew scriptures and two different terms to describe them: *zona* for the female harlot practicing secular or common prostitution; and *quades/qedesa* (hallowed one) for the hierodule, male or female, who practiced sacred or cult prostitution in the ancient religious fertility rites. The two terms were often interchanged in the narrative and prophetic writings, so that females, prostitutes, and idolatry became closely identified. The term "prostitute" or "harlot" was also used metaphorically by several of the prophets to describe Israel's recalcitrant relationship with God or a husband's relationship with an errant wife. This extended the negative image of women well beyond the prostitute or prostitution so that women in general, particularly those of a different religion or culture, suffered gender discrimination beyond that which was already there.

◇ **Lectionary Reading**

Now Jephthah was the son of a prostitute.
He was also a mighty warrior.
Gilead, his father, had sons by his wife,
and when these sons were older,
they drove Jephthah away, saying,
"You shall not inherit in our father's house,
for you are the son of another woman."
So Jephthah fled from his brothers to the land of Tob
where he headed a band of outlaws
who went out with him on raids. (Judg 11:1–3)

◇ ◇ ◇

Once Samson went to Gaza
where he saw a prostitute,
and he went and slept with her.
The men of Gaza were told,
"Samson has come here."
So they circled around
and lay in wait for him all night at the city gate.
They kept quiet, thinking,
"Let us wait until morning, and then we will kill him."
But Samson lay with her only until midnight.
Then he got up,
took hold of the doors of the city gate
and its two posts
and pulled them up, bar and all,
put them on his shoulders,
and carried them to the top of the hill
that stands in front of Hebron. (Judg 16:1–3)

◇ ◇ ◇

The temple was filled with debauchery
and reveling by the Gentiles
who dallied with prostitutes
and had intercourse with women
within the sacred precincts. (2 Macc 6:4)

◇ **Points for Shared Reflection**

• Prostitution is both condemned and condoned in biblical tradition. Compare this mixed signal with attitudes today. When and for whom is prostitution usually acceptable, or unacceptable, and why?

• Fertility cults flourished in the ancient Near East and continued uninterrupted throughout ancient Israel. Why were these religions so popular and so difficult to eradicate? You might want to assign someone to bring some factual information to consider the next time you meet.

• What negative impact does the Bible's association of female prostitutes with idolatry still have on women today?

• Women have so much guilt and negative feelings about their bodies. In what ways is biblical tradition responsible for this? What can women do to overcome their innate feelings of guilt, low self-esteem, and shame?

◇ **A Psalm of Reconciliation** (see p. 334)

◇ **Prayer**
Reconcile us
to changing times
and changing ways,
O One Who is Ever Changing
yet Whose love remains the same,
steadfast
and eternal
and wholly encompassing us.
Reconcile us
to one another
and especially to ourselves,
now and forever.
Amen.

◇ A PSALM OF RECONCILIATION ◇

Choir 1   Be reconciled
to a world that is different
from the way you would have
the world behave.

Choir 2   Be reconciled
to a way of life
that is different
from the one you know.

Choir 1   Be reconciled
to people and places
whose cultic ways
may seem bizarre.

Choir 2   Be reconciled
to the one next door
whose lifestyle shocks you
and challenges you
to refrain from condemnation.

Choir 1   Be reconciled
to a loss of power
as it passes to the other side.

Choir 2   Be reconciled
to changing rites
and changing prayers
to a God you no longer recognize.

Choir 1   Be reconciled
above all
to yourself
as opposing forces
continue to clash
in a climate of liberation.

Choir 2   God can help us
reach down deep
into wells of reconciliation.

Choir 1   When we are reconciled to life,
someone will rearrange it.

Choir 2   Be reconciled to that
and be at peace,
because no one but God
can change it.

    By M. T. Winter, Crossroad Pub. Co., © 1992 Medical Mission Sisters

MAIDS, SERVANTS, SLAVES

◇ **Scripture Reference**   See lectionary texts

◇ **Biography**

Female slaves, servants, maids, and nursemaids were commonplace in the households of the rich in ancient Israel. Whether young or old, house-born or acquired, temporary or permanent, Hebrew or foreign, their legal status was that of a piece of movable property owned by another. They could be bought, sold, leased to another, exchanged, and inherited. They had no genealogical history. The Bible rarely records their names.

◇ **Context**

Slavery was part of the fabric of life in ancient Israel. Female slaves were acquired in various ways: as a bridal dowry, as captives of war, as children born to household slaves, as the result of defaulting on a debt, or through purchase or inheritance or gift. Women of various cultures were among the many slaves to whom the biblical texts refer. They were considered the personal property of their owner and were often treated like objects. Their activities were mainly domestic, and in addition to the usual household chores, it was customary for a female slave to be used for sex by male members of the house. She could also be used to breed children, who would not belong to her, and she achieved her highest status when she carried the master's child. Biblical law offered the female slave some protection. Although she was inferior, she was to be treated as part of the household, invited to share in its religious activities and participate in the sabbath rest. According to Deuteronomy, after serving in bondage for six years, in the seventh year she was to be set free (15:12). A slave could voluntarily opt to remain; she would then be enslaved for life. Except for the wet nurse and the nursemaid assigned to an individual child, the various terms used to represent these women — handmaiden, bondwoman, maidservant, maid, attendant, female slave — do not indicate clear distinctions.

Personal maids of individual females often had a devoted loyalty. Rachel's nursemaid Deborah, who remained with her, and Judith's maid whom she put in charge of all she possessed shared a deep and lasting bond. The nursemaids who cared for Jonathan and Joash were dedicated, determined women who protected their charges at the risk of their lives. Slaves who became childbearers were given more privileges, although there was always the possibility of rivalry, as in the case of Hagar. It is hard to know how female slaves really felt about their status. Women were accustomed to bondage and to belonging to somebody else, and for some of these women, the household and its security were all they had ever known. See the following stories featured in this lectionary series: Hagar (p. 36), Zilpah and Bilhah (p. 106), the Slave to Naaman's Wife (p. 329) in *WomanWisdom;* and Sarah's Maid (p. 308) in this volume.

◇ **Lectionary Reading**

Narrator: We remember **Abraham's female slaves**

Reader
When Abram and Sarai entered Egypt,
the Egyptians were taken with her beauty.
Pharaoh's officials praised her,
so Pharaoh took Sarai into his house
and was generous with Abram because of her,
giving him sheep, oxen, donkeys, camels,
and male and female slaves. (Gen 12:14–16)

◇

They left for the land of the Negeb
and settled between Kadesh and Shur.
While they were there in Gerar,
once again Abram said of Sarai his wife,
"She is my sister,"
and Abimelech king of Gerar had Sarai brought to him.
But God appeared to Abimelech in a dream, saying,
"You are about to die because you have taken a married woman."
Abimelech summoned Abram and said to him,
"What have you done to us?

How have I offended you
that you should bring such guilt
on me and my kingdom?
What possessed you to do such a thing?"
Then Abimelech took sheep, oxen,
male and female slaves,
and gave them to Abram
and returned his wife, saying,
"My whole land lies before you.
Settle wherever you will." (Gen 20:1–2, 9, 14–15)

◇

"I am Abraham's servant," he said.
"God has greatly blessed my master,
and he has become wealthy,
with flocks and herds, silver and gold,
male and female slaves,
camels and donkeys." (Gen 24:34–35)

◇ ◇ ◇

Narrator: We remember **Jacob's female slaves**

Reader
Jacob grew exceedingly rich and had large flocks,
and male and female slaves,
and camels and donkeys. (Gen 30:43)

◇

Jacob sent messengers to say to his brother Esau,
"I have lived with Laban as an alien,
and stayed with him until now;
and I have oxen, donkeys, flocks,
male and female slaves;
and I have sent ahead to tell you this,
that I might find favor in your sight." (Gen 32:4–5)

◇ ◇ ◇

Narrator: We remember **Deborah,** Rebekah's nursemaid,
and we remember **Rebekah's maids**

Reader
So they sent Rebekah and her nursemaid
with Abraham's servant and his men,
and they blessed Rebekah and said to her,
"Sister of ours, may you increase
to thousands and tens of thousands!
May your descendants gain possession
of the gates of their enemies!"
Then Rebekah and her maids mounted the camels
and followed Abraham's servant. (Gen 24:59–61)

◇

Jacob came to Luz (which is Bethel)
in the land of Canaan,
he and all those who were with him,
and there he built an altar
and called the place El-Bethel,
because it was there that God was revealed to him
when he had fled from his brother.
And Deborah, Rebekah's nursemaid, died there,
and she was buried under an oak below Bethel.
So it was called Allonbacuth. (Gen 35:6–8)

◊ ◊ ◊

Narrator: We remember the **maid of Pharaoh's daughter
and the women who attended Pharaoh's daughter**

Reader
Pharaoh's daughter came to the river to bathe
while her attendants strolled along its banks.
She saw the basket among the reeds
and sent her maid to fetch it.
She opened the basket and saw the child
and he began to cry.
"This must be one of the Hebrew children," she said,
and she took pity on him. (Ex 2:5–6)

◊ ◊ ◊

Narrator: We remember the **female servants of Boaz**

Reader
Then Boaz said to Ruth,
"Listen to me, my daughter.
Do not go to glean in another field.
Stay here among my women.
Wherever the reapers are at work in the field,
follow close behind them."
When she beat out and gathered what she had gleaned,
she had quite a bit of barley.
She shared it with her mother-in-law,
who said, on seeing how much she had,
"Where did you glean today?
Blessed is the man who took notice of you."
Ruth told her all that had happened and said,
"The name of the man is Boaz."
Then Naomi said to her daughter-in-law,
"Blessed be God, whose kindness
has not forsaken the living or the dead.
The man you met is a relative,
one of our nearest of kin."
Then Ruth said to Naomi,

"He even said, 'Stay with my servants
until all my harvest is done.' "
Naomi advised her daughter-in-law,
"Stay with his women, my daughter.
There is danger of being molested
if you move to another field."
So Ruth remained close to the women of Boaz,
gleaning beside them daily,
until the barley harvest and wheat harvest
finally came to an end. (Ruth 2:3, 8–9, 17–23)

◊ ◊ ◊

Narrator: We remember the **women who served at the tent of meeting**

Reader
In constructing the sanctuary — the ark of the covenant —
Bezalel made the bronze basin and stand
from the mirrors of the women
who served at the entrance to the tent of meeting. (Ex 38:8)
Now Eli was very old.
He knew what his sons were doing to Israel,
and how they lay with the women who served
at the entrance to the tent of meeting. (1 Sam 2:22)

◊ ◊ ◊

Narrator: We remember **Abigail's maids**

Reader
Abigail arose quickly and rode away on her donkey,
with her five maids in attendance.
She followed the messengers of David
and she became David's wife. (1 Sam 25:42)

◊ ◊ ◊

Narrator: We remember **Jonathan's nursemaid**

Reader
Saul's son Jonathan had a son who was crippled.
He was five years old when the news about the death
of Saul and Jonathan came from Jezreel.
His nursemaid picked him up and fled,
and in her haste to get away,
the child fell and became lame.
The boy's name was Mephibosheth. (2 Sam 4:4)

◊ ◊ ◊

Narrator: We remember the **servant girl of En-rogel**

Reader
Abiathar's son Jonathan
and Zadok's son Ahimaaz
were waiting at En-rogel.

A servant girl was their go-between.
She would come and deliver the message
and they would go and tell King David,
for they could not risk being seen
going in and out of the city. (2 Sam 17:17)

◇ ◇ ◇

Narrator: We remember **Joash's nursemaid**

Reader
When Athaliah, mother of King Ahaziah of Judah,
saw that her son was dead,
she set out to destroy all the royal family.
But Jehosheba, Ahaziah's sister,
took Joash, Ahaziah's son,
and the boy's nursemaid
and hid them in a bedroom
when the purge began
so the child would not be killed.
For six years Joash hid in the temple
while Athaliah reigned over Judah. (2 Kings 11:1–3)

◇ ◇ ◇

Narrator: We remember **Esther's maids**

Reader
When the king's order and his edict were proclaimed,
and when many young women were gathered
in the citadel of Susa,
Esther was also taken into the palace of Ahasuerus
and put in the custody of Hegai, the king's eunuch,
who had charge of the women.
Hegai favored Esther.
He planned her cosmetics and diet,
gave seven palace maids to her,
and then advanced her and her maids
to the best place in the harem. (Esth 2:8–9)

◇

When Esther's maids and her eunuchs told her
what Mordecai had done,
the queen was deeply distressed.
She sent garments to clothe Mordecai,
so that he might take off his sackcloth,
but he would not accept them.
Then Esther said to Mordecai,
"Gather all the Jews in Susa
and hold a fast on my behalf.
Do not eat or drink for three full days.
I and my maids will also fast.

After that I will go to the king,
even though it is against the law,
and if I perish, I perish." (Esth 4:4, 15–16)

◇ ◇ ◇

Narrator: We remember the **servants and maids of Edna and Raguel**

Reader
When they had finished eating and drinking
and were ready to retire,
they escorted Tobias to the room
where Sarah his bride was waiting.
Tobias remembered Raphael's words.
He took the fish's liver and heart
and put them on embers of incense.
The odor so repelled the demon
that he fled to the ends of Egypt
where Raphael, having followed him there,
bound him hand and foot.
When Raguel and Edna had left the room
and shut the door behind them,
Tobias said to Sarah,
"My sister, get up and let us pray,
imploring God for mercy
and for safety through the night."
So Sarah got up and together they prayed,
then they went to sleep for the night.
But Raguel that night summoned his servants
to go out and dig a grave.
"It is possible he will die," he said,
"and we will be marked for derision
and for ridicule by everyone."
When the grave was dug,
Raguel called for Edna,
"Send one of the maids to look in on them," he said,
"to see if he is alive.
But if he is dead,
let us bury him
without anyone knowing of it."
So they sent a maid who lit a lamp
and opened the bedroom door.
She went in and found the two of them
sound asleep together.
She came out and informed them
that nothing was wrong,
that Tobias was alive. (Tob 8:1–5, 9–14)

◇ ◇ ◇

Narrator: We remember the **female slaves of Tobias and Sarah**

Reader
Raguel gave Tobias his daughter Sarah
who was his wife,
as well as half of all his property:
male and female slaves,
oxen and sheep, donkeys and camels,
clothing, money, and household goods. (Tob 10:10)

◇ ◇ ◇

Narrator: We remember **Susanna's maids**

Reader
One day Susanna went into the garden
accompanied by her two maids.
Susanna was hot, she wanted to bathe
in the privacy of her garden.
"Bring me olive oil and ointments,"
Susanna said to her maids,
"and shut the gates to the garden."
The maids did as Susanna had asked
and left her there alone.
They did not know, however,
that the elders were hiding there,
watching Susanna,
waiting to get her by herself.
When the maids had left,
the elders ran to Susanna and said to her,
"Look, the garden gates are shut
and there is no one to see us."
[Later] the elders told their story.
"While we were walking alone in the garden,
this woman came in with her two maids,
shut the garden gates, and sent her maids away.
Then a young man who had been hiding there
came and lay with her." (Sus 15–19, 36–37)

◇ ◇ ◇

Narrator: We remember **Judith's female slaves**

Reader
Judith was very beautiful,
and her husband Manasseh had left her
gold and silver,
male and female slaves,
livestock and fields;
and she maintained this estate. (Jdt 8:7)

◇ ◇ ◇

Narrator: We remember **Judith's maid**

Reader
When Judith heard the harsh words of the people
who were desperate for water
and Uzziah's oath to surrender in five days
if God did not come through,
she sent her maid to summon Uzziah
and the elders of the town.
"Listen to me," said Judith,
"for I have come up with a plan.
Stand tonight at the gate of the town
so that I might go out with my maid.
Within those days which you have promised,
God will deliver us by my hand.
Do not ask what I am doing.
I can only tell you when I am through."
Uzziah and the rulers said,
"Go in peace, and may God go before you."
At the very time when the evening incense
was being offered in Jerusalem,
Judith, in sackcloth and ashes,
cried aloud to God.
When Judith's prayer was ended,
she rose and called her maid —
the one in charge of all she possessed —
and went into the house where she lived on sabbaths
and other festal days.
She took off her widow's garments,
put on a tiara, and dressed in festive attire.
She gave her maid a skin of wine,
a flask of oil and a bag of roasted grain,
dried fig cakes, fine bread,
and her dishes wrapped in a cloth.
They went to the gate of Bethulia
and found Uzziah standing there
with the elders of the town.
When they saw her transformed appearance,
they were astounded at her beauty and said,
"May the God of our ancestors favor you
and fulfill your expectations,
that the people of Israel may glory
and Jerusalem may be exalted."
And she bowed down to God.
"Open the gate of the town," she said,
"that I may go out and accomplish

the things you said to me."
So they opened the gate as she requested
and Judith went out with her maid.
They watched her go down the mountain
and enter into the valley
and there they lost sight of her.
As the women were walking through the valley,
they were taken into custody.
The Assyrian patrol asked them,
"Where are you coming from?
Where are you going?
To what people do you belong?"
"I am a daughter of the Hebrews," said Judith,
"but I am fleeing from them,
for they are about to be handed over to you
to be devoured.
I am on my way to Holofernes,
commander of your army,
to give him a true report.
I will show him a way he can enter in
to capture all of the region
without losing one of his men."
When the men heard her words and saw her face —
she was oh, so beautiful —
they said to her, "You have saved your life
by coming over to us.
Go at once to the commander's tent.
Some of us will escort you and hand you over to him.
When you stand before him, have no fear,
just tell him what you have said,
and he will be good to you."
Judith said to Holofernes:
"The food and water supplies are exhausted.
When my people eat forbidden meat
and consume the tithes consecrated to God,
they will be handed over to you.
I will remain here with you,
but at night I will go into the valley to pray.
God will tell me when they have sinned,
then I will come and tell this to you
so that your strength may prevail."
Holofernes and his servants marveled
at her wisdom and her beauty.

On the fourth day Holofernes
held a banquet for his personal attendants.

He did not invite his officers.
He said to the eunuch in charge of his affairs,
"Go and persuade the Hebrew woman
to eat and drink with us.
It would be a disgrace to be near such a woman
and not have intercourse with her.
If we do not seduce her, she will laugh at us."
The eunuch said to Judith,
"Come to my lord, enjoy his presence,
and become like one of the Assyrian women
who serve in the royal palace."
"Who am I to refuse my lord?" said Judith.
"Whatever pleases him, I will do,
and it will be a joy."
So she dressed in all her finery.
Her maid went ahead and spread on the ground
the lambskins for reclining.
Judith came into the tent and lay down,
and Holofernes was wild with passion,
for he had waited for this opportunity
from the day he laid eyes on her.
"Have a drink. Be merry!" he said.
"I will gladly drink, my lord," said Judith,
"for this is the greatest day of my life,"
and she ate and drank what her maid had prepared.
Holofernes was so delighted with her,
he drank an enormous amount of wine,
more than he had drunk on any one day
since the day that he was born.
When evening came, his servants withdrew.
Judith was left with Holofernes
sprawled in a drunken stupor across his canopied bed.
Her maid waited outside the tent,
for Judith had said they would go to pray
as on every other night.
Judith stood beside the bed
and prayed within her heart.
She took the sword from the bedpost
where it hung by Holofernes' head,
grabbed hold of his hair
and struck his neck, twice, with all her might,
and with that, cut off his head.
She pushed the body off the bed
and rolled it in the canopy.
The head of Holofernes
she put into the bag with her food.

Then she and her maid went out to pray
as they had been accustomed.
They passed through the camp, circled the valley,
went up the side of the mountain,
and came to Bethulia's gate.
Judith called out to the sentries,
"Open the gate! Our God is with us,
overpowering our enemies yesterday and today."
When the people of Bethulia heard her voice,
they summoned the elders of the town
and all ran to the gate,
astounded that she had returned.
"Praise God," she said, "whose mercy abounds,
for God has destroyed our enemies
this very night by my hand."
She pulled the head from the bag and said,
"Here is the head of Holofernes,
commander of the Assyrian army.
He died by the hand of a woman!"
For the rest of her life Judith was honored
throughout all of Israel.
Many desired to marry her
but she never wed again.
She grew more and more famous
and she grew old,
to the age of one hundred and five.
She set her maid free
and died in Bethulia,
and they buried her beside her husband Manasseh.

                    (Book of Judith, chaps. 8–16, condensed)

◇ ◇ ◇

Narrator: We remember **all female servants and slaves in Israel**

Reader
The heads of ancestral houses were chosen
to go up to Jerusalem, according to their tribes,
with their wives and sons and daughters,
and male and female servants,
and their livestock. (1 Esd 5:1)

◇

The whole assembly together
that was gathered in Jerusalem
[after the return from exile]
was forty-two thousand three hundred sixty,
besides their male and female slaves,
of whom there were seven thousand three hundred thirty-seven;

and they had two hundred forty-five singers,
male and female. (Ezra 2:64–65; Neh 7:66–67; 1 Esd 5:41–42)

◇

Antiochus sent Apollonius, the captain of the Mysians,
with an army of twenty-two thousand,
and commanded him to kill all the grown men
and to sell the women and boys as slaves. (2 Macc 5:24)

◇ **Points for Shared Reflection**

- Comment on the fact that slavery was condoned in biblical tradition. How has this contributed to racial subjugation in our own times?

- Domestic chores are one thing, sexual services quite another. Comment on the male's free and easy use of a woman's body in the past and in the present. How can we effect a change?

- How do you think God felt about the institution of slavery in biblical times? What do you say to someone who insists, it's in the Bible so it must be all right?

- In what ways are women enslaved today? What will bring about their liberation?

◇ **A Psalm on Labor** (see p. 348)

◇ **Prayer**

We labor for You
in our labors of love
and our lives of labor,
Shekinah-Shaddai,
labor to sow the seeds
of Your promise,
labor to share a sense
of Your Presence,
labor to know and proclaim
Your intentions
for us
and for all
who would live by Your will
and be led by Your wisdom,
now and forever.
Amen.

◇ A PSALM ON LABOR ◇

Choir 1   We labor at so many menial jobs
in the world which we inhabit.

Choir 2   We labor in so many different roles
in public and in private.

Choir 1   We labor on so many different levels
and in so many different networks.

Choir 2   We labor at achieving so many goals
and addressing so many issues.

All   We are building the new society
as we labor to change our social structures.
Bless our interaction, Shaddai.
Bless the work of our hands.

Choir 1   We labor at bringing ourselves into line.

Choir 2   We labor at helping our loved ones to grow.

Choir 1   We labor at our own maturing
in the soul of our becoming.

Choir 2   We labor at loving one another,
labor at loving ourselves.

All   We are building a firm foundation
for the transforming of our culture.
Bless all our labors of love, Shaddai.
Bless the work of our heart.

Choir 1   We labor at working for justice and peace.

Choir 2   We labor at forging bonds of equality
for race and class and gender.

Choir 1   We labor to overcome all oppression
here at home and abroad.

Choir 2   We labor at dealing with poverty,
with hunger and with homelessness,
challenging structures,
pushing for change,
praying for a change of heart.

All   We are building a future of hope for all
within a new world order.
Bless our lives of labor, Shaddai.
Bless the work of Your heart.

   By M. T. Winter, Crossroad Pub. Co., © 1992 Medical Mission Sisters

WOMEN

◇ **Scripture Reference** See lectionary texts

◇ **Biography**

There is little that can be said about the kaleidoscope of women of all ages and various cultures who span the centuries of biblical tradition and are included here. They are remembered because they once lived among us. The texts do not do justice to the reality of their lives but the words do ensure that these women of the Bible will never again be forgotten.

◇ **Context**

Those women whose stories are not featured elsewhere in this lectionary series or whose presence is not noted under some other classification are among the women included here. Much has already been said about the women of biblical tradition in the pages preceding this section. While individual narratives add flesh to facts and a bit of passion to memory, there is also value in collectively recalling women of past faith and courage, ordinary women who lived and suffered and eventually died within the context of biblical tradition. May women of all ages, cultures, and religions stand in solidarity with the sisters here. They represent a cross-section of the female gender and they tell us that there are many facets to herstory that have yet to come to light. Perhaps in remembering the lives of these women we may remember more of our own.

◇ **Lectionary Reading**

Narrator: We remember **women of the Exodus**

Reader
Then the prophet Miriam, Aaron's sister,
took a tambourine in her hand,
and all the women followed after her
with tambourines and dancing. (Ex 15:20)

◇

God said to Moses,
"Tell the people that every man and every woman
is to ask their neighbor for objects of silver and gold."
So they came, women and men;
all who were of a willing heart
brought brooches and earrings
and signet rings and pendants,
all sorts of gold objects.
Everyone brought an offering of gold to God
to be used in the tent of meeting
for its service and its sacred vestments.
All the skillful women spun with their hands
and brought what they had spun
in blue and purple and crimson yarns and fine linen;
all the women whose hearts moved them to use their skill

spun the goats' hair.
All the Israelite men and women
whose hearts made them willing to bring anything
for the work that God had commanded by Moses to be done,
brought it as a freewill offering to God. (Ex 11:1–2; 35:21–22, 25–26, 29)

◇

God spoke to Moses saying,
"Command the Israelites to put out of the camp
everyone who is leprous, or has a discharge,
and everyone who is unclean through contact with a corpse;
put both male and female outside the camp.
They must not defile the camp where I dwell among them."
The Israelites did as God commanded through Moses,
putting those people outside the camp. (Num 5:2–4)

◇ ◇ ◇

Narrator: We remember **ordinary women**

Reader
As David and his troops were returning
from successfully killing the Philistines,
the women came singing and dancing
out of all the towns of Israel
to meet King Saul with songs of joy
and tambourines and other musical instruments.
And the women sang to one another
as they made merry,
"Saul has killed his thousands,
and David his ten thousands." (1 Sam 18:6–7)

◇

They brought in the ark of God
and set it inside the tent that David had set up for it,
and they offered before God burnt offerings
and offerings of well-being.
When David had finished offering,
he blessed the people in the name of God,
and he distributed to every person in Israel —
man and woman alike —
to each a loaf of bread, a portion of meat,
and a cake of raisins. (1 Chr 16:1–3)

◇

The children gather wood, the fathers kindle fire,
and the women knead dough to make cakes
for the queen of heaven;
and they pour out drink offerings to other gods
to provoke me to anger. (Jer 7:18)

◇

Then the hand of God brought me
to the entrance of the north gate of God's house;
women were sitting there, weeping for Tammuz. (Ez 8:14)

◇

As for you, mortal, set your face
against the daughters of your people
who prophesy out of their own imagination;
prophesy against them and say,
Thus says God:
Woe to the women
who sew bands on wrists
and make veils for the heads of persons of every height,
in the hunt for human lives! (Ez 13:17–18)

◇

All the people gathered in the square before the Water Gate.
Ezra the priest read to the assembly from the book of the law
which God had given to Israel.
On the first day of the seventh month,
he read to both women and men
and to all who could hear with understanding.
He read from early morning until midday
in the presence of the men and the women
and those who could understand,
and the ears of all the people
were attentive to the book of the law.
                    (Neh 8:1–3; 1 Esd 9:38–41)

◇

They offered great sacrifices and rejoiced
on the day of the dedication of the wall of Jerusalem,
for God had filled them with joy.
Women and children also rejoiced. (Neh 12:27, 43)

◇

Because the holy place was about to be dishonored,
women, girded with sackcloth under their breasts,
thronged the streets.
Some of the young women who were kept indoors
ran together to the gates, and some to the walls,
while others peered out of the windows;
and holding up their hands to heaven,
they all made supplication. (2 Macc 3:18–20)

◇

In all Judea they mourned for Josiah.
The prophet Jeremiah, the principal men,
with the women,
have lamented for him to this day. (1 Esd 1:32)

◇ ◇ ◇

Narrator: We remember **young girls and virgins**

Reader
Moses said to the army officers,
"Kill every Midianite woman who has slept with a man,
but all the young girls who are still a virgin
keep alive for yourselves."
The booty from the spoil the troops had taken
totaled thirty-two thousand women
who had never slept with a man. (Num 31:17–18, 32, 35)

◇

Jephthah's daughter said to him,
"Let this thing be done for me:
Give me two months to wander the hills
and bewail my virginity, I and my female friends."
"Go," he said, and sent her away.
Two months later she returned to her father
who kept the vow he had made.
Now she who died a virgin
became a tradition in Israel. (Jdg 11:37–39)

◇

As Saul and his companion went up the hill to the town,
they met some girls coming down to draw water,
and they asked them, "Is the seer [Samuel] here?"
"Yes," they answered, "there he is just ahead of you.
Hurry, he has just come into town
because the people have a sacrifice today at the shrine.
You will find him as soon as you enter the town,
before he goes up to the shrine to eat.
The people will not eat until he comes,
since he must bless the sacrifice;
then those who are invited will eat.
Go up now, quickly, and you will meet him." (1 Sam 9:11–13)

◇

King Ahasuerus loved Esther more than all the other women;
she won his favor and devotion above all the other virgins. (Esth 2:17)

◇ ◇ ◇

Narrator: We remember **sisters and sisters-in-law**

Reader
Then Rahab said, "Give me a sign of good faith,
that you will spare my father and mother,
my brothers and sisters
and all who belong to them,
and deliver our lives from death."
The men said to her,
"We will be released from this oath

that you have made us swear to you
if we invade the land
and you do not tie this crimson cord
in the window through which you let us down,
and you do not gather into your house
your father and mother,
your brothers, your sisters,
and all your family."
Joshua said to the two men who had spied out the land,
"Go into the prostitute's house,
and bring the woman out of it
and all who belong to her, as you swore to her."
So the young men who had been spies
went in and brought Rahab out,
along with her father, her mother, her brothers, her sisters
and all who belonged to her —
they brought all her kindred out —
and set them outside the camp of Israel.
Then they burned down the city and everything in it.
Only the silver and gold, and the vessels of bronze and iron,
they put into the treasury of the house of God.
But Rahab the prostitute,
with her family and all who belonged to her,
Joshua spared.
Her family has lived in Israel ever since.
For she hid the messengers whom Joshua sent
to spy out Jericho. (Josh 2:13, 17–18; 6:22–25)

◊

After a while, at the time of the wheat harvest,
Samson went back to see his wife,
and he brought a kid for her.
"Let me visit my wife in her room," he said,
but her father would not allow it.
"I was sure you had rejected her,
so I gave her to your companion," he said.
"Consider her younger sister instead.
Look, she is prettier than her." (Jdg 15: 1–2)

◊

Hadad found favor with Pharaoh,
who gave him his sister-in-law for a wife,
the sister of Queen Tahpenes.
The sister of Tahpenes gave birth by him to their son Genubath,
whom Tahpenes weaned in Pharaoh's house;
Genubath was in Pharaoh's house among Pharaoh's children.
                    (1 Kings 11:19–20)

◊

God restored the fortunes of Job
when he had prayed for his friends;
and God gave Job twice as much as he had before.
Then his brothers and sisters
and all who had known him before
came to his house and ate with him.
They were sympathetic to him and comforted him
for all the evil that he had endured;
and each of them gave him money and a gold ring.

(Job 42:10–11)

◇

Their concern for their wives and their children,
and for their brothers and sisters and relatives,
lay upon them less heavily than their concern
for the consecrated sanctuary,
which was their first and greatest fear. (2 Macc 15:18)

◇ ◇ ◇

Narrator: We remember **women of other cultures**

Reader
While Israel was encamped at Shittim,
the men entered into sexual relationships with the women of Moab,
who invited them to attend sacrifices to their gods.
Consequently, Israelites ate sacrificial meals
and bowed down before Semitic gods;
and God's anger flared against Israel
because it had yoked itself to the Baal of Peor. (Num 25:1–3)

◇

Ezra prayed and wept before the house of God
and a very large assembly of men, women, and children
wept bitterly with him.
"We have broken faith with our God
and have married foreign women from the peoples of the land,
but still there is hope for Israel," said Shecaniah son of Jehiel.
"So now let us make a covenant with God
to send away all these wives and their children,
and let it be done according to the law.
Take action, for it is your duty; be strong and do it."
Then Ezra stood up and made the chief priests,
the Levites and all Israel swear
that they would do as had been said. (Ezra 10:1–5)

◇ ◇ ◇

Narrator: We remember **women who were captives**

Reader
When Abram heard his nephew had been taken captive,
he took three hundred eighteen of his trained men

and pursued them as far as Dan.
He divided his forces, routed them,
and followed them to the north of Damascus.
Then he brought back all the material goods,
his nephew Lot, and the women and other people. (Gen 14:14–16)

⋄

The Israelites took the women of Midian and their little ones captive;
and they took their cattle, their flocks, and all their goods for themselves.
(Num 31:9)

⋄

Abimelech put Thebez under siege,
and all the men and women and elders of the city
fled to the tower and shut themselves in,
then went up to the roof of the tower.
When a certain woman threw a millstone
and crushed Abimelech's head,
the people all went home. (Jdg 9:50, 53, 55)

⋄

The Amalekites had attacked Ziklag
and burned it down and taken the women
and all its inhabitants captive.
They did not kill them but carried them off.
David recovered all that the Amalekites had taken. (1 Sam 30:1–2, 18)

⋄

The people of Israel took captive
two hundred thousand of their kin,
women, sons, and daughters;
they also took much booty from them,
and brought the booty to Samaria. (2 Chr 28:8)

⋄

The king of Babylon appointed Gedaliah governor in the land,
and committed to him men, women, and children,
those of the poorest of the land
who had not been taken into exile to Babylon. (Jer 40:7)

⋄

Johanan and all the leaders of the forces with him
took all the rest of the people
whom Ishmael had carried away captive from Mizpah
after he had slain Gedaliah —
soldiers, women, children, and eunuchs
whom Johanan brought back from Gibeon.
Johanan and all the commanders of the forces
took all the remnant of Judah
who had returned to settle in the land of Judah
from all the nations to which they had been driven —
the men, the women, the children, the princesses,

and everyone whom Nebuzaradan the captain of the guard
had left with Gedaliah; and also the prophet Jeremiah
and Baruch son of Neriah —
and they came into the land of Egypt,
for they did not obey God's voice. (Jer 41:16; 43:5–6)

◇

A collector of tribute sent by Antiochus
came to Jerusalem with a large force.
He plundered the city, burned it,
tore down its houses and surrounding walls
and took captive the women and the children. (1 Macc 1:29, 31–32)

◇

When Timothy learned of the approach of Judas,
he sent off the women and the children and the baggage
to a place called Carnaim;
for that place was hard to besiege and had difficult access
because of the narrowness of its approaches. (2 Macc 12:21)

◇ ◇ ◇

Narrator: We remember **women who were massacred**

Reader
Moses said to the army officers
who had returned from battle with the Midianites,
"Have you allowed all the women to live?
These women here, on Balaam's advice,
made the Israelites act treacherously against God
in the affair of Peor,
so that the plague struck the congregation of God.
Kill every male among the little ones,
and kill every woman who has slept with a man." (Num 31:14–17)

◇

We captured all of King Sihon's towns,
and in each town we utterly destroyed
men, women, and children.
We left not a single survivor.
God gave everything to us, from Aroer as far as Gilead.
But we did as God commanded
and did not encroach on Ammonite land.
King Og of Bashan and his troops
also came out to battle against us,
and we utterly destroyed them and their cities,
their men, women, and children. (Deut 2:31, 34, 36–37; 3:1, 6)

◇

Every one of the troops cut a bundle of brushwood
and set it against the stronghold
following the lead of Abimelech,

and they set the stronghold on fire,
so that all the people in the Tower of Shechem died,
about a thousand women and men. (Jdg 9:49)

◇

The house was full of men and women.
All the lords of the Philistines were there,
and on the roof about three thousand women and men
were watching Samson perform.
Then Samson said, "Let me die with the Philistines."
He pulled with all his strength, and the house fell,
killing everyone in it. (Jdg 16:27, 30)

◇

Doeg the Edomite put Nob, the city of priests, to the sword,
killing men, women, children and infants,
oxen, donkeys, and sheep. (1 Sam 22:18–19)

◇

David and his men went up and made raids
on the Geshurites, the Girzites, and the Amalekites.
David struck the land, leaving neither man nor woman alive.
Against the Negeb of Judah, of the Jerahmeelites,
or of the Kenites, David left neither man nor woman alive
to be brought back to Gath, thinking, "They might tell about us."
Such was his practice all the time
he lived in the country of the Philistines. (1 Sam 27:8–11)

◇

At that time Menahem sacked Tiphsah
and all who were in it
and its territory from Tirzah on.
Because they did not open it to him,
he sacked it and ripped open
all of its pregnant women. (2 Kings 15:16)

◇

Antiochus commanded his soldiers
to cut down relentlessly everyone they met
and to kill those who went into their houses.
They massacred young and old,
boys, women, and children,
and slaughtered young girls and infants.
Within three days, eighty thousand were destroyed
and as many were sold into slavery. (2 Macc 5:12–14)

◇ ◇ ◇

Narrator: We remember **women not recorded in scripture**
       whose presence is implied
- **women destroyed in the flood**
- **women destroyed in Sodom and Gomorrah**
- **women who were victims of the plagues in Egypt**

- all women destroyed in all the wars
- women raped, abused, and molested in the occupation of the land
- women who married Jewish husbands and were constantly condemned
- women who left home, culture, religion to follow their men
- women who made significant contributions and whose story has been lost
- every woman who contributed herstory and whose name and story are lost

⬦ **Points for Shared Reflection**

- What can we do to demonstrate our solidarity with women of every culture, race, and religion around the world? Be specific.

- How can we sensitize ourselves to culturally different ways of being in the world? How can we become more accepting of other religious views? Be specific in your response.

- If you had one wish for women as we approach the turn of the century, what would that wish be? What steps might we women take to see that your wish comes true?

- What are you prepared to do to see that the stories of biblical women are told and that their lives are remembered?

⬦ **A Psalm about Taking Time** (see p. 360)

⬦ **Prayer**

O Thou eternally present,
timeless Existence
beyond all time,
we are always present to You,
even when we have forgotten You
or simply turned away from You
because we ran out of time.
Give us the sense
to take the time
for what is really important:
those deep, sustaining relationships
that bind us to the ones we love
and the sacred, Spirit-fed,
live-giving bond
we know we share with You.
Be present to us
all of the time,
now and forever.
Amen.

◇ A PSALM ABOUT TAKING TIME ◇

Choir 1   I wanted to say
I love you,
but I didn't take the time.

Choir 2   I wanted to say
I believe in you,
but I didn't have the time.

Choir 1   I wanted to share
some things with you,
but I couldn't find the time.

Choir 2   I wanted just to be
with you,
to share a piece of me
with you,
but I couldn't spare the time.

All   The days of our months
and the months of our years
are filled with so many trivial things
that take so much of our time.

Choir 1   Let me say
how much I love You, Shaddai.
Yes, I have the time.

Choir 2   Let me say
I believe in You, Shaddai.
Yes, I have the time.

Choir 1   Let me share
some things with You, Shaddai.
Yes, I have the time.

Choir 2   Let me just come and be
with You
and share a piece of me
with You.
Right now.
I have the time.

All   If projects, programs
swallow us up,
life will pass us by.
Time, take time
to love and be loved
in the Spirit of Shaddai.

   By M. T. Winter, Crossroad Pub. Co., © 1992 Medical Mission Sisters

Psalm Index

References to the three volumes in the series are as follows:

I: *WomanWisdom: Women of the Hebrew Scriptures: Part One*
II: *WomanWitness: Women of the Hebrew Scriptures: Part Two*
III: *WomanWord: Women of the New Testament*

Index of Women

References to the three volumes in the series are as follows:

I: *WomanWisdom: Women of the Hebrew Scriptures: Part One*
II: *WomanWitness: Women of the Hebrew Scriptures: Part Two*
III: *WomanWord: Women of the New Testament*

Daughters (cont.)
  Joash's, **II** 280
  Job's, **II** 259
  king's, the, **II** 281
  Lot's, **II** 215
  Machir's, **II** 281
  Meshullam's, **II** 281
  Peninnah's, **II** 281
  Philip's, **III** 218
  of the priests, **II** 281
  Rehoboam's, **II** 281
  Shallum's, **II** 282
  Sheshan's, **II** 282
  Shimei's, **II** 282
  who returned from exile, **II** 284
  who suffered, **II** 283
  Zelophehad's, **II** 226
David
  Concubines of, **I** 177
  Daughter of, Tamar, **II** 253
  Daughters, **II** 279
  Mother of, **II** 159
  Wives of, **I** 177
Deborah, **II** 32
Deborah (Tobit's mother), **II** 201
Deborah (Rebekah's nursemaid), **II** 337
Delilah, **II** 46
Dinah, **II** 221
Dorcas (Tabitha), **III** 187
Drusilla, **III** 273
Edna, **II** 179
Eglah, **I** 177
Elect Lady, **III** 286
Elisheba, **I** 133
Elizabeth, **III** 2
Endor, Witch of, **I** 294
Ephah, **I** 278
Ephrath, **I** 255
Esau's Wives, **I** 113
Esther, **II** 95
Eunice, **III** 280
Euodia, **III** 224
Eve, **I** 2
Eve's Daughters, **II** 210
Female Slave of Philippi, **III** 206
Girls, **II** 353
Gomer, **I** 208
Hagar, **I** 36
Haggith, **I** 177
Hammolecheth, **II** 201
Hamutal, **II** 193
Hannah, **I** 163
Hazzelelponi, **II** 273
Helah, **I** 256
Hephzibah, **II** 192
Herodias, **III** 90
Heroine of Thebez, **I** 290
High Priest's Maid, **III** 139
Hodesh, **I** 255
Hoglah, **II** 226
Huldah, **I** 335

Hushim, **I** 255
Ichabod's Mother, **II** 154
Isaiah's Wife (The Prophet), **I** 203
Iscah, **II** 274
Jael, **II** 41
Jairus's Daughter, **III** 62
Jambri, Bride of, **I** 242
Jecoliah, **II** 191
Jedidah, **II** 193
Jehoaddin, **II** 191
Jehosheba, **II** 288
Jemimah, **II** 259
Jephthah's Daughter, **II** 237
Jerioth, *see* Azubah
Jeroboam's Wife, **I** 197
Jerusha, **II** 191
Jewish Mother, **II** 171
Jezebel, **II** 77, 195
Joanna, **III** 148
Job's Daughters, **II** 259
Jochebed, **II** 134
Judith, **II** 110
Judith (Esau's wife), **I** 113
Julia, **III** 240
Junia, **III** 240
Keren-happuch, **II** 259
Keturah, **I** 103
Keziah, **II** 259
Leah, **I** 57
Levite's Concubine, **I** 142
Lo-ruhamah, **II** 266
Lois, **III** 280
Lot's Daughters, **II** 215
Lot's Wife, **I** 95
Lydia, **III** 200
Maacah (Caleb's concubine), **I** 278
Maacah (David's wife), **I** 177
Maacah (Jeiel's wife), **I** 256
Maacah (Machir's wife), **I** 256
Maacah (Queen Mother), **II** 189
Maacah (Reumah's daughter), **II** 274
Mahalath (Esau's wife), **I** 113
Mahalath (Rehoboam's wife), **I** 257
Mahlah (Zelophehad's daughter),
  II 226
Mahlah (Hammolecheth's daughter),
  II 274
Maid
  Bilhah, **I** 106
  Deborah (Rebekah's), **II** 337
  High priest's, **III** 139
  Joash's, **II** 340
  Jonathan's, **II** 339
  Judith's, **II** 343
  Rhoda, **III** 191
  Sarah's, **II** 308
  Zilpah, **I** 106
Maids, **II** 335
  Abigail's, **II** 339
  Edna's and Raguel's, **II** 341
  Esther's, **II** 340

Maids (cont.)
 Pharaoh's daughter's, **II** 338
 Rebekah's, **II** 337
 Susanna's, **II** 342
Martha, **III** 125
Mary, **III** 11
Mary (Cleopas's wife), **III** 163
Mary (James and Joseph's mother), **III** 148
Mary (John Mark's mother), **III** 195
Mary of Bethany, **III** 125
Mary Magdalene, **III** 156
Mary of Rome, **III** 240
Mary's Sister, **III** 119
Matred, **II** 274
Mehetabel, **II** 274
Merab, **II** 247
Meshullemeth, **II** 193
Micah's Mother, **II** 149
Michal, **I** 340
Midwives, **II** 325
 Hebrew, **II** 326
 Ichabod's mother's, **II** 327
 Puah, **II** 16
 Rachel's, **II** 326
 Shiprah, **II** 16
 Tamar's, **II** 326
Milcah (Nahor's wife), **I** 31
Milcah (Zelophehad's daughter), **II** 226
Miriam, **I** 74
Miriam (Bithia's daughter), **II** 273
Mothers, **II** 199
 Abraham's, **II** 202
 Aiah (Rizpah's), **II** 200
 Canaanite Woman, **III** 84
 David's, **II** 159
 Deborah (Tobit's), **II** 201
 Edna (Sarah's), **II** 179
 Elisha's, **II** 204
 Eunice (Timothy's), **III** 280
 Herodias, **III** 90
 Hiram's, **II** 204
 Ichabod's, **II** 154
 Jabez's, **II** 205
 Jephthah's, **II** 332
 Jeremiah's, **II** 205
 Jewish, **II** 171
 Jochebed (Moses'), **II** 134
 Lois (Eunice's), **III** 280
 Mary (James and Joseph's), **III** 148
 Mary (John Mark's), **III** 195
 Micah's, **II** 149
 not recorded in scripture, **II** 206
 Phinehas's, **II** 203
 Rahab's, **II** 203
 Rebekah's, **II** 202
 Rufus's, **III** 240
 Salome (Zebedee's sons'), **III** 95
 Samaritan, **II** 167
 Samson's, **II** 143
 Shaul's, **II** 203
 Shelomith, **II** 138

Simon Maccabee's, **II** 205
Sisera's, **II** 204
Susanna's, **II** 205
Two, **II** 163
 who were persecuted, **II** 205
Naamah (Queen Mother), **I** 189
Naamah (Zillah's daughter), **II** 274
Naarah, **I** 256
Nain, Widow of, **III** 53
Naomi, **II** 52
Nehushta, **II** 194
Nereus, Sister of, **III** 240
Noadiah, **II** 292
Noah (Zelophehad's daughter), **II** 226
Noah's Wife, **I** 88
Nympha, **III** 248
Oholibamah, **I** 113
Orpah, **I** 286
Paul's Sister, **III** 267
Peninnah, **I** 257
Persis, **III** 240
Peter's Mother-in-law, **III** 44
Pharaoh's Daughter, **II** 20
Philip's Prophetic Daughters, **III** 218
Phoebe, **III** 228
Pilate's Wife, **III** 135
Poor Widow, **III** 80
Potiphar's Wife, **II** 9
Prisca (Priscilla), **III** 233
Prophet, The (Isaiah's wife), **I** 203
Prophets
 Anna, **III** 40
 Deborah, **II** 32
 Huldah, **I** 335
 Isaiah's Wife, **I** 203
 Miriam, **I** 74
 Noadiah, **II** 292
 Philip's Daughters, **III** 218
Prophet's Widow, **I** 318
Prostitutes, **II** 331
 Gomer, **I** 208
 Jephthah's mother, **II** 332
 Rahab, **II** 24
 Samson's, **II** 332
 Tamar, **II** 2
 Temple, **II** 333
 Two mothers, **II** 163
Puah, **II** 16
Queen Mothers, **II** 187
 Abi, **II** 192
 Athaliah, **II** 88, 190
 Azubah, **II** 190
 Bathsheba, **I** 177; **II** 62, 189
 David's Mother, **II** 159
 Hamutal, **II** 193
 Hephzibah, **II** 192
 Jecoliah, **II** 191
 Jedidah, **II** 193
 Jehoaddin, **II** 191
 Jerusha, **II** 191
 Jezebel, **II** 77, 195

Wife (cont.)
Cain's, **I** 84
Dathan's, **I** 260
Elisheba (Aaron's), **I** 133
Ephraim's, **I** 261
Ezekiel's, **I** 265
Gilead's, **I** 262
Gomer (Hosea's), **I** 208
Hannah (Elkanah's), **I** 163
Hodiah's, **I** 262
Isaiah's, **I** 203
Ishmael's, **I** 259
Jeroboam's, **I** 197
Joanna (Chuza's), **III** 148
Job's, **I** 264
Lot's, **I** 95
Mary (Cleopas's), **III** 163
Mered's (Judean), **I** 261
Naaman's, **I** 262, 329
Noah's, **I** 88
Peninnah (Elkanah's), **I** 257
Pilate's, **III** 135
Potiphar's, **II** 9
Samson's, **I** 156
Wives, **I** 252
Abijah's, **I** 263
Ahab's, **I** 264
Belshazzar's, **I** 265
Benjaminites, **I** 149
of Daniel's Accusers, **I** 266
David's, **I** 177, 340, 347; **II** 62, 189
Esau's, **I** 113
of the Exodus, **I** 268
Faithful, **I** 273
Foreign, **I** 270
Gideon's, **I** 262
of Jacob's sons, **I** 260
Jehoram's, **I** 263
Joash's, **I** 263
of Noah's sons, **I** 258

not recorded in scripture, **I** 274
Priests', **I** 264
Priests' (of Bel), **I** 267
Rehoboam's, **I** 263
Solomon's, **I** 190
who suffered and died, **I** 268
Woman
of Abel-beth-maacah, **I** 309
Accused of Adultery, **III** 48
of Bahurim, **I** 355
Crippled, **III** 75
in the Crowd, **III** 100
Cushite, **I** 129
with the Flow of Blood, **III** 57
Shunammite, **I** 322
of Tekoa, **I** 302
of Thebez, **I** 290
at the Well, **III** 105
Who Anoints Jesus' Feet, **III** 70
Who Anoints Jesus' Head, **III** 66
Women, **II** 349
of the Exodus, **II** 350
in the Church, **III** 293
in ministry in Rome, **III** 240
not recorded in scripture, **II** 358
ordinary, **II** 351
of other cultures, **II** 355
at Pentecost, **III** 174
who accompanied Jesus, **III** 148
who were captives, **II** 355
who were massacred, **II** 357
Zarephath, Widow of, **I** 313
Zebidah, **II** 193
Zeresh, **I** 257
Zeruah, **II** 194
Zeruiah, **II** 201
Zibiah, **II** 191
Zillah, **I** 254
Zilpah, **I** 106
Zipporah, **I** 124

Lectionary Calendar

The women of the Bible invite us into a rhythm of reading and reflection on the remnants of their lost lives, promising to be there with us to push us to new possibilities in reinterpreting tradition and in understanding ourselves.

The women stand solidly at the center of biblical faith, yet we know so little about them. Seldom are they the subject of our preaching or our prayer. With very few exceptions, they are absent from our lectionaries, missing from our commentaries, left out of the liturgical cycles of our churches and synagogues. The following calendar is a rudimentary lectionary that will guide us as we seek to establish the bonds of shared sisterhood. Feminist communities may find it fruitful to plan their celebrations around these heroines of the past. Individuals are encouraged to use the calendar as a framework for a program of personal prayer.

The calendar is arranged in seasons. We begin with Women of Winter, but one can enter in anytime. The cycle is more flexible than the ancient calendar of saints. Women are not assigned to particular days, but are grouped according to months. Within a given month, one chooses one's own days for reflective prayer, allowing for a number of open days to accommodate the busy pace of contemporary life. Through reflective reading, listening, and prayer, we will experience a deeper integration between the planetary seasons, the seasons of woman's life, and the seasons of the heart. Christians can also connect to the primary seasons of their liturgical year: Advent/Christmas, Lent/Easter, Pentecost.

It is important to establish a rhythm of continuity through the year. A small amount of time, consistently taken, will reap untold rewards. Set aside fifteen minutes on definite days each week. Try to establish a pattern: the same amount of time, at the same time of day, the same days of the week. Once you are seen to be serious, family and friends will honor your need for sacred space and sacred time. The place you choose is important. So is the time of day. Both have to be right for you. You have to feel like you are visiting with friends, not doing what "ought" to be done. If you are a morning person, you may prefer to reflect by a window. Choose a comfortable chair. Or sit with a cup of herbal tea in the middle of the afternoon. Or withdraw late in the evening and reflect by candlelight.

Set a routine, but be flexible. Let the calendar serve as a guide. If you find in the bleak mid-winter that you come with a summer mood, or feel drawn to a particular woman's story, rearrange the order. Mary, a woman for all seasons, reappears seasonally. Read the selections indicated, or read her entire story each time, focusing your reflection on the passages assigned. Prayers and psalms are interchangeable. Use the index to help you find a psalm to match the theme of your personal prayer when it differs from the theme of the day. Such prayer is governed by circumstances and the season of your heart. As you integrate your own story with the biblical woman's story, listen to the intuitive wisdom stirring deep within you and be open to the Spirit.

Finally, this lectionary calendar is structured on the seasonal symbols of the northern hemisphere and on North American realities. Women in other areas and cultures are encouraged to create an appropriate seasonal calendar for local use. A note to everyone, everywhere: the prayers are only a guide. Be sure to add your own words and the wordless prayer centered in the silent movement of the heart.

References to the three volumes in the series are as follows:

I: *WomanWisdom: Women of the Hebrew Scriptures: Part One*
II: *WomanWitness: Women of the Hebrew Scriptures: Part Two*
III: *WomanWord: Women of the New Testament*

◇ WOMEN OF WINTER ◇

Winter... a time of drawing in, digging deep, letting go ... of keeping secrets, spinning dreams, living behind a mask. Winter earth is barren and cold, the winter solstice fleeting. Storms penetrate inside and out, cutting us off from our deepest connections, interrupting reflective repose. Just when it seems that everything worthwhile is hidden, hard, lifeless, when the heart is closed, the will unyielding, the Spirit silent, the future unknown, the wellspring within us empty, we feel the persistent pulse of life penetrating our inertia, inviting us into mystical communion, teasing us with Her song.

Women of winter are women of faith, women of strength and courage. Alone, they embrace the loneliness with singlehearted purpose. Violence will never destroy them because they are survivors. Women of winter, like mystics, are drawn into the Mystery, content to sojourn there. Listening to the sounds in the silence, learning to let go and let life be, they hover on the edge of the now in a covenant with the stars. Trusting the process of death to life, bravely enduring the long hiatus, they wait for dormant energies to rise and live again. Patient, confident, determined, they have faith in tomorrow because they are already pregnant. A vision no eyes but theirs have seen promises new beginnings. Their intuitive wisdom sings of things no other heart has heard.

DECEMBER/JANUARY

*Mary, **III** 16–22
*Anna, **III** 40
 Eve's Daughters, **II** 210
 Cain's Wife, **I** 84
 Keturah, **I** 103
 Leah, **I** 57
 Asenath, **I** 119
 Cushite Woman, **I** 129
 Shelomith, **II** 138
 Virgin Daughter, **II** 242
 Wives of the Benjaminites, **I** 149
 Woman with the Flow of Blood, **III** 57
 Crippled Woman, **III** 75
 Poor Widow, **III** 80
 Heroine of Thebez, **I** 290
 Samson's Wife, **I** 156
 Ichabod's Mother, **II** 154
 Mothers not recorded in scripture, **II** 206

FEBRUARY

Witch of Endor, **I** 294
David's Daughter Tamar, **II** 253

Michal, **I** 340
Solomon's Wives, **I** 190
Two Mothers, **II** 163
Wife of Jeroboam, **I** 197
Foreign Wives, **I** 270–73
Women not recorded in scripture, **II** 358–59
Samaritan Mothers, **II** 167
Jezebel, **II** 77
Women who were massacred, **II** 357–58
Esther, **II** 95

MARCH

Women in Ministry in Rome, **III** 240
Chloe, **III** 258
Paul's Sister, **III** 267
Huldah, **I** 335
The Prophet, **I** 203
Lo-ruhamah, **II** 266
Daughters who suffered, **II** 283–84
Cleopatra, **I** 236
Arsinoe, **II** 312
Faithful wives, **I** 273
Midwives, **II** 325
Elizabeth, **III** 2

---

*During Advent

◇ WOMEN OF SPRING ◇

Spring... a time when the world awakes and sets its house in order, liberally spilling seed and sun on a burgeoning universe. Torrents test the will to live, fostering transformation, making all things new. Beginnings are always tentative. Mists mask insecurity as fragile, fertile, inexperienced life looks to its own potential to liberate and bless. Love blooms, the heart sings, the chastened spirit rises up and dances on the waters. Nature in her myriad ways adorns our sacred spaces, saying, enjoy the rites of spring.

Women of spring are women of hope, women of adventure. Lighthearted, their sheer delight in the process of becoming sparks a spontaneity that is hallmark of the young. Fun-loving, optimistic, their passion for possibilities puts them at ease with beginnings. They rejoice in bringing to birth. Women of spring are risk takers who believe in the new creation and are eager to bring it about. Vulnerable, unpredictable, they bare their sensitivity to encourage free expression of both laughter and tears. They are fire and flame, women of spirit, rising from the ashes with wide, welcoming wings.

MARCH/APRIL

Eve, **I** 2
Noah's Wife, **I** 88
Sarah, **I** 15
Tamar, **II** 2
Woman Accused of Adultery, **III** 48
Widow of Nain, **III** 53
Jairus's Daughter, **III** 62
Canaanite Woman and Her Daughter,
   III 84
*Pilate's Wife, **III** 135
*High Priest's Maid, **III** 139
*Daughters of Jerusalem, **III** 143
*Mary's Sister, **III** 119
*‡Mary, **III** 26–27
†Women Who Accompanied Jesus,
   III 148
†Mary Magdalene, **III** 156
†Mary, Wife of Cleopas, **III** 163
†Dorcas, **III** 187
Shiprah and Puah, **II** 16
Jochebed, **II** 134
Zipporah, **I** 124

MAY

Mahlah, Noah, Hoglah, Milcah, Tirzah,
   II 226
Women of the Exodus, **II** 349–51
Deborah, **II** 32
Jephthah's Daughter, **II** 237
Samson's Mother, **II** 143
Bathsheba, **II** 62
Abishag, **I** 360
Widow of Zarephath, **I** 313
Shunammite Woman, **I** 322
‡Women at Pentecost, **III** 174
‡Female Slave of Philippi, **III** 206
‡Philip's Prophetic Daughters, **III** 218
Women in the Church, **III** 293

JUNE

Mothers whose names we know, **II** 199–202
Wives whose names we know, **I** 252–58
Slave to Naaman's Wife, **I** 329
Prostitutes, **II** 331
Temple Singers, **II** 297
Daughters who returned from exile,
   II 284–85
Ordinary Women, **II** 351–52

---

*During Holy Week
†During Easter season
‡During Pentecost Octave

◇ WOMEN OF SUMMER ◇

Summer is synonymous with serenity, shalom. It is a time for healing, an opportunity for making whole. The bountiful earth conceals the scars of earlier indiscretions, and fields of dreams invite us to forget the wounds of war. Summer is more than a season. It is slowing time, growing time, a time when the cup of life overflows to nurture all who sojourn in its furrowed fruitfulness. Summertime. Loving is easy, expectations high.

Women of summer are women of peace . . . compassionate . . . productive. They are self-possessed and inventive. They know how their garden grows. Resourceful and resilient, they have borne the heat of the day and they have managed to survive. They cherish their independence, standing firm in the freedom that defines them inside and out. Summer women are warm women who learn from their experience, consistently seeking wholeness in the center of their soul.

JUNE/JULY

Milcah, **I** 31
Rebekah, **I** 44
Rachel, **I** 68
Esau's Wives, **I** 113
Wives whose names we do not know,
 I 258–67
Potiphar's Wife, **II** 9
Pharaoh's Daughter, **II** 20
Miriam, **I** 74
Rahab, **II** 24
Jael, **II** 41
Delilah, **II** 46
Concubines, **I** 277
Orpah, **I** 286
Sisters and sisters-in-law, **II** 353–55
Mary, **III** 22–25
Peter's Mother-in-law, **III** 44
Salome, Mother of Zebedee's Sons, **III** 95
Woman in the Crowd, **III** 100
Woman at the Well, **III** 105
Sisters of Jesus, **III** 112

AUGUST

Achsah, **II** 232
Daughters whose names we know, **II** 271–75

Daughters whose names we do not know,
 II 275–82
Abigail, **I** 347
David's Wives, **I** 177
Queen of Sheba, **II** 72
Prophet's Widow, **I** 318
Micah's Mother, **II** 149
Mothers whose names we do not know,
 II 202–5
Rhoda, **III** 191
Phoebe, **III** 228
Prisca (Priscilla), **III** 233
Nympha, **III** 248
Drusilla and Bernice, **III** 273

SEPTEMBER

Maids, Servants, Slaves, **II** 335
Jehosheba, **II** 288
Athaliah, **II** 88
Noadiah, **II** 292
Queen Vashti, **II** 303
Sarah's Maid, **II** 308
Susanna, **II** 316
Young Girls and Virgins, **II** 353
Judith, **II** 110

◇ WOMEN OF AUTUMN ◇

Autumn is a season of dual identity. The endtime is the goal of life. All is brought to fulfillment, as the heart, ripe for harvest, senses maturity. Savor the fullness of being before the winds of disintegration blow us from here to eternity, before our choice achievements once again go up in flames. First the reaping, then the pruning, the stripping away of all excess and even necessities, as everything meaningful falls to earth in a cyclical returning we cannot comprehend. The pain of deprivation is softened by the memory of promises to keep. The soul digs deep down into darkness, burrows into a blessing place, preparing to keep vigil until love comes again.

Women of autumn, women of wisdom, walk in the comforting shadow of the everlasting hills. They are about thanks giving. Given a glimpse of glory, they have come to accept diminishment as prelude to reward. They trust their own experience, trust the rhythm of life after life pulsating within them. Faith-filled...faithful...they look to their heart's abundance for comfort in their grieving, transcending self-destructing pain as they learn to live with loss. Women of autumn are weavers who fold the strands of their stories into patterns for handing on. They are traditional healers and the healers of their tradition. They, the keepers of its flame, know more than they can tell.

SEPTEMBER/OCTOBER

Woman Who Anoints Jesus' Head, **III** 66
Woman Who Anoints Jesus' Feet, **III** 70
Martha and Mary, **III** 125
Herodias and Her Daughter, **III** 90
Sapphira, **III** 182
Hagar, **I** 36
Lot's Wife, **I** 95
Zilpah and Bilhah, **I** 106
Elisheba, **I** 133
Wives of the Exodus, **I** 268
Ruth and Naomi, **II** 52
Woman of Tekoa, **I** 302
Wise Woman of Abel-beth-maacah, **I** 309
David's Mother, **II** 159
Edna, **II** 179
Widows, **I** 248
Mary, Mother of John Mark, **III** 195
Lydia, **III** 200
Damaris, **III** 212
Euodia and Syntyche, **III** 224

NOVEMBER

Apphia, **III** 253
Claudia, **III** 263
Lot's Daughters, **II** 215

Dinah, **II** 221
Daughters of the Exodus, **II** 282
Cozbi, **I** 137
Levite's Concubine, **I** 142
Rizpah, **I** 170
Merab, **II** 247
Gomer, **I** 208
Bride of Jambri, **I** 242
Wives who suffered and died, **I** 268–70
Women who were captives, **II** 355–57
Jewish Mother, **II** 171
Mothers who suffered persecution,
   II 205–6
Woman of Bahurim, **I** 355

DECEMBER

Elect Lady, **III** 286
Lois and Eunice, **III** 280
Queen Mothers, **II** 187
Women of other cultures, **II** 355
Sarah, Wife of Tobias, **I** 215
Job's Daughters, **II** 259
Daughters of cross-cultural marriages, **II** 283
Anna, Wife of Tobit, **I** 228
Hannah, **I** 163
*Mary, **III** 13–15

---

*During Advent